T0376919

AFRICAN ETHNOGRAPHIC STUDIES OF THE 20TH CENTURY

Volume 15

UMBUNDU KINSHIP AND CHARACTER

UMBUNDU KINSHIP AND CHARACTER

GLADWYN MURRAY CHILDS

LONDON AND NEW YORK

First published in 1949 by Oxford University Press for the International African Institute.

This edition first published in 2018
by Routledge
2 Park Square, Milton Park, Abingdon, Oxon OX14 4RN

and by Routledge
711 Third Avenue, New York, NY 10017

Routledge is an imprint of the Taylor & Francis Group, an informa business

© 1949 International African Institute

All rights reserved. No part of this book may be reprinted or reproduced or utilised in any form or by any electronic, mechanical, or other means, now known or hereafter invented, including photocopying and recording, or in any information storage or retrieval system, without permission in writing from the publishers.

Trademark notice: Product or corporate names may be trademarks or registered trademarks, and are used only for identification and explanation without intent to infringe.

British Library Cataloguing in Publication Data
A catalogue record for this book is available from the British Library

ISBN: 978-0-8153-8713-8 (Set)
ISBN: 978-0-429-48813-9 (Set) (ebk)
ISBN: 978-1-138-49597-5 (Volume 15) (hbk)
ISBN: 978-1-351-02274-3 (Volume 15) (ebk)

Publisher's Note
The publisher has gone to great lengths to ensure the quality of this reprint but points out that some imperfections in the original copies may be apparent.

Disclaimer
The publisher has made every effort to trace copyright holders and would welcome correspondence from those they have been unable to trace.

UMBUNDU
KINSHIP &
CHARACTER

BEING A DESCRIPTION OF THE SOCIAL
STRUCTURE AND INDIVIDUAL DEVELOP-
MENT OF THE OVIMBUNDU OF ANGOLA,
WITH OBSERVATIONS CONCERNING THE
BEARING ON THE ENTERPRISE OF
CHRISTIAN MISSIONS OF CERTAIN PHASES
OF THE LIFE AND CULTURE DESCRIBED

By GLADWYN MURRAY CHILDS

Published for the
INTERNATIONAL AFRICAN INSTITUTE *and*
the WITWATERSRAND UNIVERSITY PRESS
by the OXFORD UNIVERSITY PRESS
LONDON NEW YORK TORONTO
1949

Oxford University Press, Amen House, London E.C.4
GLASGOW NEW YORK TORONTO MELBOURNE WELLINGTON
BOMBAY CALCUTTA MADRAS CAPE TOWN
Geoffrey Cumberlege, Publisher to the University

PRINTED IN GREAT BRITAIN

PREFACE

THAT Chief of California Indians who told Dr. Benedict of the power of his people in the old days when they had eaten 'the health of the desert' made a profoundly interesting observation.

In the beginning, he said, God gave to every people a cup, a cup of clay, and from that cup they drank their life. . . . They all dipped in the water but their cups were different. Our cup is broken now. . . .[1]

The African peoples also have had their cups of clay or wood, or their gourd dippers. They have worked out their intricate and appropriate adaptations to their particular environments, a social structure well suited to their needs, and a remarkably successful system of education.

Now that Africa has come under Western influences, however, the environment has changed. In many cases the changes have been so rapid that the Africans by their own unaided efforts, and within the pattern of their cultures, are no longer able to make the necessary adaptations. The results in social disintegration are well described by the Umbundu proverb:

Where the pot breaks, there also the potsherds remain.[2]

The broken pot no longer has either utility or beauty—is no more a pot, but only broken and scattered sherds. So it is also with a broken social group—only scattered individuals remain. This proverb refers primarily to a broken family, but thoughtful Ovimbundu are now applying it to their whole social structure.

Since the life of Africa has been thrust thus suddenly into the world's life, 'it becomes a problem of urgent importance, how, while introducing the European system . . . to conserve the very real values of the indigenous African system'.[3] The solution of this problem is a responsibility of Christian missions inasmuch as theirs is the responsibility for the greater part of the education of the Africans.

The Ovimbundu,[4] the people chosen for the present study, are

[1] Ruth Benedict, *Patterns of Culture*, p. 21 f. (Boston and N.Y.: Houghton Mifflin, 1934).

[2] *Pa fila ombia, haipo oviyo pa siala.*

[3] E. W. Smith, *Essays presented to C. G. Seligman*, p. 334, quoted in the *Year Book of Education, 1938*, p. 697 (London: Evans).

[4] For explanation of terms see note on Orthography, p. xi.

vi   PREFACE

a Bantu-speaking group numbering about one and one third million, whose home is the Benguela Highland of Angola (Portuguese West Africa). Christian missions have worked among them since 1881, the date of founding of the W.C.A.M. of the A.B.C.F.M., with which work the writer has been connected since 1924.

Umbundu mentality. It is not the purpose of this study to appraise Bantu or Umbundu mentality. Every new description of a Bantu culture gives a new angle or vantage point from which to view the versatile mentality of that interesting group of people. All available objective views unite to show us, as Driberg holds for primitive man in general, 'a being as human as ourselves, affected by the same emotions . . . with thoughts, responses, and actions differing in no essential way from our own'[1]—neither the noble savage of Rousseau nor the subhuman creature of more recent doctrinaires. 'The grouping of savages with children and idiots is but another symptom of an attitude which, when faced with a different type of culture, insists on assuming a lower type of mentality to account for that culture.'[1]

It must be owned that different views of primitive mentality are held, but it would seem that those which hold primitive man to be incapable of reasoning logically, his mentality in some way inferior or 'pre-logical', base their conclusions too largely on theoretical or library material and too little on results of actual field work.[2] It is not the purpose of the present study to examine these theories, but a word of protest must be raised against some who, basing their view of the mentality of Bantu peoples on some such theories as those mentioned above, and with or without sup-

[1] J. H. Driberg, *The Savage as He Really Is*, pp. 2, 3 (London: Routledge, 1929).

[2] Cf., for example, L. Levy-Bruhl, *Les Fonctions Mentales dans les Sociétés Inférieures, La Mentalité Primitive*, &c. The seriousness with which these and similar theoretical studies have been taken is surprising. Cf. e.g., R. Allier, *Mind of the Savage* (London: Bell, 1929); J. W. C. Dougall, *Characteristics of African Thought* (London: International Institute of African Languages and Cultures, 1932); N. S. Booth, *Teaching a Bantu Community* (MS. copy). Dr. Max Gluckman of the Rhodes-Livingstone Institute told me that I had wrongly interpreted Levy-Bruhl, and he kindly loaned me a copy of a paper by Evans-Pritchard which sets forth a different interpretation of Levy-Bruhl's thesis with regard to the 'pre-logical' mentality. It is not my intention here to combat the thesis of the 'pre-logical' mentality, but rather a common interpretation of it (Evans-Pritchard, 'Levy-Bruhl's Theory of Primitive Mentality', *Bulletin of the Faculty of Arts of the Egyptian University*, vol. i, pt. ii).

PREFACE

port from intelligence tests of doubtful suitability, have called in question the 'educability' of some Bantu groups.[1]

I shall not examine these theories but rather leave to descriptions of Umbundu culture given in the main part of the study, the task of showing that the mental capacity of the Ovimbundu is sufficient to enable them to assimilate the education placed at their disposal. Educators who really believe otherwise would hardly waste their time in attempting to educate a people who, after all, may be incapable of education.

If we do not believe in the logic of the savage and in the identity of his processes of thought with our own, then we should be proved illogical ourselves in attempting to develop along logical lines peoples of an alien mentality, and in attempting to transmit our civilization to peoples mentally incapable of assimilating it.[2]

The capacity of the Ovimbundu and their 'educability' are assumed.

The Approach. All the various types of approach to African education have been classed under one of the two aims: Assimilation, which has represented Latin colonial policy; and Adaptation, which has been more representative of the British and Belgian point of view. *Assimilation* would make African Frenchmen, African Portuguese, &c., of the natives. *Adaptation* would take what is best in both the African and the European cultures in order to produce a better African civilization'.[3]

Within the aim of *assimilation* there may be distinguished at least two policies. One ignores indigenous culture, presents the European culture quite without reference to it, and treats the African as though he had no cultural background—as though he were a *tabula rasa*. The other may study the indigenous culture, but only in order to be able to uproot it the more thoroughly and efficiently.

Within the aim of *adaptation* at least three distinct policies may

---

[1] See discussion in Malherbe (ed.), *Educational Adaptations*, Chap. XVIII (*N.E.F. Conference Report*, Cape Town, 1937); also P. A. W. Cook, *The Education of a South African Tribe* (Cape Town, 1934).

[2] Driberg, op. cit., p. 4.

[3] There is an interesting discussion of these two policies by H. Dubois, 'Assimilation ou Adaptation?' in *Africa*, 1929, pp. 1 ff. See also the discussion in the Preface of *Western Civilization and the Natives of South Africa*, by I. Schapera (London, 1934). There are other policies for dealing with the Africans such as repression, exploitation, &c., but since they cannot be classed as educational theories I have not included them in this analysis.

a 3

viii PREFACE

be recognized. *First*, there is a sympathetic but entirely unsystematic use of the culture in question which collects folk-lore, customs, or other single items to use them as illustrations, as lesson or sermon material, &c., but without reference to their context in the fabric or pattern of the culture. *Second*, there is an attempt to rebuild those functions or institutions which *a priori* are judged essential and to leave untouched those judged unessential. Still, whatever is done, is done without reference to the pattern of the culture in question and the criteria are predetermined. *The third method* is that advocated by the present study. It begins with a systematic study of the culture in question, especially its characteristic patterns of behaviour, significant attitudes, beliefs and customs; and the effect of its contact with other cultures; in order

To determine and describe the content;

To analyse and evaluate this content with reference to its bearing upon present local needs; and

To make suggestions for tentative procedures which shall build upon indigenous patterns of behaviour, make adjustment to approved attitudes from the outside as easy as possible, and work toward a continuous and self-functioning process of self-adjustment.

The view-point assumed is a composite of practical anthropology, progressive education, and the newer approach to Christian missions. The criteria have been evolved in part through a study of the local situation and its needs.

Sources. More documentary material has been sifted than the references indicate. The historical account which has finally been incorporated as Chapter XII was written before the main part of this study and served as an important part of its background.

The chief sources, however, are original materials descriptive of certain phases of Umbundu life and culture—materials gathered on the field over a period of years, especially between 1933 and 1938. Much of it consists of traditional 'literature' (folk-tales, proverbs, riddles and songs). More of it, however, consists of descriptions of customs, beliefs, institutions and other culture traits secured from personal observation, from descriptions by natives, from schedules collected and written up by trained natives, and Umbundu autobiographical data. Much of this is given in direct translation, certain parts in summary or by reference, while the rest has served as background.

PREFACE

Limits of time and space have made it necessary to restrict the study to the two major fields of social structure and education. These two phases were chosen because description of them seems to be pre-requisite to treatment of other areas of the culture, and also because of their inherent importance both anthropologically and educationally. In order to provide background and make for better understanding, an introductory chapter on 'Habitat' has been provided. I hope to illustrate the remaining phases of the culture at a later date.

It is not possible adequately to thank, nor even to mention by name, all those for whose help I am indebted. It would never have been possible to organize this study had it not been for a generous provision of fellowships and of many facilities by Union Theological Seminary in New York City, and also for the necessary allowance of time during two furloughs by the American Board of Commissioners for Foreign Missions. For extraordinary facilities put at my disposal, I am grateful to the Missionary Research Library and to its Director, Mr. C. H. Fahs. Among my many teachers at Union Seminary, Teachers' College, and in the Anthropology Department of Columbia University, for whose help I am indebted, I must name Professors I. L. Kandel, D. J. Fleming, A. L. Swift, Jun., Gene Weltfish, George Herzog, and Ralph Linton, who have freely given me much advice, counsel, and encouragement. For an especially high order of help I am very deeply indebted to Dr. Ruth Fulton Benedict and to Professor Harrison S. Elliott. Dr. Benedict not only gave freely of her time and wisdom as teacher and counsellor, but she also gave much encouragement and assistance in the task of arranging publication. For help with the German source material, I am indebted to my wife. To these whom I have named, and to many others, go my sincere thanks.

UNION THEOLOGICAL SEMINARY
NEW YORK CITY
May 1939

G. M. C.

THE manuscript was revised in Africa in 1940 and the typing, done by J. C. Lasaro, African secretary of Currie Institute (Dondi), was completed in March 1941. It is now nearly six years later that the opportunity for publication has finally been realized. It is not

PREFACE

possible to make a new revision at this time nor do I feel this necessary. Many changes have taken place, but I feel that the tendencies here outlined in 1939–40 continue to operate. A few notes have been added, especially with regard to matters on which the 1940 Census of Angola, published 1941–43, has thrown new light. For much original material, and for suggestions and help in revision, I am very grateful to many of my African friends and colleagues, especially the Rev. P. Ngonga Liahuka, Rev. Abraham Ngulu, Rev. R. Kavita Evambi (deceased, 1946), Sr. Pedro Paulo, and Sr. H. Kapiñalã Sukuakueche; and also to Dr. and Mrs. Merlin W. Ennis. I wish to thank Mr. Lewin and Professor Doke of the University of the Witwatersrand, Professor Schapera of the University of Cape Town, and Dr. Max Gluckman of the Rhodes-Livingstone Institute (Northern Rhodesia) for their helpful interest. I am grateful, indeed, to the International African Institute and to the University of Witwatersrand Press, under whose auspices this study appears.

AUBURNDALE, MASSACHUSETTS,

January 1947

G. M. C.

NOTE ON ORTHOGRAPHY OF AFRICAN WORDS USED

Ovimbundu (pl.) is the name of the people (sing. *Ocimbundu*). *Umbundu* is the name of the language, of the culture, and the form of the descriptive adjective.

The orthography used in most particulars follows recommendations of the International African Institute.[1] The sounds of Umbundu are relatively simple. Each vowel has a single value—for practical purposes the same as in Spanish. The tilde over a vowel indicates nazalization; with *ñ* it indicates the velar *n*, i.e. the value of the English (or German) *ng* in 'singer'. The sound of the English *ch* in 'church' is represented by *c*. The consonants *g* and *j* are always hard; these two and also *d* appear always and only preceded by *n*,—*nd*, *ng*, and *nj*. Likewise *b* never appears alone but preceded by *m*,—*mb*. The other consonants have approximately the same values as in English; *w* and *y* are only used as consonants; *r*, *x* are not found except in foreign words.

I have retained the prefixes Oci-mbundu, Ovi-mbundu, and U-mbundu in accordance with the correct Umbundu usage and because it seems that in no other way can confusion with regard to the identity of this people be avoided. When the truncated form of 'Mbundu' is used even great scholars are led to confuse the Ovimbundu with the 'Kimbundu' of the Luanda hinterland.[2] These two peoples must not be confused: they are entirely distinct and even belong to different linguistic zones. An Umbundu Grammar by Dr. Merlin W. Ennis is to be published shortly by the University of Witwatersrand Press.

[1] *A Practical Orthography of African Languages* (London: International Institute of African Languages and Cultures, 1927); *Short Guide to the Recording of African Languages* (London: ibid., 1933).

[2] See, for example, *Bantu Studies*, 1937, p. 375; E. W. Smith, 'Africa: what do we know of it?' *J.R.A.I.*, 1935, p. 71; D. W. Westermann, 'Study of African Languages', *Africa*, 1939, p. 20.

CONTENTS

Preface v

Note on Orthography of African words used . . . xi

INTRODUCTION

Chapter I. HABITAT 1
  Morphology 1
  Climate 3
  Environmental Factors 5
  Neighbouring Peoples 8
  European Administration, Communications, Missions . . 9
  Widespread Use of Umbundu 11
  Bibliography 11

Part One

SOCIAL STRUCTURE

Chapter II. POLITICAL AND SOCIAL LIFE . . 17
  The Tribe 19
  The King (royal office and functions) 20
  Sub-Tribes 23
  The Village 25
  The Village Plan 27
  The Villagers 28
  Social Life of the Village 32
  The Village Headman 36
  Moving a Village 37

Chapter III. KINSHIP 40
  The Household 40
  Kinship: Blood Relatives 42
    Classificatory System of Relationship . . . 46
    Umbundu Terms of Blood Relationship . . . 47
  The Kin: Relatives by Marriage 51
    Umbundu Terms of Relationship by Marriage . . 55
    Relatives with whom Marriage is Preferred . . . 56
  Sorcery 56
  The Hierarchy of Age 58
  Umbundu Social Structure: Summary . . . 59
  Genealogical Table 62

xiv CONTENTS

CHAPTER IV. SIGNIFICANCE OF THE SOCIAL STRUC-
TURE 63
The Village Work 65
Kinship Ties 67
The Household Attitudes, their use and extension . . 69
Leadership 70
Summary 72
Cultural Disintegration 73
BIBLIOGRAPHY, Chapters II & III 74
Chapter IV 77

PART TWO

INDIVIDUAL DEVELOPMENT AND EDUCATION

CHAPTER V. THE UMBUNDU BABY . . . 81
Birth 81
Twins 85
Naming 86
The Period of Lying-in 87
Babyhood Proper 89
The Sitting Baby or Toddler (*ocisembe*) . . . 92
Crawling 92
Teething 92
Weaning 93
Cleanliness 95
Language 96
Manners, Physical Development 96–7

CHAPTER VI. CHILDHOOD 98
The Child (*oneñe* or *omõlã*) 98
Psychological Education 99
Social Usage 100
Training in Skills 104
Later Childhood (from nine years) 105
Acquiring Skills 106
Cultivating 106
Side-line professions 109

CHAPTER VII. ADOLESCENCE . . . 111
From Puberty until Marriage 111
Girls congregate in kitchens, boys build own houses . . 111
The Trial Marriage 112
Certain Other Factors in Adolescent Development . . 114

CONTENTS   XV

Associations of Coevals (*vakuacisoko*)   115
Initiation   115
Adolescence a Time of Preparation for Marriage   .   117
Adult Life and Old Age   117
Summary   118

CHAPTER VIII. ANALYSIS OF UMBUNDU DEVELOPMENT   119
Theory of Personality   119
Education and Society   121
Social Adjustment   123
    Adjustments in Anger   .   .   .   124
    Adjustments in Family Life .   .   .   125
      Between Parents and Children   .   .   126
      Between Siblings   128
    Identification   129
    Inferiority Conflict   129
Umbundu Estimate of Character   .   .   130
Statement of the Problem   .   .   .   132

CHAPTER IX. EDUCATIONAL EVALUATIONS   .   134
Results of Umbundu Education   .   .   134
Character   134
Educational Method   .   .   .   135
Educational Content   136
Instrumentalities   .   .   .   137
Educational Policy   .   .   .   137
Problems of Organization, School, and Community   .   139

CHAPTER X. PARTICULAR FIELDS OF EDUCATION   .   141
Method and Content   141
    Social Behaviour   .   .   .   141
    Language Teaching   .   .   .   142
    Physical Education and Recreation .   .   144
    Music   144
    Christian Education   .   .   .   145
Treatment of other Umbundu Material   .   147
    Initiation Camps   .   .   .   148

CHAPTER XI. EDUCATION AND LIFE   .   .   150
Can Umbundu Knowledge and Practice yet be adapted?   150
What should be Central for the Umbundu Curriculum?   150
Community Education   .   .   .   152

BIBLIOGRAPHY, Chapters V–VIII   .   .   156
      Chapters IX–XI .   .   .   158

xvi CONTENTS

PART THREE

CHAPTER XII. HISTORICAL	164
Pre-history	164
Tribal Divisions of the Ovimbundu	167
Independent Kingdoms	168
Tributaries	168
Tribal Origins	169
Language Affinities	169
Traditional Histories	170
Ndulu (Andulu)	170
Bailundu	171
Viye (Bie or Bihe)	172
Ngalangi (Galangue)	174
Wambu (Huambo)	176
Ciyaka (Quiaca)	176
Other Groups	178
Border Groups	179
Neighbouring Peoples	180
Historical Evidence	181
The 'Jagas' and the Migrations . . .	181
Place-Names	188
Attitudes toward other Tribes . . .	189
Conclusion	189
Historical Development	190
Dominant Tendency: Trade	190
European Influences, 1600–1770 . . .	192
,, ,, 1770–1840 . . .	195
Dominant Tendencies, 1840–1874 . . .	199
The Rubber Trade, 1874–1911 . . .	207
'First Class Rubber', 1874–1886 . . .	207
'Red Rubber', 1886–1900	208
Decline, 1900–1911	211
Recent Developments: Currency . . .	215
Taxation	215
Land Tenure	216
Health	217
Religion	219
CHRONOLOGICAL CHART	224
BIBLIOGRAPHY, Chapter XII	232
Index of Authors and Sources	236
INDEX	239

LIST OF ILLUSTRATIONS

facing page

PLATE I. *a.* Rock outcrop beside the Keve River. *Photo. R. S. Webb* . . . .
b. Rapids of the Kuvale River (Katombela system). *Photo. M. W. Ennis* . . } 16

PLATE II. *a.* Court procedure: the King and his counsellors (Bailundu) . . . .
b. Mortuary rites at Ngendo . . . } 17

PLATE III. *a.* The inquest at a funeral. *Photo. R. S. Webb*
b. On the woman's side of the dancing floor during the celebration of funerary rites at Ngendo . . . . } 32

PLATE IV. *a.* A new village (*itula*) near Elende .
b. A granary (*osila*) also used as a guest-house *Photo. M. W. Ennis* . . } 33

PLATE V. *a.* An Esele village. *Photo. R. S. Webb* .
b. Hulling coffee (Bailundu Mission). *Photo. R. S. Webb* . . . . } 48

PLATE VI. *a.* Harvesting peanuts (Bailundu). *Photo. R. S. Webb* . . . . .
b. Road-workers. *Photo. M. W. Ennis* . } 49

PLATE VII. *a.* Communal fishing party (Talenge River, Elende). *Photo. M. W. Ennis* .
b. Women grinding meal (Bailundu). *Photo. R. S. Webb* . . . . } 64

PLATE VIII. *a.* Umbundu pots (before firing), baskets, and hoes. *Photo. R. S. Webb* . .
b. Umbundu basketry with native-woven tapestry. *Photo. M. W. Ennis* . . } 65

PLATE IX. *a.* A potter at work (Dondi) . . .
b. Fetish charms and diviner's rattle. *Photo. M. W. Ennis* . . . . } 128

PLATE X. *a.* Wounded bull eland (Malolo). *Photo. M. W. Ennis* . . . . .
b. Head of wart-hog (Bailundu). *Photo. R. S. Webb* . . . . } 129

xviii   LIST OF ILLUSTRATIONS

facing page

PLATE XI.   *a.* Musicians of Luanda with xylophone. *Photo.* ⎫
              '*Minerva*'   .   .   .   . ⎬ 144
              b. Musicians with flutes. *Photo. M. P. Childs* ⎭

PLATE XII.   *a.* A baby clinic (Dondi). *Photo. D. G. Ridout* ⎫
              b. Bringing a patient in a hammock (*owanda*) ⎬ 145
              (Bailundu). *Photo. R. S. Webb* .   . ⎭

PLATE XIII.   *a.* Baptismal service by the Rev. J. H. Cilūlū. ⎫
              Photo. D. G. Ridout   .   . ⎪
              b. Umbundu wedding, new style: Elende church ⎬ 154
              in the background   .   .   . ⎭

PLATE XIV.   *a.* Woman (educated) carrying baby (*oku veleka*). ⎫
              Photo. R. S. Webb   .   . ⎬ 155
              b. Old age. *Photo. M. W. Ennis*   . ⎭

PLATE XV.   Bailundu: town of Teixeira da Silva .   . 176

PLATE XVI.   *a.* Ruins at Usengo: section of wall between ⎫
              stone outcrops   .   .   . ⎬ 177
              b. Rock tomb of the va Sela (Kasongi)   . ⎭

MAPS   Habitat of the Ovimbundu   .   .   . 1
              Angola: Zonas Climatologicas .   .   . 8
              Tribal divisions and history of the Ovimbundu 167

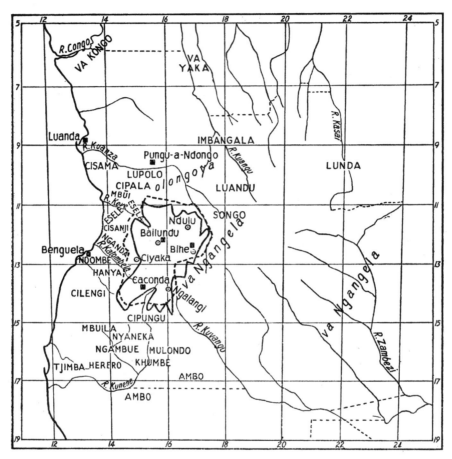

HABITAT OF THE OVIMBUNDU
AND THEIR POSITION WITH REGARD TO THEIR NEIGHBOURS
Heavy continuous line indicates elevation of 1,500 metres (4,920 ft.).
Broken line indicates limits of Umbundu territory.
⊙ Leading capital villages (*olombala*).　■ Portuguese presídios.

INTRODUCTION

CHAPTER I

HABITAT

Morphology

THE homeland of the Ovimbundu is the Benguela Highland in central Angola. Strictly speaking the Highland comprises those regions which have an elevation of 1,500 metres (about 4,920 feet) or more. A glance at the accompanying map will show how closely the territory inhabited by the Ovimbundu corresponds with the extent of the Highland proper. The adjoining regions, in which the Ovimbundu also live, nowhere have an elevation inferior to 1,000 metres (about 3,280 feet). Geographically the region of the Highland is a part of the South African sub-continental plateau. The ridges of the Highland form the plateau's highest north-western portion.

Geologically this sub-continental plateau is one of the oldest parts of the earth's surface. The north-western portion, with which this study is concerned, has remained above sea-level from before the time of fossils. The vast slab of primeval crystalline rock which forms the foundation of the plateau often outcrops in the form of isolated rocks of unusual appearance,[1] or in massive peaks, the highest of which, in the western escarpment, reach an elevation of nearly 9,000 feet (2,850 metres).[2] Some of these outcrops remain bare, some are hidden by laterite and some by soil formed from decomposition of rock.

Among the sediments which overlie these primeval rocks there are unfossiliferous sandstones, conglomerates, and others, all of which are considered to be of Palaeozoic age. Deposits of iron are numerous, many of which were once worked by the Ovimbundu or by their predecessors. Much of the soil has been greatly im-

---

[1] Several of these rocks have caught the attention of travellers and writers. *Luvili* (north-west of Bailundu) is perhaps the most striking of all. Cameron said that the natives called it 'The Devil's Finger', a name I have not been able to verify. *Nganda* and *Kawe* are near the railway between Nova Lisboa and Vila Robert Williams. A journalist recently gave them the name of 'Cleopatra's Breasts'.

[2] One of the peaks of the ridge called *Moko* (The Knife) is the highest, but no complete survey has been made.

poverished both by use and by the action of the weather. The most productive soil areas consist of alluvial deposits, but the precipitate nature of much of the region precludes the formation of such deposits. The bulk of the soil is rather poor, but still it is of better quality, on the whole, than in adjoining regions to the north, east, and south.[1]

In common with several of the African plateaux the Benguela Highland rises very precipitately from the sea. This is one of the most striking features of African geography. The steepness of the ascent forces the Benguela Railway to use a cog-line for a short distance. The village of Ngendo, described in the section dealing with the social structure, has an elevation of about 1,650 metres (5,400 feet) but is situated at only about 60 miles from the ocean.[2] That part of the intermediate zone which adjoins the Highland on the west consists of river valleys between mountain ridges and is well watered, but between that and the sea the country is very arid. This arid region is in reality a northern extension of the Kalahari, Omaheke, and Namieb deserts. Much of this arid stretch is exceedingly rough mountainous country. All along the African coast there is a coastal plain, but in the region under consideration it is very narrow. Plain and mountain are equally arid and this desert country generally has an elevation of less than 1,000 metres (about 3,280 feet). This intermediate zone is well known to the Ovimbundu and played an important role in the history of their commercial developments since they were obliged to cross it to reach the European stations on the coast.

Other adjoining regions have also been of importance to the Ovimbundu. It was from the region to the north between the Highland and the Kuanza River that some of the principal ruling families came. Across this same region the Ovimbundu had their first European contacts—with the Portuguese establishments on the Kuanza River. In the regions to the south live cattle-raising people whence the Ovimbundu got cattle, whether by raiding or by trading. East of the Kuanza River valley the elevation drops gradually toward the basins of the Congo and the Zambezi. When the slave- and rubber-trades led the Ovimbundu into this region

---

[1] i.e. of all adjoining regions only on the north-west are there valleys of superior soil. No complete survey of the soils of Angola has been made. Most books overrate the qualities of the soils of the colony.

[2] See *infra*, Chap. II.

HABITAT 3

they came to call it *ofeka yonjala*, 'The Hungry Country' or better 'The Country of Hunger', since it was without inhabitants and consequently without the possibility of purchasing provisions.[1] Much of the soil in all three of these adjoining regions is very sandy and comparatively unproductive.

Many rivers find in the Benguela Highland a great catchment basin. The two largest are the Kuanza (Kuanja) and the Cunene (Kunene), both flowing into the Atlantic. Between them are the Queve (Keve, also marked 'Cuvo'), the Balombo, and the Catumbela (Katombela), which also reach the ocean. A peculiar stream is the Cubango (Kuvango or Okavango), which rises near the source of the Cunene, and after becoming a great and free-flowing river loses itself in the Kalahari desert. Some authorities hold that through the Chobe swamp it maintains a seasonal connexion with the Zambezi. In this event the springs of the Benguela Highland feed the waters of both oceans. The part played by the Mbuluvulu plain in Bié (Viye) has often been noted by travellers and writers, for it drains into the Kuanza and also into the Cubango. As with most of the Southern Bantu,[2] rivers have had little directly to do with building the material culture of the Ovimbundu. Watersheds have furnished trade-routes, and fishing has become a side-line occupation for those who live conveniently near the streams. The rivers themselves, however, have always been of the greatest importance to the mass of the people who are dependent upon them for water, whether it comes in the form of rainfall or is taken more directly from the streams.

Climate

The regions under consideration in this study belong to the South Central African zone of summer rains. Coming on the monsoon from the Indian Ocean, the rains are precipitated by cold winds from the south-western antarctic current.[3] The Benguela Highland constitutes a distinct climatic zone, as the fact of the altitude would lead one to infer. The adjoining and coastal regions

[1] Cf. H. W. Nevinson, *A Modern Slavery*, chap. vi (New York: Harpers, 1906); also M. Burr, *A Fossicker in Angola* (London: Adelphi, 1933).

[2] A. J. H. Goodwin, 'Habitat', p. 34, in Schapera, *The Bantu-Speaking Tribes of South Africa* (London: Routledge, 1937).

[3] See C. E. P. Brooks and S. T. A. Mirrlees, *A Study of the Atmospheric Circulation over Tropical Africa*. Meteorological Office. Geophysical memoirs no. 55 (London: H.M.S.O., 1932).

4 UMBUNDU KINSHIP AND CHARACTER

are divided into several sub-zones. A glance at the map reproduced herewith will give a fairly good idea of the climatic regions. This map, apparently based entirely upon temperature averages and relative humidity in the localities for which such data are to be had,[1] is useful for an approximation of the principal zones and sub-zones. The names given to the several zones and sub-zones, however, are somewhat misleading, and the data on which the map is based are insufficient to assure accuracy.

The mean annual rainfall varies from 1,000 mm. (40 inches) to 1,500 mm. (60 inches) according to region[2] and locality. In the Highland the rains begin with a few showers during September and usually set in heavily during October. During November they increase in intensity and then suffer a break of from two to four weeks in December, January, or February. Then they continue until the end of April with sometimes a few showers in May. The heaviest fall is often in November or December, but sometimes in March. There seems to be some sort of cycle of morning, afternoon, and night rains, but I know of no study on this subject. Afternoon and evening rains are more common. Night rains seem to be more common towards the end of the season. Morning rains are least frequent. A day in which rain begins near (or before) daybreak and continues well into the day is called in Umbundu *ulembi*. On such a day agricultural work and travel are suspended. There is a custom that on such a day the first, after greeting, to speak the word *ulembi* can claim a gift from the one to whom he says it. The number of days in which work or travel may be suspended on account of rain is relatively not large. The working day is customarily from early morning until mid-afternoon. Men often continue field-work later in the day than do women. The connexion of the working day with weather conditions is readily seen.

Whether the heavier rainfall occurs in November–December or in February–March, it is in March and April that transportation is most likely to be interfered with. That is the time of swollen

---

[1] See Dr. José de Oliveira Ferreira Diniz, 'As características climatológicas de Angola' (*Boletim Geral das Colónias*, 1930, no. 62, 63, pp. 3–15).

[2] See maps and charts of rainfall in H. F. Shantz and C. F. Marbut, *The Vegetation and Soils of Africa* (New York, 1923); also some figures on rainfall and temperature in J. C. B. Statham, *Through Angola, a Coming Colony* (London, 1922) and in O. Letcher, *South Central Africa*, chap. xiii (Johannesburg, 1932). More detailed treatment of the whole subject is given by Marquardsen u. Stahl, *Angola*, chap. v (Berlin, 1928).

HABITAT 5

streams and washed-out bridges. Electrical discharges in connexion with storms are very common and often cause property and personal damage. In connexion with mean annual rainfall figures, the cycle of rainy and dry seasons is of importance. An annual rainfall of 50 or 60 inches may not seem unduly heavy save when it is realized that practically all of it falls during seven or even six months. It is this heavy seasonal rainfall which has made much of the Highland into what is known in South Africa as 'sour veld'—a type of pasturage relatively ill-suited for cattle raising.

The Benguela Highland is well within the tropics (between 11° and 14° 30' South), but the altitude and the effect of the antarctic current combine to produce a decidedly moderate climate. The variations of temperature, however, are quite unlike those found in most regions having a 'temperate' climate. The régime of the rains, tropical position, altitude, and other factors combine to produce a peculiar set of temperature variations. The annual variation of temperature is relatively slight, a day's maximum is seldom above 90° F., it may be as low as 60°, but the more usual maximum is around 80°. The minimum of 32° or even 30° is sometimes reached in the winter (about 20 May–20 July),[1] but it seldom goes quite so low. A day's minimum has been registered as high as 63°, more usually the minimum goes to about 40° or 45° in winter and between 50° and 55° during the rest of the year. Daily variations are important. Greatest variations occur in winter with differences of as much as 42° often registered. During the rest of the year there is a considerable range of daily variation—sometimes as much as 40° and sometimes as little as 7° with usual variation of from 20° to 30°.[2] On the days when it rains or remains cloudy all day the slightest variations are registered. Such days are cold and disagreeable and a grate fire is almost a necessity.[3]

Environmental Factors

Differences of characteristic vegetation as between the Highland and the lower zones are striking. The most characteristic feature

[1] Ice forms nearly every winter—at least in small pools along the streams, and sometimes more generally. There are Umbundu words for hoar-frost (*ocikokoto*) and for hail (*ocive*), but not for ice nor, of course, for snow.

[2] Figures compiled from records of the weather station of Currie Institute, Ndondi—elevation 1,800 metres (5,900 feet).

[3] Grate fires are agreeable mornings and evenings during ten to eleven months of the year. In the winter they are a real necessity.

6   UMBUNDU KINSHIP AND CHARACTER

of the lower zones between the plateau and the coast is the baobab (*Adansonia digitata*). Where these lower zones are well watered, especially along the streams, dense tropical forests are the rule.

The Highland proper until quite recent times was well covered with a good variety of trees. This gave a pleasing aspect not lost upon travellers. Commander Cameron, who crossed from Zanzibar to Benguela in 1875, was greatly impressed by the rustic beauty of the country-side:

As we went forward the scenery increased in beauty, and at last I was constrained to halt and surrender myself to the enjoyment of the view which lay before me.

I will content myself with asserting that nothing could be more lovely than this entrancing scene, this glimpse of Paradise. To describe it would be impossible. Neither poet, . . . nor painter . . . could by pen or pencil do full justice to the country of Bailundu.

In the foreground were glades in the woodland, varied with knolls crowned by groves of large, English-looking trees, sheltering villages with yellow thatched roofs; . . . plantations with the fresh green of young crops and the bright red of newly hoed ground in vivid contrast, and running streams flashing in the sunlight; while in the far distance were mountains of endless and pleasing variety of form, gradually fading away until they blended with the blue of the sky. . . .

That evening we camped in a wood, a clear space having literally to be cut out of the masses of sweet-scented creepers which festooned the trees.[1]

Some of this natural beauty still remains in Bailundu and other parts of the country, but much of it has gone, as grasslands have taken the place of forest and woodland. Native agriculture and the annual fires have caused much deforestation and much has also come about from the demands of European settlement and the needs of the railway, which up to the present time uses only wood for fuel. The question as to whether the rainfall has yet been much affected is often discussed.

The Benguela Highland is within the tropics and therefore subject to many tropical diseases. Malaria is prevalent owing to the presence of the *Anopheles* mosquito, one of the two essential hosts in the life-cycle of the malaria germ, man being the other. Infant mortality owing to malaria seems to be high among the Ovimbundu. It seems probable, however, that many of the

---

[1] V. L. Cameron, *Across Africa* (New York: Harpers, 1877), p. 410 f.

HABITAT

survivors acquire at least a limited immunity. Many observers have noted the comparative rarity among African natives of that chronic complication of malaria known as black-water fever, although it frequently attacks Europeans. Another disease, which has been found largely among Africans, and was at one time considered as a possible malarial complication, is now classified by most observers as a variety of scurvy. This disease is known to medical science by the Umbundu name of *onyalãi*.[1] Among other common diseases are yaws, tick fever, tropical ulcers, common sores, infections, intestinal parasites, and pneumonia. Others, such as bilharzia and leprosy, are less common but well known. The comparatively recent introduction and spread of pulmonary tuberculosis and the venereal diseases give cause for alarm.[2] Neither sleeping-sickness nor the cattle nagana are found. There are a number of cattle diseases, such as scab, carbuncle, quarter evil, pleuro-pneumonia, and gall-sickness.

Termites are a tropical pest present in large numbers. Their depredations require the periodical replacement of woodwork, unless made of the very few species of hard wood which they seem unable to attack. In common with all of South Africa, locusts are always to be found and they increase greatly at irregular intervals.

The *fauna* of the country under consideration includes nearly all of the commoner south and central African species. Some of the rarer and more localized species are not present, but on the other hand this is the home of certain rare species, as, for example, the giant sable.[3] The elephant, the rhinoceros, and other large species are no longer to be found in the Highland proper, but only in adjoining comparatively unpopulated regions to the west, south, and south-east. All game is comparatively scarce, which is not surprising considering that the Ovimbundu have possessed firearms for about 250 years, and considering also the extent of European settlement during the past fifty years.

[1] First reported by Dr. F. C. Wellman, a missionary physician who worked among the Ovimbundu.

[2] No figures on the incidence of any disease with reference to the population of the colony are available. Nor are population movements known, for previous to the first general census, which was taken in 1940, such figures on population as there were, were hardly more than guess-work. Results of this first census were published in 10 volumes, 1941–3. (Colónia de Angola, Repartição de Estatística Geral: *Censo Geral da População*. Luanda: Imprensa Nacional.)

[3] *Hippotragus niger varianii.*

8 UMBUNDU KINSHIP AND CHARACTER

The Highland is evidently well suited to the particular type of agriculture which the Ovimbundu carry on with upland fields for the principal crops of maize and beans growing in the rainy season and with river gardens for secondary cultures in the dry season. The purpose of the latter is to piece out between the principal harvests. The situation of the Highland across principal watersheds and therefore on convenient trade routes has been noted. This is doubtless one factor in commercial development among the Ovimbundu. Cattle-keeping with them seems to be largely a commercial development. While cattle may live on the Highland, they thrive better in the less well-watered lands to the west and the south where the neighbouring peoples are cattle-keepers.

Neighbouring peoples

The cattle-keeping peoples who live just west and south of the Ovimbundu are the Nganda, the Ndombe, the Hanya, the Cilenge, the Cipungu, the Muila, the Nyaneka, the Mulondo, and the Khumbi.[1] These peoples all seem to be related to each other and in some way to some, at least, of the Ovimbundu.[2] Still further south beyond these peoples are the Ambo and the Herero, also cattle-keepers. All these, together with the Ovimbundu, have been classified linguistically as making up the 'Western Province' of the Southern Bantu.[3] There are also a few Bushmen on the southern borders.

The peoples to the east and south-east of the Umbundu country are probably Lunda emigrants and so belong to the Congo group (Cokue and Songo) and to the Zambezi or Central group (Luimbi, Lucazi, Nyemba, Ngonzelo, &c.).[4] These people are lumped together by the Ovimbundu under the somewhat deprecatory term of *va Ngangela*.

The northern neighbours belong to the Western or Angola 'cluster' of the Congo group (Esela, Cipala, Lupolo, Ndongo or

---

[1] See C. Estermann, 'Notas Etnográficas sôbre os povos indígenas do Distrito da Huila' (*Boletim Geral das Colónias*, Fev. 1935, pp. 41–69). He groups some of these people together under the name 'Bangala' or 'Ovambangala'.

[2] Information from Nganda, Mulondo, Cilenge, and Ovimbundu individuals.

[3] See R. A. Dart, 'Racial Origins', p. 23, in Schapera, op. cit., 1937; C. M. Doke, *Bantu Linguistic Terminology* (London: Longmans, 1935); Sir H. H. Johnston, *Comparative Vocabulary of the Bantu and Semi-Bantu Languages*, 2 vols. (Oxford: Clarendon Press, 1919, 1922).

[4] Johnston, op. cit.

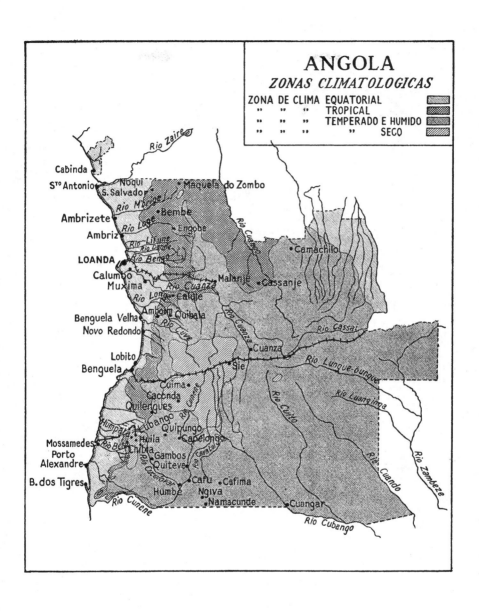

HABITAT 9

'Kimbundu', Imbangala, &c.). The Esele and the Mbuï, on the north-west, may belong to the Western Province but they have not yet been surely classified.[1]

These neighbouring peoples have been listed only as background for studying the Ovimbundu. Linguistically the Ovimbundu belong to South Africa even as their country geographically is a part of it. 'In respect of climate and vegetation Angola is essentially a borderland and may be regarded as the area of mergence of several distinct zones which attain their fullest development outside the Colony.'[2] Since the Benguela Highland comprises the north-western ridges of the South African sub-continental plateau, it is not surprising that its inhabitants should be the northernmost of the Southern Bantu.[3]

European Administration, Communications, Missions

As a Portuguese colony, Angola is governed under the Ministry of Colonies in Lisbon by a Governor-General whose residence is Luanda, the capital of the colony since 1576. For administrative purposes the colony is divided into five provinces, each with a governor in charge. These are divided into thirteen districts which in turn are divided into circumscriptions and these again into administrative areas. The country of the Ovimbundu is divided between the provinces of Benguela, Bié, and Huila in the districts of Benguela, Huambo, Cuanza-Sul, Bié, and Huila. 'Direct rule' is the method of administration and native political

---

[1] Ibid.

[2] Walter Fitzgerald, *Africa, a Social, Economic and Political Geography of its Major Regions* (London: Methuen, 1934).

[3] The general census of 1940 (*vide supra*, p. 7, note 2) showed the population as follows:

Whites	. .	44,083
Mixed	. .	28,035
Blacks	. .	3,665,829
Others	. .	63

3,738,010 (op. cit., vol. i, p. 78 f.)

Of the various tribal divisions, the Ovimbundu ('Mbundo') are listed with 1,331,087 (op. cit., vol. ix, p. 23). Owing to the mistaken inclusion of several small tribal groups, this number should probably be reduced by at least 150,000, but on the other hand there are without doubt more Ovimbundu than this last number who have emigrated to neighbouring colonies and to the Union of South Africa.

UMBUNDU KINSHIP AND CHARACTER

institutions or divisions have had little consideration in drawing administrative boundaries.

Systems of communications have been developed during the last forty years. The Benguela Railway, built by Sir Robert Williams and the Tanganyika Concessions, Ltd., was completed in 1931 from Lobito to Elisabethville in the Katanga region, where direct connexion is made with the South, Central, and East African systems of rail and water transport. This railway serves as the most direct outlet for the mines of the Congo and Northern Rhodesia. The great majority of native employees of the railway are Ovimbundu and it has also brought this people their first contact with the mines and with industrialized South Africa. Regular steamship connexion between Lobito and Europe includes Portuguese, Belgian, German, and British lines with occasional calls from American, Japanese, and Scandinavian ships.[1] Recent years have seen considerable extensions of telegraphic and radio service throughout the colony. Motor roads have been built extensively, especially on the plateau and along the watersheds. In addition there are many wagon-tracks for ox-wagons which were introduced by the voortrekkers almost seventy years ago. In many cases the routes followed are those first used by native caravans.

There are eleven missionary societies at work among the Ovimbundu: five Protestant and six Roman Catholic.[2] There is only one fully organized Umbundu Church. It includes the work of three Protestant societies. It is the work of this Church and of the Missions of the A.B.C.F.M.[3] and of the United Church of Canada with which the evaluations of this study are concerned. The Mission of the A.B.C.F.M. was founded in 1880, as the first Christian work undertaken among the Ovimbundu.[4]

---

[1] This was the situation in 1939. During the period of the war the Portuguese services were maintained, although with less regularity than before. The U.S. Maritime Commission maintained a cargo service. There were occasional calls by cargo vessels of various nationalities. The Belgian line is reopening its service (1946) and the Portuguese lines have acquired additional vessels.

[2] Pères du Saint-Esprit began work among the Ovimbundu in 1890; the Padres Seculares have been working in the towns; the Benedictines and several orders of nuns also have stations.

[3] American Board of Commissioners for Foreign Missions.

[4] The two missions mentioned conduct their work in most respects as a single mission. The other Protestant societies do not have very extensive work among the Ovimbundu.

HABITAT 11

Widespread use of Umbundu

While the home of the Ovimbundu is in the Benguela Highland, the use of their language is now more widespread. The va Nganda and the va Hanya are increasingly using Umbundu. The mixed populations at the coast towns of Lobito, Catumbela, and Benguela use it almost exclusively. It is also used in Novo Redondo, in Mossamedes, and along the Benguela Railway to the interior. There is a considerable *diaspora* of Ovimbundu at widely separated points owing to very recent movements.

For more extensive treatment of the various aspects of the problems touched upon in this introductory chapter, works listed in the bibliography may be consulted. A complete description of the habitat has not been attempted but only sufficient to provide the necessary background for the study as a whole.

BIBLIOGRAPHY

FOR PREFACE AND INTRODUCTION

Africa, Journal of the International African Institute, London. Quarterly.

ANDRADE, ALFREDO DE. *Relatorio da Viagem de exploração geográfica no districto de Benguella e Novo Redondo, 1898–1899* (Lisboa: Imprensa Nacional, 1902).

Angola, Delegação à Exposição Colonial Internacional de Paris, 1931 (Luanda).

ANGOLA, GOVÊRNO GERAL. *Documentário comemorativo . . . do 1° cruzeiro de estudantes das Colónias, à Metrópole* (Luanda: Imprensa Nacional, 1937).

Angola nos últimos anos, Alguns números acerca do desenvolvimento da Colónia de (Lisboa: Agência Geral das Colónias, 1936).

Angola: Relatório da Repartição dos Serviços de Cadastro e Colonização, 1933 (Lisboa: Agência Geral das Colónias, 1933).

Annuaire de Documentation Coloniale Comparée. Année 1936 (Bruxelles: Institut Colonial International).

ARNOT, F. S. *Garenganze* (New York: Revell, 1888).

—— *Bihe and Garenganze* (London, 1893).

Bantu Studies, a journal devoted to the scientific study of Bantu, Hottentot, and Bushmen (Johannesburg: The University of Witwatersrand Press. Quarterly).

BARKER, H. W. *The Story of Chissamba* (Toronto, 1904).

BARNS, T. ALEXANDER. *Angolan Sketches* (London: Methuen, 1928).

BAUM, H. *Kunene-Sambesi Expedition* (Berlin, 1903).

12 UMBUNDU KINSHIP AND CHARACTER

BEAVER, S. H., and STAMP, L. D. *A Regional Geography, Part II, Africa* (London: Longmans, 1934).

BEBIANO, JOSÉ BACELAR. *Geologia e Riqueza Mineral de Angola* (Lisboa: Museu Comercial, 1923).

BLEEK, D. F. 'Bushmen of Central Angola', *Bantu Studies*, vol. iii, 1928, pp. 105-25.

Boletim Geral das Colónias (Lisboa: Agência Geral das Colónias), Government publication, monthly. The following articles touch upon the subject of this chapter:—

1926, February:
Bebiano, José Bacelar: Subsídios para o estudo geológico e mineiro da Provincia de Angola.

1930, August-September:
Ferreira Diniz, Dr. José de Oliveira: As características climatológicas de Angola, pp. 3-15.

1935, February:
Estermann, Padre Carlos: Notas Etnográficas sôbre os povos indígenas do Distrito da Huila, pp. 41-69.

Melo, Geraldes C. de: A Protecção da Flora nas Colónias, pp. 3-15.
Monard, A. A.: Fauna Africana, pp. 36-43.

1936, January:
Schwalbach, Luiz: A Colonização perante os Climas Convencionais e os Climas Reais, pp. 3-11.

Carrisso, Dr. L. Wittnich: A História Natural e o Ultramar Português, pp. 60-84.

BORCHARDT, P. *Bibliographie de l'Angola, 1500-1910* (Bruxelles: Institut Solvay, 1912).

Breve Método da Língua Lunyaneka (Huila, Angola: Missão Católica, 1938).

British Museum. *Catalogue of African Plants collected by Frederick Welwitsch*, 4 vols., 7 parts (Pub. for the Museum, 1896-1902).

BROOKS, C. E. P., and MIRRLEES, S. T. A. *A Study of the Atmospheric Circulation over Tropical Africa*, Geophysical Memoirs, No. 55 (London: H.M.S.O., 1932).

BURR, MALCOLM. *A Fossicker in Angola* (London: Adelphi, 1933).

BUSSETO, MARIO. *Una Colónia di grande avvenire, l'Angola* (Milano, 1920).

CAMERON, COMMANDER V. L. *Across Africa. Vide* Chaps. 30-3 (New York: Harpers, 1877).

CAMPBELL, D. *In the Heart of Bantuland. Vide* Chaps. 1, 2 (Philadelphia: Lippincott, 1922).

Colónia de Angola, Repartição de Estatística Geral: *Censo Geral da População*, 10 vols., 1941-3 (Luanda: Imprensa Nacional).

COOK, P. A. W. *The Education of a South African Tribe* (Cape Town: Juta, 1934).

CORDEIRO, LUCIANO. *L'Hydrographie Africaine.*

CUNNINGHAME, CAPT. BOYD A. 'A Pioneer Journey in Angola', *Geog. Jour.*, vol. xxiv, pp. 152-68 (London, 1924).

BIBLIOGRAPHY TO PREFACE AND INTRODUCTION 13

CURRIE, W. T. 'Explorations in West Central Africa', *Missionary Herald*, August 1887.

DART, R. A. 'Racial Origins', in Schapera, *The Bantu-Speaking Tribes of South Africa* (London: Routledge, 1937).
DAYE, PIERRE. *Congo et Angola* (Bruxelles: La Renaissance du Livre, 1929).
DOKE, C. M. *Bantu Linguistic Terminology* (London: Longmans, 1935).
—— 'Language', in Schapera, 1937.
—— *Bantu: Modern Grammatical, Phonetical and Lexicographical Studies since 1860* (London: International African Inst., 1945).
DRIBERG, J. H. *The Savage as He Really Is* (London: Routledge, 1929).
DU TOIT, ALEXANDER L. *Geology of South Africa* (London, 1926).

Encyclopedia Britannica, 14th Edition. Article on 'Africa'.
—— Article on 'Angola'.

FERREIRA DINIZ, Dr. J. DE O. *Populações indígenas de Angola* (Coimbra: Typ. da Univ., 1918).
—— 'Une Étude de l'Ethnographie d'Angola', *Anthropos*, 1925, pp. 321–31. (Based on the study listed above, but neither is very reliable.)
—— *Une Étude de l'ethnographie d'Angola*. Réponse au questionário etnográfico. 754 pp. (Lisboa, 1926).
—— 'Contribuição para o estudo da demografia indígena de Angola', *Boletim de Antropologia*, vol. 4, 1929.
FITZGERALD, WALTER. *Africa, a Social, Economic and Political Geography of its Major Regions* (London: Methuen, 1934).

GIBSON, A. G. S. *Between Capetown and Loanda* (London: Wells Gardner, 1905).
GOODWIN, A. J. H. 'Habitat', in Schapera, 1937.
Great Britain, Department of Overseas Trade. *Economic Conditions in Angola* (London: H.M.S.O., 1929).
—— Foreign Office, Historical section, 1920. Peace Handbooks no. 120, *Angola* (London: H.M.S.O.).
GREGORY, J. W. *Contributions to the Geology of Benguela* (Edinburgh: Trans. R. S., 1915).

HAHN, C. L., *et al. The Native Tribes of South West Africa* (Cape Town: Cape Times, 1928).
HAILEY, LORD. *An African Survey* (London: O.U.P., 1938).

JENSEN, O. *Reisen und Forschungen in Angola* (Berlin, 1936).
JOHNSTON, SIR H. H. 'On the Races of the Congo and the Portuguese Colonies in Western Africa', *Journ. Anthr. Inst.*, vol. xiii, 1883.
—— *A Comparative Vocabulary of the Bantu and Semi-Bantu Languages*, 2 vols. (Oxford: Clarendon Press, 1919–22).
—— *The Opening up of Africa* (New York: Holt, n.d.).

14 UMBUNDU KINSHIP AND CHARACTER

LETCHER, O. *South Central Africa.* An Outline of the History, Geography, Commerce, and Transportation Systems of the Congo–Zambesi Watershed, with special reference to the Mineral Industry (Johannesburg: African Publications, 1932).
LIMA VIDAL, Dom J. E. DE. *Por Terras de Angola* (Coimbra, 1916).

MARQUARDSEN, HUGO, und STAHL, A. *Angola* (Berlin: Reimer, 1928).
MEINHOF, CARL. *An Introduction to the Phonology of the Bantu Languages.* Tr. N. J. van Warmelo: revised and enlarged with the help of the author and Dr. A. Werner (Berlin: Reimer, 1932).
Mission of the A.B.C.F.M. to West Central Africa (pamphlet) (Boston, 1882).
MONARD, A. 'Voyage de la mission scientifique suisse en Angola', *Soc. Neuchâteloise de géographie, Bulletin*, 1930, tome 39, pp. 1–99.
MONTEIRO, J. J. *Angola and the River Congo*, 2 vols. (London: Macmillan, 1875).
MOUTA, F. (ed.). *Generalidades sôbre Angola* (Luanda: Imp. Nacional, 1935).
—— et O'DONNELL, H. *Carte Géologique de l'Angola*, Notice Explicative (Lisboa: Ministério das Colónias, 1933).

O Mundo Português (Lisboa: Agência Geral das Colónias). Govt., publ. monthly.

NASCIMENTO, J. PEREIRA DO. *A colonização do planalto de Benguela* (Lisboa, 1913).
NEVINSON, H. W. *A Modern Slavery* (New York: Harpers, 1906).
NORTON DE MATOS, GEN. J. J. R. *A Província de Angola* (Pôrto, 1926).

PORTUGAL, Commissão de cartografia das colónias. *Valores normais dos principais elementos meteorológicos dos observatórios e postos das colónias* (Coimbra: Imprensa da Universidade, 1933).
—— —— *Atlas colonial português* (ibid., n.d.).
A Practical Orthography of African Languages (London: International Institute of African Languages and Cultures, 1930).

RAHIR, M. 'A propos de la carte de Congo et de l'Angola', *Soc. Royal Belge de Géographie, An. 49*, pp. 234–8, 1925.
Report of the Deputation to the West Central Africa Mission, Topography and Resources, pp. 7–11 (Boston: A.B.C.F.M., 1911).
Revista Portugueza Colonial e Maritima (Lisboa: 1897–9).
ROHAN-CHABOT, J. DE. 'Notes sur l'Angola' (Paris: *La Géographie*, t. 35, pp. 1–26, 1921).

SCHACHTZABEL, ALFRED. *Im Hochland von Angola* (Dresden, 1923).
SCHAPERA, I. *Select Bibliography of South African Native Life and Problems* (London: O.U.P., 1941).

BIBLIOGRAPHY TO PREFACE AND INTRODUCTION 15

SCHATTEBURG, H. Fr. *Angola–Westafrika von Heute!* Gesichtspunkte afrikanisch-kolonialen Aufbaues: Beilage:Sprachschatz der 'Umbundu' Eingeborenen–Hauptverkehrssprache in Angola! (Munich: Datterer, 1933). (A handbook of Angola for prospective colonists with a separate language guide which quite outdoes the familiar type of 'Spanish at a glance'. In thirty pages it conveniently (?) reduces the Umbundu language to a sort of 'Kitchen Kaffir'. Little attention is paid to the transcription or pronunciation and none at all to the grammar.)

SELIGMAN, C. G. *Races of Africa* (London: Butterworth, 1930).

SHANTZ, H. L., and MARBUT, C. F. *The Vegetation and Soils of Africa* (New York: American Geographical Society, 1923).

SMITH, E. W. *Africa: What do we know of it?* (London: Royal Anthropological Institute, 1935).

Sociedade de Geografia de Lisboa, *Boletim*, monthly. Note the following articles:—

1885–6 (Series 5 and 6):
Novas Jornadas de Silva Porto, pp. 3 ff.

1894 (Series 14):
Expedição ao Bié, Relatorio . . . do Maj. A. de Paiva, pp. 5 ff.

1896 (Series 16):
Lecomte, Padre E.: Planalto do Sul, Missões portuguezas, pp. 223 ff.

1915 (Series 35):
Nascimento, J. P. do: La colonisation du plateau sud d'Angola, pp. 253–351.

1916 (Series 36):
Mello e Atayde, Luiz de: O perigo do despovoamento de Angola, pp. 227 ff.

1921–2 (Series 39–40):
Angola, Temperaturas, Quadro de Synthese, p. 166.

1923 (Series 41):
Colónias portuguesas, Elementos para a sua climatologia, p. 11.
Notas sôbre os rios Cubango e Cunene, p. 112.

1925–6 (Series 43–4):
Roque, Antonio Bernardino: Contribuição para o estudo do clima do planalto de Angola sob o ponto de vista meteorológico e médico.

1929 (Series 47):
Caminho de Ferro de Benguela (several articles on the Benguela Railway).

STATHAM, J. C. B. *Through Angola, a Coming Colony* (London: Blackwoods, 1922).

TARUFFI, DINO. *L'Antiplano di Benguela (Angola) ed il suo avvenire agricolo.* Relazioni e monografie agrario-coloniali (Florence, 1916).

TUCKER, JOHN T. *Drums in the Darkness* (Toronto and New York: Doran, 1927).

—— *Angola, The Land of the Blacksmith Prince* (London: World Dominion, 1933).

16 UMBUNDU KINSHIP AND CHARACTER

TYRELL, S. W. *A Contribution to the Petrography of Benguella* (Trans. R.S. of Edinburgh, 1915).

VALDEZ TOMAZ DOS SANTOS, A. C. *Angola, Coração do Império* (Lisboa: Agência Geral das Colónias, 1945).

VARIAN, H. F. 'The Geography of the Benguela Railway', *Geog. Journal*, London, vol. lxxviii, pp. 497–523.

VEDDER, Dr. H. *South West Africa in Early Times*, tr. and ed., Dr. C. G. Hall (London: O.U.P., 1938).

WHITTLESLY, D. S. 'Geographic Provinces of Angola', *Geog. Review*, New York, vol. xiv, pp. 113–26, 1924.

PLATE I

Photo. R. S. Webb
a. Rock outcrop beside the Keve River

Photo. M. W. Ennis
b. Rapids of the Kuvale River (Katombela system)

PLATE II

Photo. D. G. Ridout

a. Court procedure: the King and his counsellors (Bailundu)

b. Mortuary rites at Ngendo

PART ONE

SOCIAL STRUCTURE

The object of Part One is (1) to describe the present social structure of the Ovimbundu, and (2) to suggest significant elements that this social structure has or may have for the programme of Christian missions among this people.

CHAPTER II

POLITICAL AND SOCIAL LIFE

HAD my historical survey revealed a detailed description of Umbundu social structure made at some former time, it would also be useful to make comparisons with the present state of affairs. Since there is no such witness out of the past, it is only possible to describe and analyse that which at present exists. For this purpose some excerpts from Umbundu narratives are presented and references made to certain folk-tales and proverbs. The basis of the analysis and description rests more especially, however, upon notes and impressions gathered in field-work over a period of years and upon a considerable number of genealogical tables and schedules of marriage arrangements.[1] These latter are referred to here only to a certain extent. I hope to treat these more fully later. The subject of marriage properly belongs to the field of social structure, but because of its importance I hope to devote a chapter to it. Only certain of the genealogical tables are presented fully and in their several aspects, while the others have served as basis and background for the whole of this part of the study.

The most significant historical allusion to the social structure of the Ovimbundu which I have found was an observation of Pinheiro de Lacerda about 1790. 'These are they of the Highlands who are made up of two "systems" the one call themselves "Quimbundos" (i.e. Ovimbundu), (these do not eat human flesh): the others are called "Quimbangalas" (i.e. the royal households of Imbangala stock), who eat it, and when they make their sacrifice, at which all together attend, then all eat the "Makongo".'[2]

[1] I have 192 of the former and 75 of the latter.
[2] *Annaes Maritimos e Coloniaes*, 5a Ser., p. 488.

C

18 UMBUNDU KINSHIP AND CHARACTER

Evidently royal persons could then be easily distinguished from the commoners.

The question naturally arises how far may a similar distinction be observed at the present time. The genealogical tables presented may answer the question. It may be seen that intermarriage of commoners and royalty has proceeded to such a degree that the differences have been greatly dimmed, if not quite erased. Furthermore, the loss of the political power which the royal families formerly held has levelled down distinctions until they have largely lost their meaning. This loss again has hastened the process of intermarriage with commoners. While there are some distinctive practices which persist, they may now pertain to or be practised by certain members of a family only, or in some instances, and not in others. These refer especially to inheritance and to the naming of children.

By 'social structure' is meant the more or less permanent framework of relationships between members of a community which manifests itself in an ordered group-life, with reciprocal rights and duties, privileges and obligations, of members, determining behaviour-patterns . . . and moulding the feelings, thoughts, and conduct of members according to these patterns, so that it is only in and through them that the individual can achieve his personal self-realization and participate in the satisfactions offered by the life of his community.

This framework of social organization, or social structure, is permanent compared with the stream of human lives that, in the succession of the generations, flows through it. Each new generation finds it there, as an inheritance from untold generations of his predecessors. Yet the framework of social structure is not absolutely rigid or fixed for all time, but is itself a thing of growth, capable of variation in detail, sometimes giving birth to new developments, at other times undergoing disintegration and decay.[1]

The genealogical tables which I have collected are fairly representative of the major divisions or 'tribes' of the Ovimbundu. The only 'tribes' not represented are those of the border regions of Namba, Sanga, Cikomba, and Kalukembe, none of which save the last are numerically important. These border groups themselves offer an interesting field of study and particularly in that they may provide cultural and linguistic bridges between the

---

[1] A. W. Hoernlé in Schapera, *The Bantu-Speaking Tribes of South Africa* (London: Routledge, 1937), p. 67 f.

POLITICAL AND SOCIAL LIFE 19

Ovimbundu and their neighbours. I have no tables representative of the Umbundu-speaking *diaspora* at the coast and in other outlying regions. There is an interesting and significant article in *Africa*[1] on those of these *diaspora* which are settled in the Mossamedes–Lubango area. The author has done all that could be expected within the limits of an article necessarily short, and it is to be hoped that subsequent writings may clear up matters left in doubt, especially with regard to the present social structure of the groups described.[2]

The social structure described in this chapter is that of the main body of the Ovimbundu. I may say that from observations and from a study of the genealogical tables collected, I have concluded that the structure of kinship and of social life is fairly homogeneous throughout the several tribes.

The Tribe

A complete enumeration of the Umbundu-speaking tribes or kingdoms with descriptions of their reciprocal relations is included in Chapter XII. Almost half of the twenty-two kingdoms were generally tributaries of one of the larger or more powerful kings, so that for practical purposes the Ovimbundu may be divided into eight or ten tribal groups. Although more than half of the Umbundu kingdoms may be said to be feudatories of the larger ones, it is nevertheless true that each of them had its own separate

---

[1] C. Estermann, 'Coutumes des Mbali du Sud d'Angola', *Africa*, Jan. 1939, pp. 74–86. The author states that their language is Kimbundu (of Luanda-Malange), but the examples which he gives show that although there are words borrowed from Kimbundu, from Portuguese, and from other sources, the structure both of verbs and of nouns and the method of 'Bantuization' of Portuguese words belong to Umbundu. These people may declare their language to be 'Kimbundu' in imitation of the European usage. So did the native 'Mohongo' taken to Paris by the Mission Rohan-Chabot (*Angola et Rhodesie*, Paris, 1914). I have personally ascertained that Umbundu is commonly spoken in Mossamedes and may also say that the samples of the language given in this article show it to be much the same as that spoken in the cities of Benguela, Lobito, &c. It would be better if an orthography more nearly like that recommended by the International African Institute were used. The term 'Mbali' (va Mbali, Mambari, Ovimbali) is an Umbundu term used for nearly one hundred years to designate those who imitate the Europeans or who live at or near the European towns which are collectively designated by the cognate term—*Lupali*. (For 'Mambari', &c., *vide* Livingstone, *Missionary Travels and Researches in South Africa*, pp. 91 f., 271, 384, &c.)

[2] e.g., who is the '*tante* de la jeune mariée ou la "marraine" des noces'? (op. cit., p. 78).

20 UMBUNDU KINSHIP AND CHARACTER

life and each could be taken as a unit complete in itself. Individual studies and comparisons of one with another would provide much valuable material. Familiarity with individuals and groups belonging to all the major tribal groups, and study of their folk-lore and customs has led me to conclude that as in language, so in social structure and in culture, the differences are of small account. In offering illustrative material, I shall give its tribal source.

The King

To describe the royal office and functions it would be necessary to use the past tense. That reason, along with others, leads me to exclude this subject from the present study. Effective European occupation of the country and government by direct rule[1] have atrophied the royal office among the Ovimbundu until to-day kings survive as hardly more than living museum pieces. This being the case, I shall only enumerate the royal functions, very briefly characterize them, and pass on to describe other and living parts of the Umbundu social organism.

The principal functions of the royal office were:

1. *Religious.* The spirits of the king's ancestors were the principal national deities. The king was not only high priest but also the visible vice-regent and incarnation of the spirits. The sacrifices at the royal shrine, *kakokoto* (literally, at the skulls), the place of the royal skulls, were for the nation in order:

(*a*) *To control the elements*, i.e. to ensure a sufficient supply of rain and avoid the dangers caused by hail, by lightning, &c. Also to control fire by providing a new fire properly (ceremonially) kindled from which everyone took his fire. A king's reign was spoken of as 'during the Water of Lord So-and-so' (*Kovava a Ñalã Ngandi*), or 'during the Fire of Lord So-and-so' (*Kondalu ya Ñalã Ngandi*).

(*b*) *To ensure fertility*, toward which desideratum the royal marriage had great influence. The queen's special province was agriculture and her kitchen was sanctified by human sacrifice to guarantee the national food supply. Ceremonially treated seed was distributed to be mixed with the seed of each granary.

---

[1] 'Direct rule' is applied in most parts of Africa where European settlement is the predominant consideration and also where centralized government is the ideal. 'Indirect rule' is best illustrated in the Gold Coast, Nigeria, Uganda, and Tanganyika Territory.

POLITICAL AND SOCIAL LIFE

(c) *In hunting*, deities other than the king's ancestors were invoked, especially *Hũvĩ*, the hunters' god, and *Kuanja*, a goddess, both of which had their own shrines and priests. These may have been connected with the country or with its earlier inhabitants (the kings being recognized as late comers). At the inaugural hunt the offices were assigned. The king's character was supposedly revealed by the sex of the animal killed at this hunt: 'If the duiker[1] is a female, then it is good indeed, but if a male, then the king is a real person but he habitually will become angry to excess' (*Nda ombambi yaco omange ciwa muēlē, puaĩ nda ulume, Soma omunu puaĩ o tema tema enene*).

2. *To represent the nation in its external relations*, i.e. (*a*) *To make agreements with other kings to promote trade*, and (*b*) *To make war on other peoples* in order to provide his court with tribute and his warriors with plunder. The war leader (*Kesongo*) had his own residence and establishment entirely separate from that of the king, whom he must not meet face to face except on certain state occasions. In Bailundu he, with certain other officials, was of the stock of the slaves of the state (*ovinduli viosoma*) who came from Luandu in the Songo country. Each king must inaugurate his reign with a war, during or after which he must ceremonially 'eat the old one' (*oku lia ekongo*)—a feast consisting of the flesh of a specially fattened slave cooked with the flesh of the principal animals commonly eaten.

3. *To dispense justice.* In point of time consumed, this question was very important, for it occupied much of the time of both rulers and ruled. Good evidence of this is in the number of proverbs used at court, second only in number to those used for the education of the young. The king's court (*olusenje*) was the supreme court of the nation where cases were continually heard and 'fines eaten' (*oku lia ovimbu*). Cases might be settled either by ordeal or by decision of the king, and there was therefore room for appeal and re-trial. The king's word, however, was final, as the proverb has it: *O popia onganji, o mãlãpo osoma.* (The advocate speaks, the king finishes [decides].) The king was not generally arbitrary in his decisions but was bound not only by the customs of his people, but also by the desires of his councillors. Among the legitimate kings of the Ovimbundu there were comparatively few of the revolting and wholesale punishments which were so

---

[1] The duiker, *ombambi* (*Silvicapra grimmii leucoprosopus*).

22   UMBUNDU KINSHIP AND CHARACTER

common at African courts. A few Umbundu rulers carried on such practices, and especially certain self-constituted robber-barons such as Samakaka, who left Viye after the military occupation and established himself first in Bimbe (Mbimbi), later in Huambo (Wambu), and then at Elende, until taken by the Portuguese authorities in 1903.

4. In order to protect himself and the nation, *the king had resort to magical means*, some of which would be accounted witchcraft or murder if practised without authority. Such were the ritual murders of *Katõkõlã* (The Strangler), *Oku ipa ukaĩ watimba avali* (killing the woman of two bodies, i.e. pregnant), of the children whose lives were required for building and furnishing the queen's kitchen, &c.

5. In order properly to carry out the functions of his office, *the king made much use of divination*, for which purpose he had his own diviner (*Citue cosoma*), who was of the blood royal. He also called in or consulted diviners of many regions and of many types, one of the commonest of which was the 'Diviner of the Basket' (*Ocimbanda congombo*).[1]

The king was a divine representative and a divine incarnation, but the mode of his succession reveals that he was also a demo-cratically chosen leader. Note has been made of the fact that the royal succession is in the male line, sometimes from father to son, but more often from elder to younger brother, to brother's son, or to one even more distantly related. The election is made by the councillors whose duty it is, ordinarily before the old king's death is announced, but these same councillors may depose an unpopular king. There have been many revolutions and *coups d'état*. This fact was noted by several early observers, among whom I cite one who wrote in 1837:

The government of 'Bailundo' is democratic. These heathen mix with the infamous humiliations of the orientals, the unbridled coarse-ness of the English people at election times in England. The kings defer to and flatter their counsellors; these are they who elevate a king to the throne and also who cast him down.[2]

---

[1] A rather cursory description of divination as practised by this type of diviner was given by Hambly, op. cit., pp. 274–6. For a fuller treatment, *vide* L. S. Tucker, 'The Divining Basket of the Ovimbundu', *J.R.A.I.* (London), 1940, vol. lxx, pp. 171–201.

[2] C. de Almeida Sandoval in *Annaes do Cons. Ultr.*, Ser. I, p. 519. The refer-ence to English elections reminds one of Dickens. See also P. M. Pinheiro de

POLITICAL AND SOCIAL LIFE

This so-called democratic streak is also abundantly attested by folk-tales which give incidental and intimate pictures of petty details in the life of kings. There is one in which a king gives instructions for caring for his field while he is absent on a war party; another which tells of a fine levied on a man who while hiding up a tree accidentally urinated on a king; another, of a king who in a time of hunger himself climbed a tree for the *epõlē* fruit and nearly starved when the prop by which he had climbed was taken away. Recent arrivals in Africa upon meeting some king just coming up from work in his fields may at first conclude, as did I, that this extreme of 'democracy' is due to the low estate to which royalty has fallen in these latter days, but these historical and legendary references show that this 'democracy', such as it is, is not a degeneration but an essential part of the picture.

With this I shall have to leave royalty. I trust that enough of the picture has been given, and enough also to show what inherent interest would lie in a study of such a Divine King who is at the same time a sort of 'democratic' leader. Should 'indirect rule' ever come to this part of Africa, a resurrection of the royal office would be the order of the day as has been the case in Tanganyika Territory and in the Belgian Congo. For this additional reason an early and a thorough treatment of the subject is to be desired.

Sub-Tribes

Each of the kings of the Ovimbundu was an overlord, for the tribe was made up of a number of sub-tribes called *atumbu* (plural), a word derived from the verb *oku tumbulula*, to transplant. Some of these princes, whether of the blood-royal or not, themselves established dynasties, while others were newly appointed and promoted from time to time. Some of the *atumbu* were ruled by court officials not of royal birth, while others belonged to separate dynasties some of which were natives of the respective regions, at least more anciently native than was the paramount royal family. The kingdom of Bailundu had about 200 *atumbu*, each of which had from 3 to 300 villages or more, and a number of the larger *atumbu* were themselves made up of several smaller

Lacerda in *Annaes Mar. e Col.*, 5 Ser., p. 488 f.; L. Magyar, *Reisen in Süd-Afrika* (tr. Hunfalvy, Pesth, 1859), p. 278.

24 UMBUNDU KINSHIP AND CHARACTER

ones. This situation was reported by Magyar, when he wrote, 'Quibanda (should be Civanda) to the east has 500 villages. The Chief has great power. He sends tribute every year to the king of Bailundu but is himself fully independent.'[1] Magyar described about 15 *atumbu* or *'ovikandscho'*,[2] as he called them, of Bailundu. He estimated the population of Bailundu at 450,000, and for all the kingdoms of the Ovimbundu 1,200,000,[3] figures which are probably not very different from present-day facts. The report and description of the 'Capitania de Benguella' in 1799 said that the king of Bailundu dominated 2,056 villages; the king of Viye, 886; and the king of Ngalangi, 900; and listed their 'feudos' respectively as 82, 54, and 78.[4] My list of the Ngalangi *atumbu* shows 112. In Bailundu about 20 *atumbu* were ruled by members of the royal family, including heirs apparent or expectant, and the queen (*Inakulu*), who also had her own establishment.[5] About 20 were ruled by other court officials.

Most of these *atumbu* are still recognized as such or as *olombala*.[6] Their decay has not been as great as that of the *ombala*[6] of their liege lord, for they still fulfil certain functions in native life. They have also been given new functions by the administrative authorities. The minor chiefs as well as village headmen are all required to assist in assessing and collecting the native tax, and also in recruiting labour for government works and for contracts. In some areas they receive in return the remission of their own taxes. In some areas they are required to wear uniforms. On the dancing floors of most of these minor *olombala* courts are still held, justice determined, and (to a limited extent) fines 'eaten'. Such judgements are not officially recognized or allowed by the European authorities. The African, however, often finds that European courts do not meet his needs or accord with his concepts of justice.

---

[1] Magyar, op. cit., p. 389.

[2] Umbundu *ovikanjo* (plural), 'branches', a term which through commercial or European influence is applied to the *atumbu*.

[3] For these figures and for descriptions of the several kingdoms, see Magyar, op. cit., chap. ix.

[4] *Annaes Mar. e Col.*, 4a Ser., pp. 155 ff.

[5] Magyar, op. cit., p. 390.

[6] *Olombala*, plural of *ombala*, a capital village or chief's residence.

POLITICAL AND SOCIAL LIFE

The Village

Among the Ovimbundu the outstanding social and political unit at the present time is the village (*imbo*, plural *ovaimbo*). The village may consist of from 5 to 500 households,[1] the heads of which are in the great majority of cases related to each other in the male line. Each village has a headman or elder (*sekulu*, literally 'grandfather' or 'elder father') who is literally, according to Umbundu kinship usage, the patriarch of the villagers. He was formerly responsible for his village to the sub-chief, and through him to the king. At the present time, the administrative authorities hold the village headmen responsible for matters relating to taxes, labour recruiting, &c. The present decay of this office and of village life varies very greatly from region to region. Nearly everywhere matters of purely local concern are not directly interfered with, and the headman continues his patriarchal government, assisted by a council of all (male) householders.

Ngendo, a typical village. The village of Ngendo lies at about 14° 40' east, 11° 40' south, about thirty-five miles south-west of the Keve, where that river crosses the fifteenth parallel, and about sixty miles in a direct line from the Atlantic Ocean. Its altitude is about 1,650 metres, and the ground on which it is built slopes down to a small stream of the Keve system. Directly across the stream to the north rises the granite outcrop on which may be seen the ruined fortress of Usengo. Ngendo belongs to the tribe of Kasongi, *etumbu* of Ekongo. It is about fifteen miles north-west of the administrative post of Cassongue and about two miles from the motor road which connects that post and points farther inland with the district capital and port of Novo Redondo.

The most striking feature of this village is the fact that it consists of four smaller units or wards (*ovitawila*, plural), each of which appears to be quite self-contained. The four together make up the village (*imbo*), which name is also applied to either of the two larger units by themselves. Each unit has its own elder, but

---

[1] Most, but not all, of the larger villages are *olombala* (q.v., *supra*), but even these are not as large now as they formerly were. In 1850 the *ombala* of Bailundu was said to have 5,000 inhabitants (Magyar, op. cit.). At the present time there is probably no village with more than 3,000 inhabitants, and few of that size. The tendency seems to be toward smaller villages, and there is even some movement toward isolated households and farmsteads after the fashion of so many of the Southern Bantu.

26 UMBUNDU KINSHIP AND CHARACTER

they recognize Sekulu Sikīlīlē, the elder of the largest unit, as the village headman. Only in his village is there a dancing floor (*ocīlã*),[1] which is the centre of village life, social, legal, and recreational. As the name indicates, it is first and foremost a place for recreation, but here also religious functions are held since they involve so much dancing and drinking, and here formal cases are tried. The *ocīlã* is the heart of the village.

The Men's Club-House. Ngendo does not have that other important Umbundu institution, the Men's Club House (*onjango*).[2] The *onjango* is, or was, hardly less important than the *ocīlã*. Perhaps before it fell to its present state of disuse, its place was of even greater importance, for in the *onjango* all the men, youths, and boys gathered day by day for the evening meal. From all the kitchens came baskets of stiff corn porridge (*iputa*), and dishes of relish (*ombelela*)[3] which all shared, from the most honoured guest or the village elders, down to the naked, ash-whitened little boys just old enough (say from seven or eight years) to leave the kitchens to their mothers and sisters. In the *onjango* guests were entertained, judicial cases of lesser import were settled, the day's work and gossip discussed, and youth was educated by precept and example in nearly everything from traditional history to etiquette. The *onjango* was dining-room, living-room, court, school, hotel, and club, all in one. For some of the Ovimbundu it continues to function. Upon inquiry I found that in all Kasonge there were hardly ten villages where the *onjango* existed and retained its former functions. The reasons which my informants assigned are that the demands for road work (in the immediate region), for contract labour (involving absences of from six months to two years), and the difficulty of securing tax-money, did not leave the leisure required for the common meal in the *onjango*. When I made wider inquiries as to localities where the *onjango* now exists and retains its former functions, it seems that this institution is widely decadent. According to my information, the regions where it continues to function are chiefly in Ngalangi, in Viye, and

---

[1] *Ocīlã* comes from the verb *oku cīlã*, to dance.

[2] *Onjango* has been traced to the verb *oku vangula*, to converse, but I am doubtful of this derivation. It has been called 'The Palaver House', but this is an evident misnomer, for the *onjango* is much more than that.

[3] *Ombelela* is a word to cover any dish which may be eaten with the porridge staple. It may be meat, beans, mushrooms, or greens, and is preferred with gravy into which pieces of the stiff porridge may be dipped (*oku miña*).

POLITICAL AND SOCIAL LIFE

perhaps in Ndulu. In Ngendo the Men's Club had taken over the rocks just behind the headman's household for its meeting-place, but the meetings were only occasional and there was no common meal.

The Village Plan

To speak of the plan of an Umbundu village may seem a contradiction in terms, so haphazard seems the relation of houses, gardens, &c., to each other. Some houses are circular, but the majority are more nearly rectangular in shape. There is a palisade of hardwood sticks surrounding all the village except that side of the headman's household which is adjacent to the rocks used for a club-house. The headman had not bothered to keep up his own part of the fence since his only garden was a small tobacco plot fenced in by itself. The village is itself divided up by the palisades which shut off one compound from another, each compound containing the houses of from one to three households. Between the palisades are paths which lead on to the dancing floor and out of the village. In the village of Sekulu Sikĩlĩlĕ there were twenty-five households with thirty-two houses in all. Each house (*onjo*) had its own granary (*osila*), and small chicken-coop built on stilts, and of all the houses only six had separate kitchens (*ociwo*). Nearly every household had separate pens for the pigs, goats, and sheep for the night. At one side of the headman's compound there was a common corral for the nine cattle which the villagers owned. Only the headman had a spirit-hut (*etambo*), used also for a storehouse, for entertaining a guest, and for his own bedroom should he sleep apart from his wives. Within the several compounds were small gardens of tobacco and of maize and beans, and just outside the village were two separate tobacco gardens. Just a few paces to the west was a small patch of wheat belonging to a man in the smallest ward. There was one household of two houses quite outside the palisades appropriately belonging to a man named *Kulika* (meaning 'Being-alone'). The water-holes and pounding rocks where meal was ground were between the several units of the village and were used in common. The fields were off to the east at from thirty minutes' to an hour's walk. The two smaller wards of Ciyanda and Kanjengo were so small that they were like two or three compounds by themselves. The former had six households with eight houses, and the latter

28 UMBUNDU KINSHIP AND CHARACTER

four households with six houses. The school village had been laid out in rectangular fashion without any palisade and with eucalyptus trees planted around the sides. The school was at the centre and the elder's house at the upper corner. These two larger buildings and one other were built of adobe, while the rest of the twelve houses were of wattle and daub, identical with those in the other wards except that all were rectangular. There were a few very small gardens watered by an irrigation ditch. The people of this village had river gardens, and their fields were mostly to the south between the village and the highway. Just to the east of the main village and beside one of the water-holes, a Roman Catholic catechist had established himself, but as yet he had neither village nor school.

The Villagers

Turning now to the people living in this village, it was interesting to find that all save the households of two former slaves and the Roman Catholic catechist, were related to each other, either by blood or by marriage. Sekulu Cipange of Ciyanda summed the matter up when he said, 'Likuluta Samikanjo (the Protestant elder) is my younger brother (*manjange*), for in our Umbundu country (we) people do not build together (i.e. in the same village) unless we are blood relatives.' In order to determine the exact relationships and other facts regarding the demography of this village, I took the names of all householders and their wives, and inquired their relationships to the elders of the respective wards. This information was supplied by Njomba, a son of Sekulu Sikīlīlẽ, and by Sekulu Likuluta Samikanjo. In addition to those of the four elders, there were twenty-four households. The relationship of each of the householders to their respective elders may be summarized as follows:

A. *Paternal relatives*

In Sikīlīlẽ's village	.	.	.	.	.	.	21
,, Ciyanda .	.	.	.	.	.	.	1
,, Kanjengo's ward	.	.	.	.	.	.	2
,, School village .	.	.	.	.	.	.	2
						—	26

B. *Maternal relatives*

In Ciyanda .	.	.	.	.	.	.	1
,, Kanjengo's ward	.	.	.	.	.	.	1
,, School village .	.	.	.	.	.	.	4
						—	6

POLITICAL AND SOCIAL LIFE

C. *Sister's sons (or daughters)*[1]

In Ciyanda 1
,, School village 4
— 5

D. *Relatives by marriage*

In Sikïlïlě's 2
,, School village 1
— 3

E. *Relationship not exactly determined*[2]

In School village 2
— 2

F. *Former slaves*

In Sikïlïlě's 1
,, School village 1
— 2

Total of householders 44

The above figures show more precisely than would several pages of explanation the family nature of the Umbundu village. That the Ovimbundu are patrilocal was noted by Hambly.[3] Whether the proportions which the above figures indicate would hold for all the Ovimbundu could only be determined by gathering similar data over widely representative areas. The same approximate distribution holds for the families represented by 192 genealogies and 74 marriage-schedules which I have collected. Matrilocal residence or residence in the wife's village has always been recognized by the Ovimbundu as a possibility, although less desirable than the ideal of patrilocal marriage and residence. Of the two householders in Sekulu Sikïlïlě's village who were related to him by marriage, one was the husband of a daughter and the other a widow of a younger brother, who should have been inherited by a younger brother or a mother's brother of the deceased. Failing that, she might have returned to her father's people, but her having settled in the village of her husband's elder brother is no cause for surprise. My experience leads me to believe that Ngendo is an approximately fair sample of the present strength of patrilocal residence among the Ovimbundu. That the Protestant school village is a real part of this kinship unit is an important fact, the significance of which will be discussed later.

[1] The two daughters were widows who had come to live with their mother's brothers.

[2] In these two cases relationship was declared to exist, but I failed to find its nature.

[3] Hambly, op. cit., p. 191.

30 UMBUNDU KINSHIP AND CHARACTER

Going on to the marital status of the villagers, I found that the forty-eight households were to be classified as follows:

Monogynous	27	(including 7 at the school)
Widowers (all formerly monogynous)	3 (	„ 1 „)
Widows	7 (	„ 4 „)
Young (unmarried) man . . .	1	(at the school)
Polygynous	10	
Total	48	

Whether a similar proportion of monogynous to polygynous households would also be found more widely among the Ovimbundu is a question which could only be settled by extensive demographic studies.[1] My impression is that the proportion of polygynous to monogynous households is higher in the region of Kasonge than in other Umbundu areas for the following reasons:

1. The proximity of Kasonge to the Esele country which has long been a source of supply for concubines (slaves). (Five of the ten polygynous householders in Ngendo included at least one Esele concubine.)
2. The comparatively low bride-price in Kasonge as compared to other areas.

The South African Census for 1921 showed that at that time only one man in eight was polygynous.[2] My impression is that the proportion among the Ovimbundu is no greater and that economic factors will soon do away with any considerable polygyny.

In each of the ten polygynous households in Ngendo save one, there were only two wives or concubines. The one exception was

[1] The census of 1940 gives more reliable figures and more details than were previously available, but it does not provide a basis for studies of this order. The number or proportion of polygamous unions among the 'uncivilized population' was not recorded. For the whole colony, the division of the native population by sex is given as follows: males, 1,733,328, females, 1,932,501 (op. cit., vol. i, p. 78 f.); and for the Ovimbundu (*Mbundo*), as follows: males, 636,583, females, 694,504 (op. cit., vol. ix, p. 22 f.). Owing to the migration of labourers, and especially to the system known as 'contract labour', certain areas (of recruitment) show a large excess of females over males (as much as 4 to 1 in the 20–29 age-groups of certain areas), while certain (receiving) areas show a corresponding excess of males over females (4 to 1 in several areas and even 22 to 1 in one area, for the same age-groups) (op. cit., vol. iii, *passim*). On this subject, *vide* R. R. Kuczynski, *Colonial Population* (London, 1937), and *Population Movements* (ibid., 1936); both summarized in the *Rhodes-Livingstone Journal*, no. 2.

[2] Quoted by P. A. W. Cook, *The Education of a South African Tribe* (Cape Town; Juta, 1934), p. 3.

POLITICAL AND SOCIAL LIFE   31

the household of the headman Sikĭlĭlĕ, who had had four wives and one young Esele concubine. At the time of my last visit (1936), however, there were only two wives and the concubine, one wife having died, and another having gone to her people.

To complete the picture of the villagers, their numbers were as follows:

Village	Men	Women	Children		Total
			Male	Female	
In Sikĭlĭlĕ's village . .	24	35	31	37	127
In Ciyanda . . .	5	8	2	4	19
In Kanjengo . . .	3	6	3	1	13
At the School . . .	10	11	10	6	37
Total . . .	42	60	46	48	
	Adults: 102		Children: 94[1]		196

In Sikĭlĭlĕ's village there were domestic animals as follows: 9 head of cattle, 13 goats, 20 sheep, 100 pigs, and about 100 chickens. There was practically no professional specialization; there were almost no specialists living in the village: no blacksmith or carpenter, no mat-maker, but only one 'hunter of meat', and three 'hunters of (bee-) hives'. As to the women, all could make baskets, and there were several who had made pottery, but were not doing so at the time.

Pigs, chickens, and dogs roamed the village, functioning as a D.S.C. and a sewer system combined. Were it not for these scavengers the villages of the Ovimbundu would present an even more untidy spectacle than is the case. There is no other regular disposal of refuse, nor are there any latrines or privies.[2]

It will be seen that there is practically no division of labour as between households: each is practically a self-contained unit. The

[1] It was reported that in addition to the children then living, these same households had lost 57 by death (29 males and 28 females).

[2] At Ngendo the school village had two or three enclosed pit privies. The Umbundu euphemism for defecate, 'go to the bush' (*oku enda kusenge*), is revealing. Even more revealing is a proverb which advises one not to burn his bridges behind him, but literally it runs as follows:

Nda wa lisinga huti, Si endi konyima onjo,
Nda o ka sŭsĭlă pi ?

If you forswear yourself saying, I shall not go behind the house,
Then will you go (to) urinate where?

There is a more shocking version which, however, may not be really authentic.

32 UMBUNDU KINSHIP AND CHARACTER

common meal was formerly a great bond of village unity. Mutual help within the village and the family group is practised on many occasions. There are a number of folk-tales designed to show the evil consequences of refusing to lend, whether beer-pots or more valued assistance. Many proverbs enjoin the necessity of prompt and effectual mutual helpfulness and co-operation, as e.g.

U o popela ukuavo ongandu ka lula.
(He who saves another (from) a crocodile does not undress.)

The mechanism of co-operation, the round of daily life in village and field, together with the cycles of food and of work, are properly subjects of further study. Here the purpose is to show the definitely family nature of the village and of its life. To the casual observer the Ovimbundu appear as severe individualists. Indeed, they are individualistic to a degree, but they have worked out mechanisms of mutual helpfulness and co-operation which functioned both on political lines under the aegis of the king and within the kinship units.

Social Life of the Village

The two foci of the village life are the Men's Club and the Dancing Floor. Even though no *onjango* may have been built, the Men's Club will find a place in which to carry on, at least when there may be fine weather. Leisure may be limited, but time for conversation will be found. Europeans often express wonder at the amount of conversation which goes on between Africans, for they cannot understand what people of apparently such limited opportunities and with what seems like so narrow an outlook may have to discuss at such great length. As for the Ovimbundu, there is nothing which is a greater hardship than lack of opportunity for conversation with their fellows. Under primitive conditions this is more especially true of the men, who, in their villages, are always surrounded by members of their own family group. Owing to their peculiar position in the village and their household pre-occupations, the women's social propensities may find less outlet in these public gatherings. When the villagers gather on the dancing floor and the gourds of beer go round, they always separate according to sex. Whether the occasion be formal or informal, I have seen the discussion carried to great lengths, with the pipe passed between the men, while the women sat silently by,

PLATE III

a. The inquest at a funeral

Photo. R. S. Webb

b. On the woman's side of the dancing floor during the celebration of funerary rites at Ngendo

PLATE IV

a. A new village (*itula*) near Elende

Photo. *M. W. Ennis*

b. A granary (*osila*), also used as a guest house

POLITICAL AND SOCIAL LIFE

some pulling on their stubby little pipes and watching the men. As the men smoke, they may pass the pipe from mouth to mouth, but not so the women.

Tobacco (*akaya*) is a great vehicle for sociability whether in the pipe or in the form of snuff. 'Snuffing is held to clear the head, to clarify the thought, to enlighten the eyes, to sharpen the hearing, and comfort the heart.'[1] 'Taking a pinch of snuff, between the forefinger and the thumb, is unknown . . . and would be considered . . . very unsatisfactory. . . . They pour about a teaspoonful into the palm of the hand, and burying their . . . nostrils in the peppery mixture snort it up loudly, aided by a rotary motion of the half-closed hand.'[2]

Beer (*ocimbombo*) is of even greater importance. Its place has long been threatened by such drinks as the stronger beer made from emmer wheat (*ekundi*), mead (*ingundu* and *ocasa*), and imported rum. Within the past thirty or forty years the Ovimbundu have themselves learned to distil rum (*okacipembe*) from sweet potatoes, sugar-cane, pumpkins, &c., and although the industry is illegal, it has grown to great proportions and nothing now seems able to stop it. It is the widespread use of this strong drink, with its concomitant evils, which is to-day the greatest enemy of the social life.

The dance is probably the most important element in the social life of the village. The Ovimbundu have many different dances and they dance on every occasion and on the slightest provocation. I have collected thirty songs to accompany dances. About three-fourths of them are sometimes used at funerals or at other ceremonial occasions, some of them are for more frivolous purposes, and most of those which are used for ceremonies are used at other times also. It is not for nothing that an Umbundu equivalent of the proverb 'Strike while the iron is hot', runs as follows:

> *Nda wa mōlã oñoma, piluka:*
> When you see a drum, dance:
> *Oñoma ka yi muĩwã luvali.*
> A drum may not be seen twice.

During one of my visits to Ngendo there was an important funeral with much dancing at Ndumba, just across the valley. At

[1] Tucker, *Drums in the Darkness* (Toronto and New York; Doran, 1927), p. 38.
[2] Monteiro, *Angola and the River Congo*, 2 vols. (London: Macmillan, 1875), vol. ii, p. 271.

D

34   UMBUNDU KINSHIP AND CHARACTER

that time I got several of the accompanying songs, the texts of which I hope may be published later. At this time I wish only to point out the important place in the social life of the village which the dance occupies, with reference both to ceremonial and to recreation. Whenever 'the moon makes a basket' (*osaĩ yi tunga ohumba*),[1] there is apt to be a great urge for rhythmic expression. The drums begin to throb, the leader's voice is heard in invitation:

> *We-lele, we-lele wiya,*
> Oh light ones, oh light ones, come,
> *Usiki woñoma Kaluyua.*
> The beater of the drum (is) Kaluyua.

Then the dancers reply with the same words as a refrain:

> *We-lele, we-lele wiya,*
> *Usiki woñoma Kaluyua.*

The invitation is not given in vain. More and more feet join the shuffling, stamping rhythm, more voices join the chorused invitation; the throbbing mounts as perhaps another drummer or two join in, and soon other songs supersede the invitation now no longer necessary. Dance follows dance, each with its appropriate song, running the gamut of the emotions from ribaldry to pathos, according to the dancers' moods. The dancing will continue nearly all the night and may be resumed on the three or four subsequent nights. After the harvest is gathered and there are no immediate agricultural labours, and if there happens to be little or no government work required at the time or in the region, dances may begin of an afternoon and last through two or three days and nights.

There are a number of games involving either agility or quick wits, or both, which are also played on moonlight nights, both by children and by adolescents. The adults do not join in except in some games which involve dancing. A simple one called *Ka limbua limbua* (Not forgotten) is played by either a large or small group. The children have many games. One which is played either by day or by night, called either *Cimbamba co lia* (The night hawk ate him) or *Mai* (Mother) *Cisangu*, has been fully described by Hambly,[2] with the transcription of its songs arranged by Dr. Herzog.

---

[1] When the moon is full it 'makes a basket', i.e. is large and round like a field-basket.   [2] Hambly, op. cit., p. 216 f.

POLITICAL AND SOCIAL LIFE 35

On nights when there is little or no moonlight, the evening gatherings in the village sometimes, although not always, follow the sex division, with the men and boys in the *onjango*, and the women and girls at one or more of the kitchens. Discussion of affairs, with youth listening to age, is the usual order, but the time is often passed in the recital of folk-tales or in propounding riddles.

Riddles are more especially a field of youth but age also enjoys hearing the answers given. A favourite occupation of the men, especially by day, is *ocela*, a game known all over Africa and in other parts of the world as well.[1] Junod calls it 'the national game of Africa'.[2]

The Ovimbundu have brought recreation to the service of their work. Europeans are often irritated by the amount of conversation which Ovimbundu carry on during working hours, but on consideration it may be found that were it not for the conversation and other psychological aids, the work might be quite unendurable. This is especially the case with regard to road work and many types of contract labour. Road songs and work songs are of real help in keeping up morale and in prolonging endurance. Most of them seem to have been developed in the days of the caravan trade, but they have not been forgotten and are now used on many occasions.

A word about ceremonial occasions before leaving the social life of the village. Some rites and ceremonies are celebrated so quietly that they are not even social occasions. Most of them, however, are very social. This is especially true of funerals and post-mortuary rites. During visits to Ngendo I was able to witness two post-mortuary rites and the funeral of an important person of a near-by village. Other ceremonial occasions, such as weddings and a return from a trading expedition, also call for much sociability, but funerals and post-mortuary rites are the social occasions which occupy the most time and attention and make for the greatest conviviality.

---

[1] Known under the name *Mancala*, which is evidently a Bantu word, or taken from one; cf. the Umbundu *oku mangala*, to play. Hambly mentions *ocela*, op. cit., p. 219. See also Nevinson, op. cit., p. 91. The *New Standard Dictionary* (Funk and Wagnalls) attributes to Arabian origin both the game and the word *Mankalah*.

[2] H. A. Junod, *The Life of a South African Tribe*, 2nd ed., vol. i, p. 345 f.

The Village Headman

The village headman (*Sekulu yimbo*) is in a very real sense the father of the villagers. Considering their relationship to him as shown by the survey of Ngendo, it is no surprise to find that to nearly all of the householders the headman is quite literally either 'father' (*tate*) or 'elder brother' (*kota*). The headman is literally the patriarch. He is also therefore the village priest. His compound is the only one in the village which has a spirit hut (*etambo*). In this hut the elder prays to ancestral spirits and holds communion (*oku felevela*) with them. In case of need, he may spend an entire night or more so occupied, but he will often offer a prayer when he awakens during the night. This hut is also used as a store-room for possessions not used every day and here are kept the insignia of office. The elder may sleep in this hut at any time when he is not sleeping with one of his wives, and here also he may lodge respected guests.

The headman functions as a Justice of the Peace for the village. The graver and more difficult cases are heard before the whole village on the dance-floor, while the simpler ones which require the attendance only of those concerned, together with their respective elders, are taken up either in the *onjango* or in the headman's own courtyard. Through all and in spite of all political and administrative changes, the village court of justice continues and will continue to function.

It is evident from the above that a headman may have much or little to do in attending to the affairs of his village, depending on several factors, such as the number of the villagers, their attitudes and disposition toward each other, relations with neighbouring villages, the demands made upon the village by the authorities, &c. However numerous may be his 'official duties', he will still find some time to attend to his own affairs, whether he be a farmer, a hunter, or a trader. In former times and before he became village headman, Sikilile was a trader and caravan leader (*ofumbelo*, Portuguese: *pombeiro*), and made many trips to the regions of Ngangela. As a headman he returned to farming and although he seemed to be quite old at the time of my visits, he had a creditable little plot of tobacco. It may be of interest to note that only the headman may speak of the village as 'my village' (*imbo liange*). The heads of the little wards may speak thus possessively only of

POLITICAL AND SOCIAL LIFE

their own wards, 'my ward' (*ocitawila cange*). The other villagers will speak only of 'our village' (*imbo lietu*).

There are, in general, two quite different and distinct types of Umbundu village according to the terrain on which they are built. The villages of the plains have room to spread out and tend toward a circular shape, with the dancing floor and men's club house near the centre. The wards may appear as quarters of a single whole or they may be added on in haphazard fashion. The villages of the mountains must conform to the possibilities of the terrain. Formerly, many villages were built on mountains for defence, and capital villages of this type may still be seen with the houses built on ledges and rocks almost one on top of the other. In this type of village, there is often not sufficient or sufficiently good soil for even small garden plots within the palisades. Occasionally one of these mountain villages may be found which has not even room within it for the dancing floor, which will in this case be found outside the palisade. If the site is not too severely confined, the wards of the mountain village tend either to string themselves out horizontally along the mountain-side, or to find successive ledges. The village of Ngendo is of an intermediate type, built as it is, on a slope. Sikĩlĩlẽ's village was first built as near the stream as possible. The wards later added themselves on, each a little higher than the one before. The school village, which was built last, got the highest and most hygienic site.

Moving a Village

Villages may be moved for any one of several reasons. When fields are worn out and others are not available[1] near by, a village may be moved to a site more conveniently located. More often, however, the reason assigned is that there has been much illness or death, that the old site is polluted, that its 'air is bad', which to the Ovimbundu means that some action displeasing to the spirits has been committed which has brought on these misfortunes. This will generally have been determined by divination, as will also the spirits' consent to the proposed new site. A site which has long been occupied is of course fertile soil. Since old sites are generally cultivated to good advantage this fact should not be overlooked as a possible additional reason for moving.

[1] Nowadays European settlement often pre-empts such lands.

38 UMBUNDU KINSHIP AND CHARACTER

A few words from the childhood recollections of Paulino Ngonga Liahuka[1] bring out the facts.

One day we noticed that Sekulu Upalandanda[2] and my father went to the mountain of Kalilonge saying, 'We go to look around (and find out) whether the spirits (*olosande*) have agreed to our moving there.' Then another day we saw that the fathers were coming out of the spirit huts (*atambo*, plural), with the sacred chests (*ovimbangu*, plural), saying, 'We go to start a new village.' When they had arrived under the mountain of Kalilonge, they said, 'The spirits have agreed.' Then when everyone had moved, the elder, whose name had been Upalandanda at Muenesi, now changed his name, declaring, 'I am *Cilembo-camunda* (Shadow of Mountain). From that time the place was called Cilembo.

On seeking a new site the headman's fire in the old village is put out and the procession starts: a girl carries the sacred chest (*ocimbangu*) containing the relics (*ociye*) and the balls of iguana skin, and a boy the sacred bows.[3] They lead the way to the site selected where they cut a pole[4] suitable for a house-wall (*ekoso*), and tie a leaf of the *upu*[5] tree to it, dig a hole into which they put mud made by rain-water (*onata yondombo*),[6] and then together they lift the stick and let it fall into the hole. This is the beginning of the spirit hut (*etambo*), the first house to be built on the new site. The boy and the girl must take part ceremonially in each operation of building the hut. After that they together ignite (*oku tiafula*)[7] the new fire. A hen and a cock are killed, cooked on the new fire, and eaten inside the *etambo* by all who have taken part in the building. The headman and his wife cannot return to the old village but must camp at the new site (*itula*) and keep the new fire alight. In building their houses, the villagers may commute (*oku usala*) from the old site, but often the distance is too great to do this, and

[1] Of Ciyaka, ordained pastor of Elende Church in 1930. He was Hambly's chief informant.

[2] Sekulu Upalandanda was the younger brother of Ngonga's father's father, and therefore grandfather to Ngonga.

[3] The bow (*ohonji*) of each ascendant who is now a guardian spirit (*osande*) of the family.

[4] When this first pole is cut, the axe should first be pointed toward the cardinal directions.

[5] A leaf of the *upu* tree is used in the divorce ceremony. Its use here is a sign of divorce from the old site.

[6] Literally, 'mud of the rainy season'.

[7] This was formerly done with a fire drill (*vide* Hambly, op. cit., Plate XXXV), but not for a number of years now. When I showed the above picture to a group of 150 young men of 17 to 25 years of age, not one of them even knew what it was.

POLITICAL AND SOCIAL LIFE 39

therefore the usual procedure is to erect temporary grass-covered huts (*olosingi*, plural) on the new site, in which they will live while building their houses. Each hearth-fire must be ignited from the headman's fire.

The houses are built by the occupants themselves. The men's club house is built by the communal labour of all men and boys with a simple ritual designed to promote concord within, and to ensure that the spirits (*olosande*) may find it a congenial abode. The spirits regularly attend the discussions in the *onjango*, and there receive their daily portions. There also they are believed to sleep.

At the first opportunity a hunt will be held and the meat brought to the spirit-hut. The girl who carried the sacred chest receives the heart and the boy the head. At this time, while a pot of sour beer (non-alcoholic) (*ocisangua*) is being brewed, the girl sits quietly in communion (*oku felevela*) with the spirits. With these physical and spiritual preparations the village community makes ready its home, a home which may seem poor and meagre to the eyes of outsiders, but to a member of the community it is home indeed and evokes in him, when absent, a feeling of great home-sickness (*ongeva*). As the Umbundu version of 'Home, Sweet Home' puts it:

Koliene, koliene, nda ku li ombambi ha yota
To your own, to your own, if there is cold you can warm yourself,

nda ku li onjala ha panga.
if there is hunger you can arrange.

CHAPTER III

KINSHIP

The Household

THE basis of the village and of the whole Umbundu kinship structure is the household consisting of a man, his wife or wives and their children, together with such other related or unrelated dependants as may be attached and live together in a single compound. The Umbundu word for the household is *ocikumba*, which includes domestic animals and possessions as well as the persons who make up the group, but nowadays this word is rarely, if ever, heard. The word *onjo*, which means 'house', is also used in the sense of household and to include the one or more 'houses' which a man has established by marriage. The housing arrangements of the household and its relation to the other households and to the headman of the village have been noted. The chief facts to remember are that each wife has her own hut, granary, chickens, and fields for her children and herself; and that the husband has no house of his own save a spirit hut (*etambo*), in case he is village headman or a family elder. There is not the same relation between the rank of the wives and the position of their houses with relation to the cattle kraal, which is found among the cattle-raising Southern Bantu, nor are there the same distinctions of precedence. The eldest child (*nuñulũ*) of his father, of whatever wife or concubine, takes precedence over all who are born later. It is nevertheless true among commoners that the first wife legally married is the chief wife. The number of persons belonging to a single household may vary greatly. Magyar stated that his father-in-law Kayaya Kayangula (king of Viye *c.* 1847–50) had seventeen sons and forty-four daughters.[1] Some recent kings have had as many as twelve wives and concubines, but I do not know of any having had even half as many children as Kayangula had. The only large household in the village of Ngendo was that of the headman, Sikĩlĩlẽ, with five wives and concubines, and fifteen children (most of whom were already grown at the time of my visits). The largest of the other households in that village had

[1] Magyar, op. cit., p. 260.

KINSHIP 41

only five children living, and the largest polygynous household had only four, but many children had died in infancy.

The attitudes within the household are much like those found universally between members of the same 'family'. Children respect and love both parents. Perhaps there is a little more respect for the father and a little more love for the mother, but this distinction is not carried to the extent which seems to be the case in more strongly patrilineal societies. The respect which a child has for his parents is plainly shown in his refusal under ordinary circumstances to speak their names. 'Even a child on being asked to tell the name of his father or his mother, will reply saying, "*Tate* (my father) indeed is his name." And if one asks again, saying, "Your mother, what is her name?" the child will reply saying, "*Mai* (my mother) indeed is her name." '[1] The sex division of Umbundu life begins within the household when very early in life the boys begin to be trained by their elder brothers, fathers, and other male relatives, while the girls remain or go about with their mothers, elder sisters, and other female relatives. Only the very small boys and girls (say under six or eight) play together. The age distinctions of Umbundu society are learned with the child's first attempts at language. Either his elder brother or sister he calls *huvange*, and he soon learns that the brother or sister younger than himself is *manjange*. Brothers and sisters, siblings or children of the same parents, 'are replicas of one another in social relationship, and . . . socially identical'[2] for practical purposes. Among Ovimbundu the principal differences are due to the two factors of age and sex. The influence of age is fundamental and is easily demonstrated by the fact that there is no word for 'brother' but instead for 'elder brother' or 'younger brother'. Within the household the factor of sex is ever present, but there is not the invidious distinction found among some of the more strongly patrilineal societies such as the Zulu[2] which reserves the more respectful term for the brother. Umbundu applies the terms *huva* and *manja*[3] to brothers and sisters without distinction of sex. There are the additional terms *kota* (elder brother), *mbuale* (sister), and the reciprocal terms *mume* (brother, spoken

---

[1] R. Kavita Evambi, from an Umbundu manuscript.

[2] E. J. Krige, *The Social System of the Zulus* (London: Longmans, 1936), p. 24.

[3] These are the root terms without the possessive suffixes.

42 UMBUNDU KINSHIP AND CHARACTER

only by a sister), and *mukãi* (sister, spoken only by a brother). In a polygynous household each of the wives is mother to all the children and each of the children is *huva* or *manja*[1] to all the others. Illegitimate children are not stigmatized but since they belong to the mother they have a distinct designation.[2] Slaves or former slaves have a status within the household and village which to the ordinary observer does not differ from that of the children: they are treated much as the children and they may carry on in all matters social and economic much as though they were members of the family. I have noticed, however, that when there is a call for labour, the lot falls oftener to one of these 'children-born-by-day'[3] whether he was a war-captive or a pawn.

Both slavery and the polygynous household, two institutions manifestly and intimately inter-related, are still a part of the Umbundu social structure, but neither the one nor the other now has the importance which it formerly had. Neither of these institutions is part of the present and personal experience of the great majority of Umbundu households.

Kinship

Blood Relatives (Epata). The relationships of the wider kinship groups are for the most part extensions of those of the household. The child learns them very early in life owing to the fact that the village community into which he is born is only a part of this larger kinship group. Nearly all of the villagers belong to the same *epata* or extended family, which includes both lines of descent. Most of them belong to the father's family (*oluse*), and the mother's family (*oluina*) may also be represented. The fact is that most of the adults of the village are father or mother to nearly every child and most of the children are brothers or sisters. Those of his coevals who do not bear this relation to him are otherwise related and are also potential spouses or potential relatives-in-law.

---

[1] This distinction *yesepakaĩ* (lit. 'of the jealousy of women') may be made but it is not applied in ordinary speech.

[2] *Omõlã a ngenda-la-ina* (lit. 'child of goes-with-mother').

[3] *Omãlã-va-citiwa-lutanya*. Cf. 'child of my calves', Luganda expression and attitudes, L. P. Mair, *An African People in the Twentieth Century* (London, 1934), p. 32 f.

KINSHIP 43

Kinship groupings: *oluse* and *oluina*.[1] Every Ocimbundu belongs to an *oluse*, i.e. his father's kin, and to an *oluina*, i.e. his mother's kin. Each of these family groupings is divided into male and female lines (*onēlē yohonji*, 'the side of the bow'; *onēlē yohumba*, 'the side of the basket'). Uterine brothers and sisters belong to the same *oluse* and *oluina*, and to the male or female 'side' respectively, according to sex. It is of great importance to get a clear idea of this bilateral nature of these kinship groupings. Every student of ethnology will note the similarity of this division to the Herero *oruzo* and *eanda*.[2] Considering the affinities between the Herero and Umbundu languages, I think that these conceptions are probably related. Further study of other peoples of this Western Bantu zone may reveal cultural and racial as well as linguistic affinities.[3] The *oluse* and *oluina* of the Ovimbundu follow their own pattern.

The *oluse* consists of a large number of local village groups, some of which recognize mutual relationships, but with no recognized headship save in the case of the several royal families. The only suggestion of any totemic relation or origin is with the royal families which have in common several taboos with regard to certain animals the flesh of which may not be eaten, nor the skins used, &c. Chief of these animals are the *ongulungu* (bushbuck, *Tragelaphus scriptus*), the *ocisema*[4] (the waterbuck, *Cobus defessa*

[1] *Olu-se*, perhaps 'the place of father', the root *se* being equivalent to the forms *sa, so, isia*; *olu-ina*, perhaps 'the place of mother'.

[2] See Vedder, pp. 185 ff. (in *The Native Tribes of South West Africa*): 'The Herero nation is divided into 2 large family groups . . . the Herero belongs to the *oruzo* of his father and also to the *eanda* of his mother.' J. Irle, *Die Herero* (Gutersloh, 1906), pp. 87–93.

[3] An interesting study of the VaNyaneka, one of the cattle-rearing people living between Ambo and Umbundu territory, was recently published: A. Lang et C. Tastevin, *La Tribu des Va-Nyaneka* (Mission Rohan-Chabot, Tome V), Corbeil: Impr. Créto. This volume was not available in England or the U.S.A. until 1940, and could not therefore have been used in the present study. I may now say, however, that the authors' treatment of the social structure is not such that it would help to solve the problem in question. The clans are described only from the standpoint of totemism. The maternal line of descent (*e-anda*) is briefly mentioned (p. 45), but not the corresponding paternal line. The authors' evident lack of familiarity with other Bantu material is a great drawback. The system used for the transcription of the vernacular is most confusing, owing to an evident lack of understanding of the Bantu phonetic and grammatical genius with consequent procrustean attempts to force it into foreign forms.

[4] The king's sons may not eat flesh of the *ocisema* lest they should *sema sema*, 'have an impediment of speech'. This may be simply a taboo on grounds of *similia similibus* (or the obverse).

44 UMBUNDU KINSHIP AND CHARACTER

penricei), and *ovinyama viakasa* (animals having paws, from the lion down). No other *oluse* has any such rules. The chief function of the *oluse* is as a local residence group. Within the *oluse* there is no inheritance of property but only succession to office, which from the king to the village headman is from father to son, or from elder to younger brother, with only as much recognition of primogeniture as belongs to the general idea of the hierarchy of age. Succession to office is further affected by the democratic tendencies already noted with regard to the kingly succession.[1] The character of the *oluse* as a series of local groups is further borne out by the character of its priesthood, which lies wholly with the village headmen.

The *oluina* is not a local group, since its members for the most part live in the villages of their several lines of paternal descent— each with his *oluse*. When an Ocimbundu speaks of his family (*epata*) in the sense of a large and widespread organization with a recognized head in some elder, it is generally his *oluina* to which he refers. This family elder (*ukulu wepata*) is generally both the legal and spiritual head of the family. He is the family high-priest in charge of the spirit-hut (*etambo*) of the family guardian spirit (*osande*)[2] of whom there may be more than one and of whom he may become one after death. This family head is generally the eldest in the maternal line. In these days the priestly and the legal functions may be divided considering the advantages of having for legal head one who knows the ways of this world, while the spiritual head needs rather to be acquainted with the spirit-world. Property is inherited through the *oluina* from mother's brother to sister's son.[3] Only the *oluina* is an organization in the wider or more than local sense, and it is to it that the children belong. Formerly the mother's elder brother had great powers over his sister's sons and was even able to pawn them or sell them into slavery to meet his own debts.[4] The patrilocal household is

---

[1] See *supra*, p. 22 f.

[2] The head of an *oluina* may or may not be a village headman. In case he is, he will be priest of two lines and have two spirit-huts. There may be more than one spirit-hut in a single village.

[3] This fact was noted by A. Bastos, *Traços Geraes sôbre a Ethnografia do Districto de Benguella* (Lisboa, 1909), p. 33 (par. 39°).

[4] This has been noted by a number of writers. Bastos, op. cit., p. 29 (par. 26°) adds that once a father has redeemed his son, the maternal uncle can never sell him again. Cf. *avunculi potestas* among the Ba-Ila, E. W. Smith and A. M. Dale, *The Ila-Speaking Peoples* (London, 1920), vol. i, p. 320.

KINSHIP

responsible for the children, especially during their early years, but they are frequently sent 'to the *oluina*', i.e. to the mother's brother for at least a part of their education. Herein has arisen a conflict between the claims of the paternal household and the maternal kinship group. Economic and other forces seem to have favoured the former so that 'During these days in which we stand, things have changed somewhat so that as between children and their parents, they work for their fathers for they say, "A child is strong with his *oluse* and less so with his *oluina*." Nowadays a man teaches a child work and also looks out for his education that he may advance properly. His mother's brothers (*va inanu*) have no longer much power as of old.'[1]

Bearing in mind their bilateral nature and the fact that every Ocimbundu belongs at the same time to his paternal (*oluse*) and to his maternal (*oluina*) groups, the functions of these kinship groups may be summarized as follows:

Oluse	*Oluina*
SOCIAL	
Consists of local residence units; succession of village and tribal offices from father to son, or elder to younger brother.	Extended family organization; office of family head descends from mother's brother to sister's son; children belong.
Marriage allowed between cross-cousins and other relatives of non-parallel descent; couple lives at groom's father's village.	*Marriage preferred* between cross-cousins and other relatives of non-parallel descent; children belong to mother's *oluina*.
EDUCATIONAL	
Responsibility for education of young children, especially in social usage.	Responsibility sometimes assumed in later childhood, especially for technical phases.
ECONOMIC	
Ownership and inheritance of land. (Passed from father to son or elder to younger brother.)	Ownership and inheritance of more largely negotiable and movable property, as e.g. trade goods, cattle, &c. (passed from mother's brother to sister's son).

[1] Raul Kavita Evambi, op. cit.

UMBUNDU KINSHIP AND CHARACTER

Oluse	*Oluina*
	RELIGIOUS
Regular village worship including agricultural festivals; village headman is also priest.	Family observances including occasional propitiations in case of illness, death, or other misfortunes; for desired economic advantages; mortuary rites. Family head is also priest.

Classificatory System of Relationship. The relationships of the wider kinship groups are quite largely extensions of those of the household, but the Ovimbundu, in common with all people who have a classificatory system, extend these relationships not only further but in quite different ways than do those who have the European (Roman) system. One who would understand the Ovimbundu must understand the Umbundu family from the inside—not as from motives of mere intellectual curiosity but as an Ocimbundu understands it. In order to demonstrate this family structure it will be necessary to present tables and diagrams. Hambly did a very creditable piece of work toward demonstrating the structure of the Umbundu family.[1] I doubt that anyone staying among them an equally short period of time, not knowing their language, could have done better in this respect unless he had come to the task with very exceptional preparation. It is only just to state this and I feel that it is necessary because so far as I am aware, in the five years since it was published, the book has received no adequate appraisal or review.[2] It must be said, however, that Hambly made some noticeable errors in his use of kinship terms owing to the fact that he did not learn the Umbundu language, and that he evidently failed to understand certain points with regard to the social structure.

For greater clarity and precision I am presenting in separate tables the terms which refer to blood relationship and those which refer to relationship by marriage.

---

[1] W. D. Hambly, op. cit., pp. 189–99.

[2] This book was reviewed in *Africa*, 1935, pp. 391–3, but the reviewer had no first-hand knowledge of the people or their language, which was perhaps his reason for taking up three-fourths of the space at his disposal with questions of orthography. E. W. Smith has taken note of the book (*Africa: What Do We Know of It?*, p. 71), but only to say that it 'is chiefly useful for its description of the material culture'.

KINSHIP

47

TABLES OF UMBUNDU TERMS OF BLOOD RELATIONSHIP

A. *Ego's Own Generation: Man or Woman the Speaker*

Term	Relation	Reciprocal term
1. *Huvange*[1]	my elder brother my elder sister mother's sister's child (if older than Ego) father's brother's child (if older than Ego) mother's mother's sister's grandchild (if older than Ego) mother's father's brother's grandchild (if older than Ego) father's father's brother's grandchild (if older than Ego) father's mother's sister's grandchild (if older than Ego)	*manjange*
2. *Kota*[2]	eldest brother (of household or of family)	*manjange*
3. *Manjange*	my younger brother my younger sister all relatives listed under '1.' (if *younger* than Ego)	*huvange* or *kota*
4. *Epalume*[2] *Upalume*[3] *Cepua*[4]	mother's brother's child father's sister's child mother's mother's brother's grandchild mother's father's sister's grandchild father's father's sister's grandchild father's mother's brother's grandchild	*epalume,* *upalume,* or *cepua*

B. *Man the Speaker*

Term	Relation	Reciprocal term
1. *Mukãi*[3]	sister all female relatives listed under 'A. 1, 2, and 3'	*mume*

---

[1] *Huvange*, my elder brother; *huvetu*, our elder brother.
   Huvove, thy elder brother; *huvene*, your elder brother.
   Huvaye, his elder brother; *huvavo*, their elder brother.
   In Viye *huva* is not now used commonly and *manja* is used without discrimination for both elder and younger brothers. This may be due to European influences. At any rate the Bantu usage has reasserted itself by appropriating *kota* (q.v. *infra*) in place of *huva*, and by using the political term *epalanga* for the true sense of *manja*.

[2] *Kota* and *epalume* belong to the sixth class of nouns, *epalume liange, kota liange*, &c.

[3] *Upalume, mukãi*, and *mume* belong to the first class, *upalume wange, mukãi wove, mume waye*, &c. Use of the three terms for cross-cousins seems to be indiscriminate.

[4] *Cepua* belongs to the fourth class, *cepua cetu*, &c.

48   UMBUNDU KINSHIP AND CHARACTER

C. *Woman the Speaker*

Term	Relation	Reciprocal term
1. *Mume*[1]	brother	*mukãi*
	all male relatives listed under 'A. 1, 2, and 3'	
2. *Mbuale*[2]	sister	*mbuale*
	all female relatives listed under 'A. 1, 2, and 3'	

D. *First Ascendant Generation: Either Man or Woman the Speaker*

1. *Maĩ*[3]	my (uterine) mother	*omolange*
	(my father's other wives)	
	mother's sister	
	mother's mother's sister's daughter	
	mother's father's brother's daughter	
	father's father's brother's daughter	
	father's mother's sister's daughter	
2. *Tate*[4]	my father	*omolange*
	(any subsequent husbands of my mother)	
	father's brother	
	father's father's brother's son	
	father's mother's sister's son	
	mother's mother's sister's son	
	mother's father's brother's son	
3. *Manu*[5]	mother's brother	*ocimumba cange*
	mother's mother's brother's son	
	mother's father's sister's son	
	father's father's sister's son	
	father's mother's brother's son	
4. *Tatekãi*[6]	father's sister	*ocimumba cange*
	father's mother's brother's daughter	
	father's father's sister's daughter	
	mother's father's sister's daughter	
	mother's mother's brother's daughter	

---

[1] See note 3, p. 47.

[2] *Mbuale* belongs to the fifth class, *mbuale yange*, &c.

[3] *Maĩ*, my mother; *inetu*, our mother.
Nyohõ, thy mother; *inene*, your mother.
Inaye, his mother; *inavo*, their mother.

[4] *Tate*, my father; *isietu*, our father.
So, thy father; *isiene*, your father.
Isiaye, his father; *isiavo*, their father.

[5] *Manu*, my mother's brother; *manu yetu*, our mother's brother.
Nyohõnu, thy mother's brother; *nyohõnu yene*, your mother's brother.
Inanu, his mother's brother; *inanu yavo*, their mother's brother.

[6] *Tatekãi*, my father's sister.
Sohãi, thy father's sister.
Apahaĩ, his father's sister.
Plural forms as for *Manu*, &c.

Hambly had only this form for the third person and dropped out a vowel with a resulting form impossible for Umbundu of *Aphai*. *Vide* op. cit., pp. 190, 196, 198, 199.

PLATE V

a. An Esele village

b. Hulling coffee (Bailundu Mission)

PLATE VI

Photo. R. S. Webb

a. Harvesting peanuts (Bailundu)

Photo. M. W. Ennis

b. Road workers

KINSHIP

49

E. *Second Ascendant Generation: Either Man or Woman the Speaker*

Term	Relation	Reciprocal term
1. *Maikulu*[1] (*Nyokulu*)	grandmother, both maternal and paternal grandmother's sister grandfather's sister	*onekulu yange*
2. *Sekulu*[1] (*Tatekulu*)	grandfather, both maternal and paternal grandfather's brother grandmother's brother	*onekulu yange*

F. *Third Ascendant Generation*

Kuku	all relatives of this generation	*onekuluila* or *omokolole yange*

G. *Fourth Ascendant Generation*

Kukululu	all relatives of this generation	*onene yange*

H. *Fifth Ascendant Generation*

Kukululua	all relatives of this generation	*onei yange*

I. *Sixth Ascendant Generation*

Ku	all relatives of this generation	*oneka yange*

J. *First Descendant Generation*

1. *Omōlãnge*	my own child woman's sister's child man's brother's child mother's sister's grandchild father's brother's grandchild	*tate* or *mãi*
nuñulũ or *uveli*	first-born child	
2. *Ocimumba*	woman's brother's child man's sister's child mother's brother's grandchild father's sister's grandchild	*tatekãi* or *manu*

The kinship terms for further descendant generations will be found in the column of 'reciprocal terms' given above. It does not seem necessary to repeat them.

The patterns of behaviour between these many blood relatives find their prototypes in the patterns of the household. Love for

---

[1] *Maikulu* and *Sekulu* are sometimes used interchangeably for persons of either sex. Each has only the two personal forms. The forms in parenthesis are but little used. *Inakulu* is used for the queen.

E

50 UMBUNDU KINSHIP AND CHARACTER

the mother who bore me and the consideration naturally expected from her cannot, in the nature of things, be given or received by *all* of the elder and younger mothers in exactly equal degree, but the type of behaviour is similar. The elder sister who carried her younger brother about on her back when she herself could hardly more than walk, or the elder brother who first taught his younger brother to make and set his little traps, has a warmth of regard which he cannot extend with just the same force to fifty or one hundred younger brothers, but nevertheless the pattern will be of the same sort if and when similar opportunity offers. The same may be said for the younger and the elder fathers, and again for the *tatekãi*, the 'female father'. But here elements other than the early household patterns enter as also with *manu*, the mother's brother. Chief of these other elements is the fact that these two classes of relatives, together with the *va cepua*, i.e. cross-cousins (mostly children of the *manu* and *tatekãi* classes), and also the *ovimumba* (plural) (one's own nephews along similar lines of descent), are all potential spouses or potential relatives-in-law.[1] The relations of *ocimumba* (sister's son) and *manu* (mother's brother) in Umbundu society follow a pattern not exactly like any other set of relationships in any society of which I know. Suggestions of this have already been given. The *manu* shares his sister's desire for the advancement of her son, and if the nephew has had a part of his education in the uncle's home or on his trading expeditions, the relationship will have become closer. It may be, however, that the uncle's own difficulties may lead him to exploit his nephew rather than to attend only to his advancement.[2] The ties of the paternal group tend to be strengthened at the expense of the maternal family and it seems that the increasing localization of the Umbundu family with the supplanting of trade by agriculture (as a man's full-time occupation) has furthered this process.

It is very important for one who would understand the Ovimbundu to look upon the Umbundu kinship structure with the eyes of an Ocimbundu. If one brought up to other ideas and other relationships finds this difficult, that is all the more reason for making the effort. I cannot better summarize the Umbundu

---

[1] See *infra*, pp. 52 ff.

[2] This is one of several points where the commercial tendencies seem to come into conflict with the patterns of the kinship group.

KINSHIP 51

attitude toward one's blood relations than by quoting Mrs. Hoernlé:

Here, then, is a large body of kin drawn intimately into contact with the lives of each generation. Looking out into the world from his own home, the Bantu child knows where he may seek hospitality and succour of every kind; where, also, he may of right be called upon to render assistance in case of need. The barriers of reserve shutting off human beings from one another are largely down so far as these classes of relatives are concerned, so that for economic assistance, for friendly counsel, in time of sorrow and in time of joy, these are the natural categories of people to turn to, the core of people with whom one is close-knit from birth in a web of reciprocal rights and duties.[1]

The Kin

Relatives by Marriage. Marriage profoundly alters the relationship of those who enter into it, that is, the two families. It must be entered into with great care and with due regard for all factors concerned in order that the balance of life may be maintained. It seems that the financial arrangements (*ilombo*) are designed to restore to the bride's family an equivalence for her loss, since marriage is patrilocal. The Ovimbundu consider mutual respect between the two families to be a necessary basis for a successful marriage. Respect (*esumbilo*) is the reason assigned by thoughtful Ovimbundu for the various avoidances (*oku liyuvuila*) enjoined upon the principals and their respective families. In the first place, the husband and wife must show their respect for each other by avoiding certain actions as, for example, either one speaking the name of the other.

This mutual respect finds its most dramatic symbol in the treatment which the husband must accord his mother-in-law, the bride her father-in-law. They must avoid seeing each other, and if it is necessary to converse, it must be done out of sight, or with gaze averted. Both husband and wife must also avoid pronouncing the names of the parents-in-law. By the principle of extended relationships, this behaviour applies to the relations of the husband and the wife with *all* their parents-in-law of the opposite sex. As all the mother's 'sisters' are 'mother', so to the husband they are all *ndatembo* (mother-in-law). Likewise, the father's 'brothers' all

[1] In Schapera, op. cit., 1937, p. 73.

52   UMBUNDU KINSHIP AND CHARACTER

being 'father', to the wife they are *ndatembo* (father-in-law). All relatives whom one considers as 'parents' are parents-in-law to one's spouse, and conversely, all whom one considers as one's 'children' are *ndatembo* (sons-in-law or daughters-in-law) to the spouse. To all these relatives-in-law is due the same pattern of respectful behaviour. Avoidance of seeing each other applies only between the *va ndatembo* of opposite sex. There is the additional prohibition that they may not eat in each other's presence. This avoidance is further extended to include one's *ndatembo* of the same sex, and also one's *nãwã* (relatives-in-law of one's own generation). With the *nãwã*, however, one is otherwise on free and easy terms.[1] The prohibition on eating does not apply to drinking beer or to other such casual refreshment, but only to 'hot food', i.e. to regular meals.

Avoidance of meeting (*oku liyuvuila kocipala*, lit. 'avoiding each other to the face') is especially difficult for the bride who comes to live in a village of her husband's people, a large proportion of the men of which may be *ndatembo* to her. The prohibition may be lifted by going through a simple ceremony in which each rubs a little oil on the other. The woman rubs oil on the breast, the face, and the right arm of her *ndatembo*, while he in turn rubs oil from the same dish on her breast and on the braids of her forehead. Avoidance of eating in each other's presence may be done away with after some months by sacrificing a chicken and feeding it ceremonially together with maize porridge to the *ndatembo* or *nãwã* (throwing it into her mouth, mouthful by mouthful), with the attendance of the immediate family. It is especially important that these ceremonies be carried through with respect (*esumbilo*).

The avoidance of the name, whether of husband and wife, or of the parents-in-law, must be maintained: the names must not be pronounced. Many euphemisms are resorted to when it becomes necessary to speak of or to these relatives-in-law. This is one reason why the parents themselves take the name of their first-born, prefixing *Na*, 'mother of', and *Sa*, 'father of'. Thus the parents of *Kambõtiã* are known as *Nakambõtiã* and *Sakambõtiã*. This name may be pronounced. This is also probably one reason for extend-

---

[1] See the folk-tale in which the man who knows the speech of the red ants gives away his knowledge by laughing out *while his sister-in-law is braiding his hair*.

KINSHIP   53

ing to the wife all the relationships which are the husband's and vice versa. Thus by courtesy the parents-in-law are spoken of not as *ndatembo*, but *Mai* (my mother) and *Tate* (my father). The same extension also applies to all of the kin of the spouse and for all kinship terms both direct and reciprocal. Another reason for this is the mutual respect which is a principal basis of the Umbundu marriage.[1]

There remains one important matter necessary to an understanding of the Umbundu concept of relationship by marriage. To the Ovimbundu the proper, or at least the most desirable, marriage is a marriage within the circle of kin. 'Formerly people never married unless they were related, that is to say, unless they touched the blood together. If in the mother's kin (*koluina*), only on the side of the bow (i.e. male line). If in the father's kin (*koluse*), only on the side of the basket (i.e. female line).'[2] Upon closer consideration it becomes evident which of the relatives one may marry. It would not be possible to marry any who are classed as brother, sister, father, mother, grandparent, child, or grandchild, for such a union would involve incest (*oku ndō*). The relatives whom one may marry are, then, those of one's own age-level who belong to classes other than the above-mentioned. An ideal mate of one's own generation is a cross-cousin classed as *Epalume* or *Cepua* (Class A. 4, p. 47). Beside this, a woman may marry one classed as her mother's brother (Class D. 3, p. 48), and a man one classed as his father's sister (Class D. 4, p. 48), if of appropriate age. One may also marry an *ocimumba* (Class J. 2, p. 49). Hambly remarked that 'cross-cousin marriage . . . is the functional form among the Ovimbundu'.[3] This is true, but only in part, for not only are there many relatives other than his cross-cousin whom an Ocimbundu may marry, but the financial arrangements are quite other than those usually associated with the cross-cousin marriage.

---

[1] While I do not pretend to believe that 'respect' is the only or even the main reason for the observances described, it seems sufficiently important to receive the attention which I have given it.

[2] Verbatim translation of statement by Likuluta Samikanjo, elder of the school village at Ngendo (Kasonge).

[3] Hambly, op. cit., p. 194. In reporting the replies of his informant as to whom he could marry, with regard to the marriage of father's sister's daughter, the reply was that it was possible but not desirable 'because the children will be stupid'. The reason assigned was evidently taken from European ideas, but the reply also indicates a preference for marriage *within* the *oluina*, which I have also had from many but not from all informants.

54 UMBUNDU KINSHIP AND CHARACTER

Cross-cousin marriage of the type practised by the Sotho[1] or Venda[2] tribes is quite foreign to Umbundu life. It is possible that the Ovimbundu formerly had some such type of cross-cousin marriage, but not for a very long time. Among the seventy-five schedules which I have collected illustrating marriage arrangements there are a few describing marriages which took place about ninety years ago. Magyar also wrote of the financial arrangements made for marriage in Viye about 1850.[3] Both of these sources, together with native tradition, indicate that, at least with regard to the financial arrangements, the cross-cousin type of marriage has not been practised by the Ovimbundu for more than one hundred years. On the other hand, the Ovimbundu know nothing of the exogamous marriage demanded by the Herero,[4] the Zulu,[5] &c. The Umbundu ideal includes marriage with a cross-cousin, but also goes out into the wider kinship group, as does the type of marriage of the Thonga,[6] which in turn is linked with that of the Ndau and the Shona group.[7]

The Umbundu principle that only 'those whose blood has touched', or who can 'count' relatives in common, has for a very long time admitted of liberal application. There are cases on record of individuals belonging to regions as widely separated as Ciyaka and Ngalangi contracting marriage *after* having properly 'counted' their common relationship. These cases refer to grandparents of the present generation. It is probable that the diverse racial and cultural elements which have fused to form the Ovimbundu people long ago made imperative the broadening of the cross-cousin type of marriage to the 'ideal' or 'classic' form of (present) Umbundu tradition. An analogous process (with modifications) has continued to operate until to-day this very ideal of marriage within the kinship group is losing its hold in favour of yet more 'liberal' practices.

In summary, the Umbundu terminology for the relative by marriage and also the connexion between the ideas of relation by marriage and relation by blood may be seen by the following:

[1] W. M. Eiselen, 'Preferential Marriage: Correlation of the various modes among the Bantu of South Africa', *Africa*, 1928, pp. 413–28.

[2] H. A. Stayt, *The Bavenda* (London, 1931), chaps. xi and xv.

[3] Magyar, op. cit., p. 282 f.

[4] Vedder in Hahn *et al.*, op. cit., p. 187; Irle, op. cit., p. 89.

[5] Krige, op. cit., pp. 34–5.   [6] Junod, op. cit., vol. i, pp. 253–64.

[7] Hoernlé in Shapera, op. cit., p. 93 f.

KINSHIP

II. Table of Umbundu Terms of Relationship by Marriage

A. *Ego's Own Generation: Man Speaking*

Term	Relationship	Reciprocal term
1. *Ukãi wange*	my wife	*veyange*[1]
2. *Nãwã*	sister-in-law every 'sister' and 'brother' of wife every *epalume* (cross-cousin) of wife in short: every relative of wife of her own generation (see Table I. A, B, p. 47 f.)	*nãwã*[2]

B. *First Ascendant Generation: Either Man or Woman the Speaker*

1. *Ndatembo*	parent-in-law every relative of spouse of this generation (see list in Table I. D, p. 48 f.)	*ndatembo*[2]
2. *Mai*	applied by courtesy to everyone whom spouse so classifies	*omolange*
3. *Tate*	applied by courtesy to everyone whom spouse so classifies	*omolange*
4. *Manu*	applied by courtesy to everyone whom spouse so classifies	*ocimumba*[3]
5. *Tatekaĩ*	applied by courtesy to everyone whom spouse so classifies	*ocimumba*

C. *Second, Third, and Further Ascendant Generations*

Each spouse applies and receives the terms respectively applied and received by the other, with corresponding sexual differentiations.

D. *Descendant Generations*

Each spouse applies and receives the terms respectively applied and received by the other, with corresponding sexual differentiations.

---

[1] *Veyange*, my husband, *veyove*, thy husband, &c.

[2] Affinal terms are applied from the time of the formal betrothal. In marriage of the preferential kinship type affinal terms replace the consanguineal. After marriage, or, more generally, after the ceremonies for doing away with avoidances, then the courtesy terms are applied.

[3] Hambly in his summary table—op. cit., p. 199—gives the meaning given here as the only meaning for *ocimumba*, but this is only a secondary meaning (see p. 47 f.). He also errs in his use of the following: *Mbuale* (used only by females), *Kulu* (not a relationship term), *Kukululu* (means great-great-grandparent), *Aphai* (should be *Apãhãi* with the two other forms, see p. 48), *Cikulume* (should be *cikuelume*).

56 UMBUNDU KINSHIP AND CHARACTER

III. TABLES OF RELATIVES WITH WHOM MARRIAGE IS PREFERRED

A. *Of Ego's Generation: Either Man or Woman*

Term	Relationship	Reciprocal term
Epalume or *cepua*	cross-cousins of all degrees (see list Table I. A. 4, p. 47)	*epalume* or *cepua*

B. *Of First Ascendant Generation: Man Speaking*

Tatekãi	father's 'sister' (see list Table I. D. 4, p. 48)	*ocimumba*

C. *Of First Ascendant Generation: Woman Speaking*

Manu	mother's 'brothers' (see list Table I. D. 3, p. 48)	*ocimumba*

D. *Of First Descendant Generation: Man or Woman Speaking*

Ocimumba	mother's 'brother's' or father's 'sister's grandchild'	*manu* or *tatekãi*

Many writers have noted that, among other purposes, the financial arrangements serve to give the bride a status in the village of her husband. In a system of preferential kinship marriage, this is a desideratum, although for other reasons than those operating in a system where the wife comes as a comparative stranger. In a system such as this of the Ovimbundu, it is evident that many of the relatives by marriage are already blood relatives. This is perhaps one reason why the avoidances with regard to 'in-laws' are less rigidly held to than in a society such as the Zulu, which holds strictly to exogamous marriage.[1]

Another factor which makes for stability of marriage is the bilineal kinship system (*epata*). This system offers to the wife an initial security not usually found where descent is unilineal, or even where there has been a one-sided development of one line of descent at the expense of the other. The bilineal system is an important factor in the preservation of social stability. Through it the household and the village are links in the chain which even yet binds the Ovimbundu into a social whole.

Sorcery

Umbundu society is subject to various forces which threaten its cohesion and stability both from without and from within. Some of the external forces have been touched upon.[2] Chief of the

---

[1] Krige, op. cit., p. 29 f. [2] *Supra*, pp. v, 26.

KINSHIP 57

internally disruptive forces is sorcery. It is apparently on the increase among the Ovimbundu, a tendency which has also been reported from other parts of Africa.[1] The extent to which sorcery operates within the kinship groups themselves makes its influence even more dangerous to social cohesion.

Any marked success achieved by an individual, especially when such success has been achieved by an individual alone or in partnership, but not in co-operation with a number of persons, often brings on suspicion of sorcery.[2] Should the results of such success be distributed widely and freely within the family or kinship group, suspicion of sorcery is less likely to arise and open accusation may be avoided. Grudges, however, whether newly built up or inherited, often find expression in suspicion or in open accusation of sorcery.[3] An open accusation of sorcery (*oku sunga owanga*) is a very serious matter and will not often be made lightly.

Such accusations are made both within and across kinship lines. Affinal relatives are quite often accused of sorcery, and suspicion frequently rests upon wives whose kinship connexions are in distant regions. Predilection for and skill in the use of sorcery is supposed to be inherited. A reputation for sorcery may be imputed to a family through a number of generations.

Somewhat less overt accusations of sorcery are made at the inquest during a funeral. The corpse in its coffin slung to a pole between two carriers responds to questions as to who 'ate him' by forward (affirmative), or backward (negative) movements. It may also cause its carriers to stop in front of a certain house during the procession through the village, meaning that one of the occupants of the house is thereby accused of having caused the death. Traditionally such accusations during inquests were exceedingly common, perhaps even usually expected.[4] Should the corpse not give a clear answer, then subsequent divination would often bring out an accusation of sorcery. Accusations such as these, involving responsibility for the death of a person, are usually made *within* the body of blood or affinal kin.

When sorcery is consciously taken up and employed, the purpose is usually economic advancement, but it often involves overt

[1] Cf. B. Malinowski, in *Africa*, 1939, p. 39.
[2] *Vide infra*, pp. 107 ff.
[3] *Vide infra*, p. 125.
[4] For an early observation of this (*c.* 1790) *vide Annaes Mar. e Col.*, 5a Ser., p. 489 f.

58 UMBUNDU KINSHIP AND CHARACTER

attacks also upon the persons or possessions of enemies. This type of sorcery in a very common form involves the enslavement of the spirit of another person, often a child of one's own family or kin.[1] The person whose spirit is used may be killed either by violent or by magical means. Sorcery of this type is much feared, but if wealth supposedly gained by this means is used for the benefit of the kin, the sorcerer may be tolerated or even protected in the exercise of his black art. Beneficiaries do not often have qualms concerning the source of the benefits received. One who, by reason of his family connexions or his own power, has secured a strong position may escape interference. Jealousy or grudges, however, often bring out accusations from within the circle of kin. Accusations may also be made by outsiders. With the decline in influence which the tribal courts have suffered, and their inability to inflict capital punishment, sorcery is less frequently punished than formerly. The consequent reductions in the number of innocent victims is a gain. This same cause has operated, however, to increase dealings in, and fear of, sorcery. Most of the cases brought to European courts, and even to the Church, under the name of 'poisoning' are in reality accusations of sorcery.

In the foregoing brief note it has not been possible adequately to treat the subject, but it will be seen that sorcery has long been a divisive influence in Umbundu life. It sometimes seriously affects the cohesion of the household and the larger kinship groups. Economic, political, and other forces now seem to be acting to increase the incidence of sorcery, the influence of which is probably a considerable factor in the present rapid disintegration of the Umbundu social structure.

The Hierarchy of Age

Passing references have been made to associations of coevals. The Ovimbundu recognize very definitely the hierarchy of age and consider orderly society quite impossible without it. One of the keenest criticisms of the European and his ways is contained in the aphorism:

> *Kundele ka ku li ukulu.*
> In 'civilization' there is no senior.

To Umbundu wisdom this is an impossible state of affairs;

---

[1] The Umbundu term is *oku andeka*; *vide* ref. *infra*, p. 107, n. 1.

KINSHIP   59

there must be a responsible senior and, hence as a matter of course, the following is accepted:

Ndalu hokuluko la Vava:
Fire is not older than water:

Ciyo wa pindikapo.
Potsherd (or frying-pan) passes between (i.e. keeps the peace).

As potsherd (or frying-pan) keeps water from putting out fire and fire from consuming water, so the elder keeps the peace between the young of relatively equal status.

The hierarchy of age is taken as a matter of course and circumcision camps or other formal 'schools' are not considered necessary to reinforce an attitude which no one would dream of disputing. At the present time there is quite a vogue for circumcision camps (*vakuevamba*) in the southern or south-eastern half of the country. Some affirm that these are new-fangled notions coming in from neighbouring tribes. Others declare the institution to be very old. The Ngalangi people say that they have always had both *evamba* for the boys and *uso wakãi* for the girls. Some tribes require *evamba* of the king before he may rule. Even where the institution is not in vogue, there are associations of coevals (*vakuacisoko*) whose members have definite rights and duties toward each other. These matters are treated more fully in a later chapter. Inasmuch as these age-grade sets are both age and sex divisions, they contain some elements of social cleavage, but their association with the economic and political sides of life makes them a strongly cohesive force for society.

Umbundu Social Structure: Summary

Summarizing the evidence of the present chapter, I wish only to tie in a few of the more important threads so that the pattern of the Umbundu social structure may be seen at a glance.

Although the Ovimbundu no longer maintain the political life which formerly existed, there are elements of cohesion which still give reality to their social organism. These elements all centre in or spring from the kinship group.

With regard to the village, two facts stand out:

1. The Umbundu village is a local kinship unit, with the villagers quite literally the children of the headman-patriarch.
2. Although its political, religious, and social functions may be

60 UMBUNDU KINSHIP AND CHARACTER

in a somewhat decadent state, the Umbundu village has up to the present maintained its status as a local kinship unit.

The household is not a solitary unit but a part of the village. Since it is constituted by marriage, it embodies the union of at least two kinship groups. The attitudes and behaviour patterns within the Umbundu household are basically those universally recognized. In common with the households of most Bantu cultures, it differs from the European model in that it extends its attitudes and behaviour patterns to the wider kinship groupings by means of a classificatory system of relationship.

In the wider kinship groupings (*epata*), the Ovimbundu recognize both the maternal (*oluina*) and the paternal (*oluse*) lines of descent. The functions of the latter have been largely local, residential, social, and religious, with succession (of status) in the male line. The function of the former has been cohesive over a larger terri-tory, with a recognized head in whom has been vested both religious and economic functions. Both his office and the inheritance of property descend in the female line. Much of the power, economic and personal, formerly held by the *oluina*, in the person of the mother's brother, seems to be passing at the present time to the *oluse*, in the person of the father. The bilineal kinship system has been a strongly cohesive social force.

The form of marriage practised by the Ovimbundu is of the two-way cross-cousin type in both lines of kin and in three generations. It seems to be an individual type developed in the particular social and economic situation of the Ovimbundu. As a contract between two families and as a new venture, the marriage relation demands that great attention be given to attitudes and behaviour patterns which emphasize mutual respect.

The hierarchy of age is a very real factor in the Umbundu social structure. Age-set 'schools' have not existed generally throughout the tribes, but there are associations of coevals. This is largely a cohesive force.

Sorcery is the most important disruptive force at work *within* Umbundu society. Working as it does, within kinship groups, and inasmuch as it seems to be on the increase, sorcery embodies a real danger to social cohesion.

Homogeneity has never been an attribute of the Ovimbundu as regards their racial or cultural make-up. The slave-trade injected other and more diverse elements, and recent movements and contacts still other. As regards social and economic status, the course of Umbundu life has seen great changes: great inequalities produced by trade booms; a severe levelling down by effective European occupation and by the application of direct rule. That the Umbundu social organism through this entire process has maintained elements of cohesion and of life speaks well for its adaptability and for the vitality of its institutions.

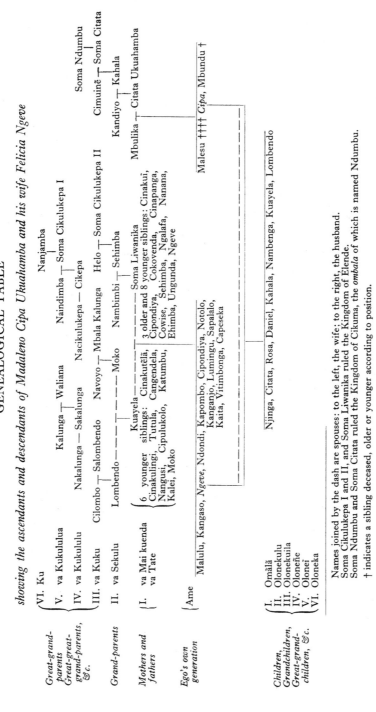

CHAPTER IV

SIGNIFICANCE OF THE SOCIAL STRUCTURE

THE first and most important factor to be considered with reference to a programme of education or culture change is the social structure of the people among whom the programme is to be set up and carried out. Few writers on missions among the Bantu have considered the significance for the work of the social structure itself. Perhaps the particular social structure and its possible reference to the programme described have been considered too obvious to merit careful consideration. I am reminded of an observation of the late Mr. Justice Holmes that the 'vindication of the obvious is often more important than the elucidation of the obscure'.[1] But formerly it was not considered at all obvious that a mission programme should take into consideration a people's social structure. So great a missionary and anthropologist as the Reverend H. A. Junod concluded with all complacency: 'Bantu collectivism is dying out. In its stead Christianity will promote a healthy and progressive individualism. . . . I see no other way in which it (the race) can escape destruction.'[2] That was written before 1929, since when advocates of individualism have been few, and fewer the students of African life who would wish to 'promote' individualism there.

The majority of missionary writers who have urged the adaptation or adoption of Bantu cultural elements have concerned themselves largely with beliefs, practices, and rites. If they so much as touch upon the social structure of the people under consideration, it is only to lay a basis for description of these other elements.[3] Although a number of writers have urged the desirability of conserving good elements believed to exist in 'Bantu communalism', 'African collectivism', and so on, few have offered concrete suggestions concerning the social structure, as designed to be of immediate or practical value. The one missionary who has

[1] Quoted in mimeographed suggestions concerning the use of *Essentials of Civilization*, by Thomas Jesse Jones (New York, 1929).

[2] Junod, op. cit., 2nd ed., vol. ii, p. 633; 1st ed. (1913), vol. ii, p. 544.

[3] The most recent work of this type which has come to my attention is *The Church and Primitive People* (The Religious Institutions and Beliefs of the Southern Bantu and their Bearing on the Problems of the Christian Missionary), by D. W. T. Shropshire (London: S.P.C.K., 1938).

64   UMBUNDU KINSHIP AND CHARACTER

addressed the burden of his writings toward saving or regenerating
the social structure of the people is Bruno Gutmann, who has
worked for many years among the Chagga on the slopes of
Kilimanjaro. Dr. Gutmann holds that our task should be to 'help
the Africans to preserve and strengthen their indigenous bonds and
their ties of kinship and of the common occupation of the soil of
their fathers, since without this solid structure the native tribal
spirit has no home'.[1] He holds that the traditional tribal culture
of the Chagga (or of any other people) is the manifestation of an
inner spirit (*Volksseele*) which is ordained by God,[2] and from this
he lays down four fundamental principles,[3] and proceeds to build
a programme for the Chagga which might also be adapted for other
people. I am not concerned here with Dr. Gutmann's theoretical,
philosophical, or theological concepts, nor even with his concrete
application of them to his own work, since the cultures of the
Chagga and of the Ovimbundu are quite different. His emphasis
on the fundamental importance of kinship ties, however, is of
great interest, and the more especially since some of his practical
conclusions are in fundamental agreement with those reached by
certain South African anthropologists faced with similar problems.
Gutmann's proposals are worthy of serious study by all African
missionaries.[4]

The problem of building a new social structure upon a solid
foundation of the structure already in existence has been faced with
all seriousness by some British African administrative officers. Expression of this attitude is found in the policy of 'indirect rule',
which, according to Sir Donald Cameron, tries 'while we endeavour
to purge the native system of its abuses, to graft our higher
civilization upon the soundly rooted native stock'.[5]

Not alone among South African anthropologists, (Mrs.) A. W.
Hoernlé has urged upon educational authorities and Missions the
necessity for respecting 'the principle of kinship, which is the basis

---

[1] *Das Recht der Dschagga*, p. 25 (quoted by G. Wagner, *I.R.M.*, 1937,
p. 511).

[2] Wagner, op. cit., p. 509.

[3] See B. Gutmann, 'Aufgaben der Gemeinschaftsbildung in Afrika', *Africa*,
1928, p. 436 f.

[4] See Bibliography for most important books and articles. It is to be hoped
that at least two or three of Gutmann's books may be made available for English
readers by translation. His German is said to be very difficult even for German
readers.

[5] Quoted by J. H. Oldham in *Africa*, 1934, p. 53.

PLATE VII

Photo. M. W. Ennis
a. Communal fishing party (Talange River, Elende)

Photo. R. S. Webb
b. Women grinding meal (Bailundu)

PLATE VIII

Photo. R. S. Webb

a. Umbundu pots (before firing), baskets, and hoes

Photo. M. W. Ennis

b. Umbundu basketry with native-woven tapestry

SIGNIFICANCE OF THE SOCIAL STRUCTURE 65

on which the social cohesion of African peoples rests'.[1] In the article here quoted, and more recently at the New Education Fellowship Conference, she summarizes her conclusions regarding 'Positive Values in the African Social Organization', with special reference to the Sotho-Tswana and Zulu-Xhosa groups of the South African Bantu.[2]

Nor have American educational authorities failed to recognize the crucial importance to educational and missionary efforts of a primitive people's social structure. Were it necessary, numerous quotations might be given. Two of the four 'Essentials of Primitive Society' listed by Dr. Thomas Jesse Jones, have to do with the social structure:

II. Power of integration with the environment, material and human:

III. A proper regard for the home and the household.[3]

Even more explicit are the counsels to be found in *The Educational Yearbook* for 1931 and 1933:

... we often find that the organization of the family and the relationships between its members are as good as, and in some cases superior to, those which are found among western peoples. ...

When it comes to other matters of social relationships, such as the communal system and the practice of sharing ... it is little less than disastrous that the western educator, brought up in a system of individualism, seems to wish to make it necessary for the indigenous peoples to go back to a social organization from which his own world is attempting to move.[4]

Social forms have got to change. But whatever changes may take place, ... the vital thing is that the sense of mutual obligation and responsibility which is found in existing relations should be conserved and express itself in the new conditions.[5]

The village is the key to an educational or mission approach to the Ovimbundu. This fact has long been recognized by the missions. The Deputation of the American Board of Com-

---

[1] M. Stauffer, ed., *Thinking with Africa* (New York, 1927), p. 86 (article by Mrs. Hoernlé), also quoted by C. T. Loram in *The Educational Yearbook, 1933* (Dr. Kandel, ed.), p. 280.

[2] See E. G. Malherbe, ed., *Educational Adaptations in a Changing Society* (N.E.F. Conference Report, Cape Town, 1937), pp. 405–7.

[3] T. J. Jones, *Essentials of Civilization* (New York, 1929), pp. 7 ff.

[4] C. T. Loram in *The Educational Yearbook, 1931*, I. Kandel, ed. (New York, 1931), pp. 10, 12.

[5] J. W. C. Dougall in op. cit., 1933, p. 159.

F

66 UMBUNDU KINSHIP AND CHARACTER

missioners for Foreign Missions which visited the Umbundu area in 1911 found some difficult problems from the great numbers of converts who had flocked to live on the mission stations. That, however, was a situation from which the missionaries had already been trying to recede for some time since 1897[1] when outstations were first undertaken by Abrão Ngulu and José Katito who went back to their own kin; and even more definitely since 1905 when Elende Station was opened with the idea that the only natives to reside there would be a small number of teachers and other leaders and boarding-school pupils who would afterwards return to their own families to form new centres of work.[2] That the village is a kinship unit has also been recognized and the description of the village of Ngendo showed that outstation work is being carried on *within* the kinship pattern of the village, and without doing violence to the Umbundu concept of social structure. The church elder and his villagers are accepted by the other villagers as kinsmen.[3] While it is evident that the way of life of the people of the school village differed from that of the elder's village, and the extent to which they mutually fulfilled kinship obligations toward each other may be questioned, nevertheless, the very fact that they mutually recognized ties of kinship and that they live side by side in harmony is of significance. It is also significant that the outstation leadership had come from within the kinship group. Likuluta Samikanjo, the elder, had attended boarding-school on a mission station, but only for a short time, and he did not pretend to be a teacher. In the beginning of the work an elder and also a teacher had been sent out from Elende Mission Station, but they had stayed only until the local people were able to carry on. The teacher at the time of my visits was Vitorino Mbambi. He belonged to the household of Likuluta's sister's son. The situation of the outstation of Ngendo is not unusual and could be duplicated many times by examples taken from various parts of the Umbundu country. It has been quite the thing for those individual Christians among the Ovimbundu who have become church elders to seek to establish villages or 'wards' of their own among their own kinsmen. Some teachers have also followed a similar bent, but if they were toc young to receive the respect due to an elder of the Ovi-

[1] *Missionary Herald*, 1898, p. 108.
[2] A.B.C.F.M., *Report of the Deputation to the W.C.A. Mission*, 1911, p. 66.
[3] See *supra*, p. 29 f.

SIGNIFICANCE OF THE SOCIAL STRUCTURE 67

mbundu, they have not, independent of some related elder, generally been very successful within the kinship group.

There is another factor in the situation of the Ngendo out-station which has tended to preserve the ties of kinship between the villagers of the two groups. The support of the two leaders is very largely found locally. Neither teacher nor elder has ever received more than a very occasional bonus from either the native church or the mission. They carry on by the help of the local people and through their own efforts. Dr. Gutmann holds that it is the schools which are most disruptive in their influence on African social structure because of their organization and the way in which they are carried on. A school, he says, should reflect the organic connexions of native society and enter into reciprocal relations with the folk group. Instead, he points out, this is being made impossible in East Africa by raising the salaries of the teachers until they are removed from the ordinary life of the rest of the people.[1] This cleavage between educated individuals who should be leaders and the masses of the people seems to have reached an even more markedly advanced stage in South Africa, according to Mrs. Hoernlé, Eiselen, and others who also seek remedies in strengthening or renewing the natural social bonds.[2] What I wish to emphasize is that the more important point is not how much salary a teacher or an elder may receive, but whether his appointment and the remuneration he receives tend to weaken the organic bonds of native society and to make difficult his relations with the folk group. Do the conditions of his position *ipso facto* place him or keep him outside the local group?

In seeking to lay among the Ovimbundu sure foundations for a truly indigenous Church, the importance of ties of kinship have probably been recognized by more than one missionary. The importance of stimulating local self-support both for its influence on building up the Church and on the development of indigenous leadership has long been stressed in mission circles, although it must be recognized that the principle has often been honoured rather in the breach than in the observance. While recognizing the value of these principles as long-term objectives, impatient of meagre immediate and visible 'results' or failing to realize how

[1] Gutmann, *Africa*, 1928, p. 443 f.

[2] e.g., see Eiselen in Schapera (ed.), *Western Civilization and the Natives of South Africa* (London, 1934), p. 81.

68 UMBUNDU KINSHIP AND CHARACTER

binding on future policy 'temporary' expedients may be, missionaries have pursued policies which may bring numbers into school and Church, but which have certainly tended to disrupt natural social bonds which ought to be conserved. The sending of young half-trained teachers into areas where they have no natural ties and where they are nearly as foreign to their prospective pupils as is the white missionary is not a policy calculated to develop either indigenous institutions or indigenous leadership. The example of or similarity with a commercial enterprise in starting branches or sending out salesmen is particularly dangerous among the Ovimbundu with their trading experience. If native workers are sent out on what may appear to them to be commercial basis, similar to that of a 'branch store', we should not be surprised if subsequently they act the part. Neither is the political heritage of the Ovimbundu a good example or pattern for the Church. A Church organized on what to the natives may appear like political lines is not likely to develop along soundly social or spiritual lines. The more fortunate pattern for Church and school is that of the household, the kinship village, and the wider kinship group.

It is fortunate that kinship still retains much of its cohesive power for the Ovimbundu and that they yet live in their kinship villages. It will be a great thing if this force can be widely utilized by the Church until a new order can be built upon the firm foundations of the old. It is fortunate that so much of the village work of the Church has already grown up within the kinship structure. The village organization of the Ovimbundu and its very plan are in favour of outstation development. It is to be hoped that the Church may make constructive use of its opportunity in the villages of the Ovimbundu. Should the Church *not* seize this opportunity and should the present disruptive forces continue to operate, the outlook for this great people must be dark indeed.

Objections will perhaps be urged against seeking to work within the kinship structure because of the influence of unprogressive elders, or inconveniences due to proximity to their villages, the prevalence of witchcraft accusations within the kinship group, &c. This last problem must be dealt with. An increased incidence of witchcraft accusations in many parts of Africa has been noted by leading authorities. These authorities agree that such increases seem to be due to insecurity.[1] Insecurity itself must certainly

---

[1] See statement by B. Malinowski in *Africa*, 1939, p. 38 f.

SIGNIFICANCE OF THE SOCIAL STRUCTURE 69

increase with disruption of the social structure, and an increase in social security should be a factor tending ultimately to loosen the hold of witchcraft. Working within the kinship group may have disadvantages, but the greater disadvantage must come in attempting to ignore, or in working against, such natural bonds.

No one would question the necessity for utilizing the attitudes of goodwill and love found within the household, between parent and child, between children of the same parents, for that is within 'the family circle' as understood by those of European culture. What missionary has not explained the love and fatherhood of God by the human parent-child relation? This is almost a commonplace of experience, but the fact which has been more generally neglected is that the Ovimbundu, in common with all the Bantu, extend the range of these attitudes beyond the household to include a great number of relatives also classified as brother, sister, father, and mother. Even though the African may not actually apply, or may but partially apply, to the larger circle of relatives the attitudes implied by the terms of relationship, is it not of potential value that the possibility exists? And if there is the possibility of extending these intimate attitudes to the wider group of kin, is there not also the possibility of extending them still further? In my opinion a classificatory system of kinship offers a splendid opportunity to the religious educator.[1] Much has been written about the new 'Tribe of God' which the Church is calling into being in Africa. My observation is, however, that unless the new tribe is rooted firmly in the soil of its own social heritage, it will not grow into a tribe at all, but rather will fall apart into its components of *deracinés*, literally uprooted individuals. Those individuals, moreover, are likely to be twofold more sons of individualism than the individualist who compassed sea and land to convert them.[2] If the 'Tribe of God' or the Kingdom of God is going to *live* among the Ovimbundu, I feel that it must find its life first in terms of the life of the household, the kinship village, the kin by blood and by marriage, until it becomes *the great fact* because it is rooted deep in the lives of the people.

[1] Some elements of the type of approach which I have in mind are illustrated for a boarding-school community by Mabel Shaw in her delightful book, *God's Candlelights* (New York: Friendship Press, 1935).

[2] The increase of denominational sectarianism by almost geometric progression among the natives of South Africa is a fact which seems to have significance in this regard. Ethiopianism is a logical outcome of religious individualism.

70 UMBUNDU KINSHIP AND CHARACTER

With regard to the larger kinship groupings, much more exact study is necessary to determine the present reciprocal relations of the two lines of descent. To what extent is the balance of *oluse* and *oluina* still maintained? Meanwhile all missionaries should seek to understand and avoid anything which might tend to disturb whatever balance may now exist. Inheritance through the maternal line has been hard for missionaries to understand, and to converts largely outside the kinship structure this type of inheritance often brings real hardship.

Marriage is to be taken up later when I shall combine all evaluations that I have to offer on the subject.

Leadership has already been mentioned with reference to the village community. It is clear that those leaders require training in schools advanced beyond the grade of the village, where they may be exposed to disruptive influences so justly feared by Dr. Gutmann, the results of which are evident from one end of Africa to the other.

Even to-day the educated people among the Bantu do not seem to be under any sense of obligation towards their sibs or their tribes. Still, it is never too late to mend, and education . . . of intelligent natives for leadership must be undertaken on a larger scale than has yet been done. The great principle involved here, common both to Christian teaching and to Bantu religion, is that man can not be truly good and truly happy unless he uses his individual gifts in the service of the community as a whole. The Christian Bantu and the educated Bantu must both have experienced the great joy which man derives from unselfish work for his fellow beings, before the Bantu people as a whole can make real progress.[1]

I am confident that the right types of leadership can be produced and that the spirit of service can be instilled. Dr. Gutmann's suggestions for retaining the kinship principle in school life are worth considering.[2] It is worth something to have the pupils definitely sent to school by their kinship groups and received back for service under the aegis of those groups once the course is finished. The problem of mediocre pupils who are members of prominent or important kinship groups is a real one, and there are many other problems which should not be glossed over. If the future leaders are to be *real* leaders, their connexion with their own

[1] Eiselen in Schapera, 1934, loc. cit.
[2] Gutmann, in *Africa*, 1928, pp. 437, 443 f.

SIGNIFICANCE OF THE SOCIAL STRUCTURE 71

folk groups must be maintained. Children of uprooted households will rarely make acceptable leaders unless some real integration or reintegration with a kinship group can be achieved.[1] The problem of the course itself is very important but too long and detailed for treatment here. Whatever else the course may have, let it include a study of the people's own culture,[2] not forgetting the social structure. Concerning the organization of the school life itself, an interesting experiment was begun at Malangali in Tanganyika.[3] It is too bad that that experiment could not have gone on. The organization of the girl's school described by Mabel Shaw also shows some very interesting features.[4] It must be said, however, that this type of organization is not unique and that such schools are going on even if they may have been but inadequately reported.

These advanced schools involve at least a limited number of communities organized on an other-than-kinship basis, for even if all the teachers of a school *could* be taken from a single group of kin, no one would attempt it. Students of Bantu society recognize the desirability of maintaining a balance between kinship groups. Villages composed of such groups of teachers and leaders if carefully constituted might offer a convenient point of departure away from the kinship system, for I do not suppose that that system can be considered as eternal. Let it not be abandoned, however, for frivolous reasons; nor until a better one has come to take its place; nor yet again until it has yielded up to its successors all that it contains of lasting worth. There are few of the Ovimbundu who are yet able permanently to reside quite out of touch with groups of their own kin, and still maintain ideals of service and a truly social morality. Close contact with and continuous employment by Europeans seems to have especially disturbing effects. It seems advisable, therefore, in most cases, to employ teachers and other leaders at

[1] It should be realized that many of those individuals who moved to the mission stations in the early days quite cut themselves off from their own kin: they became *deracinés*. Unless a subsequent reintegration was achieved, they passed that status on to their descendants who, by that fact, may be quite unsuitable as leaders.

[2] This emphasis is necessary because of the disrepute of Umbundu culture which westernized schooling has produced. The culture should, of course, not be taught by westerners, but rather by those of the students who know it, by native teachers and by elders brought in for special topics.

[3] W. B. Mumford, 'Education and Social Adjustment of Primitive Peoples of Africa', *Africa*, 1929, pp. 138–61.

[4] Mabel Shaw, op. cit.

72 UMBUNDU KINSHIP AND CHARACTER

the mission stations for limited periods of time, after which they may return to serve those of their own kin. Such rotation of employment increases the difficulty of carrying on institutions with a strictly limited European personnel, but it has the additional advantage of spreading further the advanced training as well as the desirable jobs.

In summary, the following suggestions are offered as a basis for discussion and action:

1. *The need for a sympathetic understanding of the social structure of the people cannot be stressed too much or too often.* For those co-operating with the Church in the village work, such an understanding is a first essential. It is of even greater importance to one who would make a significant contribution to the training of leaders.

2. *For the village work:*

(*a*) It is taken for granted that all village work will be undertaken by and through the native church in order that division of approach, of leadership, and of policy may be avoided. This applies to all lines of endeavour whether agricultural, educational, medical, or religious. This suggestion claims no originality: it has been made before.

(*b*) Local self-support is very much to be desired. Before outside funds are used, it should be determined that their use will not disturb the social balance, nor be a divisive force— as, for example, by setting the leader apart from those to be led, or by making the recipient dependent on the missionary and so above the discipline of those who should be responsible for him. Pauperization of the local group is also a very real danger.

(*c*) In opening new work, let every effort be made to keep it within or closely allied to present forms of the constituted social structure. For outstations this will mean proximity to and relations with a village of kin.

(*d*) For the outstations now constituted a kinship census could be taken in order that the present situation may be known. Data could be collected little by little, but efforts should be organized and results co-ordinated. The religious education department of the central training institute could assist in such a project.

SIGNIFICANCE OF THE SOCIAL STRUCTURE 73

(*e*) In everything pertaining to the native church and the village work let its bearing upon the social structure be weighed, and let Umbundu kinship principles be taken into consideration.

3. *In constructing programmes of religious education* and in the actual teaching let us seek to utilize the attitudes of the household and the principle of their extension to the wider groups of kin through the classificatory kinship system.

4. *In the selection and training of leaders* may we:

(*a*) Endeavour to use those who would be natural leaders by arranging their selection by and within the kinship groups.

(*b*) Other things being equal, avoid the use of *déracinés* and of partially uprooted persons. They will rarely be able to lead, for those whom they try to lead are unlikely to accept them. This doubt also applies to persons from other tribes and other language areas unless they have been regularly integrated in their place of service.

(*c*) In the organization of courses and the administration of schools for training leaders, the constitution of the social structure and of its component kinship groupings should be given major consideration.

(*d*) The above also applies to constitution and conduct of mission villages.

Cultural disintegration and possible reintegration with reference to mission work has received penetrating analysis at the hands of Archibald G. Baker.[1] He points out that a period of disintegration is the opportunity of the reformer, but warns 'that any movement of disintegration, excessively speeded up by high pressure tactics of government or of reformer, produces a state of social anarchy, cultural chaos, and personal disintegration, which in the long run postpones the day of permanent reform . . . '.[2] What such 'social anarchy, cultural chaos, and personal disintegration' may mean for an African tribe needs no demonstration. It may mean annihilation, as has been or is becoming the case with various groups such as the 'Strandloopers' and Bushmen (of Cape Colony and the Southwest), the Mpongue, and other Bantu tribes of the French Congo.

---

[1] A. G. Baker, *Christian Missions and a New World Culture* (Chicago: Willet, Clark & Co., 1934).

[2] Ibid., p. 215.

74 UMBUNDU KINSHIP AND CHARACTER

The least that can happen will be a centrifugal throwing off of groups of *diaspora*—a process actually taking place from among the Ovimbundu. These uprooted groups, *déracinés, ovimbali*,[1] whether they settle in the towns or move to other territories, are far less promising material from every standpoint than they were when in their former cultural and social state. In view of the many and important adaptations which the Ovimbundu have made in the past, their ability to adapt themselves to yet greater innovations may be confidently affirmed, if only the movement is not 'excessively speeded up'. Plainly, it is the duty of everyone who is interested in the social welfare of this great people to do what may be in his power to arrest the process of disintegration, and to strengthen existing social bonds lest the latter state be worse than the former.

BIBLIOGRAPHY

FOR CHAPTERS II AND III

Titles previously listed are not repeated although these chapters may contain references to them.

Angola et Rhodesie: Mission Rohan-Chabot (Paris: Ministère de l'Instruction Publique, 1914).

Annaes do Conselho Ultramarino, 1854–61 (Lisboa: Imprensa Nacional, 1867).

Annaes Maritimos e Coloniaes, Parte não-oficial, 1844–46 (ibid.).

Anuário Estatístico de Angola, 1935 (Luanda: Imprensa Nacional, 1936).

BASTOS, AUGUSTO. *Monografia de Catumbella* (Lisboa, 1912).

—— *Traços Geraes sôbre a Ethnografia do Districto de Benguella* (Lisboa, 1909).

BAUMANN, H. 'Vaterrecht und Mutterrecht in Afrika', *Zs. Ethnol.*, vol. 58, pp. 62–161 (1926).

BENEDICT, RUTH. *Patterns of Culture* (Boston and New York: Houghton Mifflin, 1934).

BROWN, G. GORDON. 'Hehe Cross-Cousin Marriage', in *Essays Presented to C. G. Seligman*, ed. by Evans-Pritchard, Firth, Malinowski, and Schapera (London: Kegan Paul, 1934).

DANNERT, E. *Zum Recht der Herero* (Berlin, 1906).

DE CLEENE, N. 'La Famille dans l'organisation sociale du Mayombe', *Africa*, 1937, pp. 1–15.

DELACHAUX, TH., and THIEBAUD, CH.-E. *Pays et peuples d'Angola* (Neuchâtel and Paris: Attinger, 1934). (Deals with peoples of the southern part of the colony.)

[1] *Ovimbali* (or *vambali*), see *supra*, p. 19.

SIGNIFICANCE OF THE SOCIAL STRUCTURE 75

EISELEN, WERNER. 'Preferential Marriage: Correlation of the Various Modes among the Bantu of South Africa', *Africa*, 1928, pp. 413–28.

ESTERMANN, C. 'Coutumes des Mbali du Sud d'Angola', *Africa*, 1939, pp. 74–86.

—— 'Cultural Changes in Ovamboland', *Zs. Ethnol.*, 1932, pp. 40–5.

—— 'La Tribu Kwanyama en face de la civilisation européenne', *Africa*, 1934, pp. 431 ff.

FIGUEIRA, LUIZ. *África Bantú* (Lisboa: Oficinas Fernândes, 1938).

GLUCKMAN, MAX. *Economy of the Central Barotse Plain* (Rhodes-Livingstone Institute, N. Rhodesia, 1941).

—— 'The Difficulties, Limitations and Achievements of Social Anthropology', *Rhodes-Livingstone Journal*, no. 1, June 1944

HAMBLY, WILFRID D. *The Ovimbundu of Angola* (Chicago: Field Museum, 1934).

HOERNLÉ, A. W. 'The Importance of the Sib in the Marriage Ceremonies of the South-eastern Bantú', *South African Journal of Science*, 1925, vol. xxii, pp. 481–92.

HUNTER, MONICA. *Reaction to Conquest* (London: International Institute of African Languages and Cultures, 1936).

IRLE, J. *Die Herero. Ein Beitrag zur Landes-, Volks- und Missionskunde* (Gutersloh, 1906).

JUNOD, H. A. *The Life of a South African Tribe*, 2nd ed. (London: Macmillan, 1927).

KRIGE, EILEEN JENSEN. *The Social System of the Zulus* (London: Longmans, 1936).

KUCZYNSKI, ROBERT R. *Colonial Population* (London: O.U.P., 1937).

—— *Population Movements* (ibid., 1936).

—— 'The Contribution of Demography to the Study of Social Problems', *Rhodes-Livingstone Journal*, no. 2, Dec. 1944.

LANG, A., et TASTEVIN, C. *La Tribu des Va-Nyaneka* (Tome V, Mission Rohan-Chabot) (Corbeil: Imprimerie Creté, 1938).

LINTON, RALPH. *The Study of Man: An Introduction* (New York: Appleton-Century, 1936).

LIVINGSTONE, DAVID. *Missionary Travels and Researches in South Africa* (London: Murray, 1857).

LOPES DE LIMA, J. J. *Ensaios sôbre a Statística d'Angola e Benguella* (Lisboa: Impr. Nacional, 1846).

LOWIE, ROBERT. *Primitive Society* (New York: Boni Liveright, 1920).

—— *An Introduction to Cultural Anthropology* (London: Harrap, 1934).

LUTTIG, H. G. *The Religious System and Social Organization of the Herero* (Utrecht, 1933).

MAGYAR, LADISLAU. *Reisen in Süd-Afrika, 1849–1857*, tr. Hunfalvy (Pesth, 1859).

76 UMBUNDU KINSHIP AND CHARACTER

MAIR, L. P. *An African People in the Twentieth Century* (London: Routledge, 1934).

MENDES CORREIA, A. A. *Antropologia angolense* (Arquivos de Anatomia e Antropologia II, Lisboa, 1916). (Chiefly concerned with physical anthropology.)

MEYER, F. *Wirtschaft und Recht der Herero* (Berlin, 1905).

OBERG, KALERVO. 'Kinship Organization of the Banyankole', *Africa*, 1938, pp. 129–58.

RADCLIFFE BROWN, A. R. 'The Mother's Brother in South Africa', *South African Journal of Science* (Nov. 1924), pp. 542–55.

RAVENSTEIN, E. G. (ed.). *The Strange Adventures of Andrew Battell of Leigh in Angola and the adjoining regions.* (Reprinted from *Purchas, his Pilgrims.*) Edited with Notes and Histories. (London: for the Hakluyt Society, 1901).

RICHARDS, AUDREY I. 'Mother Right among the Central Bantu', *Essays presented to C. G. Seligman* (London: Kegan Paul, 1934).

—— 'The Village Census in the Study of Culture Contact', *Africa*, 1935, pp. 20–33.

ROSCOE, J. *The Baganda* (London: Macmillan, 1911).

—— *Immigrants and Their Influence on the Lake Regions of Africa* (Cambridge: University Press, 1924).

SCHAPERA, I. (ed.). *The Bantu-Speaking Tribes of South Africa*, Chap. IV: 'Social Organization' by A. W. Hoernlé.

—— 'The Present State and Future Development of Ethnographical Research in South Africa (with a select Bibliography)', *Bantu Studies*, vol. viii, no. 3.

SMITH, E. W., and DALE, A. M. *The Ila-Speaking Peoples of Northern Rhodesia*, 2 vols. (London: Macmillan, 1920).

STAYT, HUGH A. *The Bavenda* (London: International Institute of African Languages and Cultures, 1931).

TONJES, HERMANN. *Ovamboland, Land, Leute, Mission* (Berlin: Warneck, 1911).

TORDAY, E. *African Races* (London: Williams & Norgate, 1930).

—— 'Dualism in Western Bantu Religion and Social Organization', *J.R.A.I*, 1928, pp. 225–45.

—— 'Notes on the Ethnography of the Bayaka', *J.R.A.I.*, 1906, pp. 39–59.

—— 'The Principles of Bantu Marriage', *Africa*, 1929, pp. 255–90.

—— and JOYCE, T. A. *Notes ethnographiques sur les populations habitants les bassins du Kasai et du Kwango oriental* (Annales du Musée du Congo, 3.2.2) (Bruxelles, 1922).

TUCKER, LEONA STUKEY. 'The Divining Basket of the Ovimbundu', *J.R.A.I.*, 1940, vol. lxx, pp. 171–201.

VAN WARMELO, N. J. *Kinship Terminology of the South African Bantu* (Pretoria: Government Printer, 1931). Pp. 119. (Union of South Africa: Department of Native Affairs—Ethnological Publications, vol. ii.)

SIGNIFICANCE OF THE SOCIAL STRUCTURE 77

VIEHE, G. 'Die Omaanda und Otuzo der Ovaherero', *Mitteil. d. Seminars f. Oriental. Sprachen*, vol. v, 1902.

WAGNER, GÜNTER. *The Changing Family among the Bantu Kavirondo*, Suppl. to *Africa*, Jan. 1939.

WEEKS, JOHN H. *Among the Primitive Bakongo* (London: Seeley, Service, 1914).

WILSON, G., and HUNTER, MONICA. *The Study of African Society* (Rhodes-Livingstone Institute, N. Rhodesia, 1939).

ZASTROW, B. v. 'Die Herero' (*Das Eingeborenenrecht*, ed. E. Schultz-Ewerth u. L. Adam, vol. ii, Stuttgart, 1930).

FOR CHAPTER IV

BAKER, A. G. *Christian Missions and a New World Culture* (Chicago: Willet, Clark & Co., 1934).

Christian Students and Modern South Africa (being a Report of the Bantu-European Student Christian Conference, Fort Hare, 1930).

DOUGALL, J. W. C. 'The Relationship of Church and School in Africa', *I.R.M.*, 1937, pp. 204–14.

GOODSELL, FRED FIELD. 'The Indigenous Church: Finance', *I.R.M.*, 1938, pp. 393–402 (contains illustrations from Umbundu Church).

GUTMANN, BRUNO. 'The African Standpoint', *Africa*, 1935, pp. 1–17.
—— 'Aufgaben der Gemeinschaftsbildung in Afrika', *Africa*, 1928, pp. 429–45.
—— *Freies Menschentum aus ewigen Bindungen* (Cassel: Bärenreiter Verlag, 1926).
—— *Gemeindeaufbau aus dem Evangelium* (Leipzig: Verlag der E.-L. Mission, 1925).
—— *Das Dschaggaland und seine Christen* (Leipzig: Verlag der E.-L. Mission, 1925).
—— *Das Recht der Dschagga* (Leipzig, 1926).
—— 'Thinking in Tribal Terms'—translation and summary by A. King, *World Dominion*, Jan. 1932, pp. 87–91.

JONES, THOMAS JESSE. *Education in Africa* (New York: Phelps Stokes Fund, 1922).

JUNOD, H. P. 'Anthropology and Missionary Education', *I.R.M.*, 1935, pp. 213–28.
—— *Essentials of Civilization* (New York: Holt, 1929).

KANDEL, ISAAC (ed.). *The Educational Yearbook 1933*. Articles: 'Missionary Education and Social Questions', by J. W. C. Dougall (pp. 139–59); 'Africa, The Place of Education in the Missionary Enterprise', by C. T. Loram (pp. 261–98).
—— (ed.). *The Educational Yearbook 1931*. Article: 'The Education of Indigenous Peoples', by C. T. Loram (pp. 3–26).

78 UMBUNDU KINSHIP AND CHARACTER

LARSEN, L. P. 'The Indigenous Church: Theological Training', *I.R.M.*, 1938, pp. 377–85.

MAIR, L. P. 'The Anthropologist's Approach to Native Education', *Oversea Education*, vol. vi, pp. 53–60.

MALHERBE, E. G. (ed.). *Educational Adaptations in a Changing Society* (N.E.F. Conference Report, Cape Town, 1937).

MALINOWSKI, B. 'Native Education and Culture Contact', *I.R.M.*, 1936, pp. 480–515.

—— 'Practical Anthropology', *Africa*, 1929, pp. 22–38.

MEINHOF, CARL. 'Changes in the African Conception of Law due to the Influence of Missions', *I.R.M.*, 1927, pp. 430–5 (summarized translation).

MUMFORD, W. BRYANT. 'Education and the Social Adjustment of the Primitive Peoples of Africa to European Culture', *Africa*, 1929, pp. 138–61.

—— 'Malangali School', *Africa*, 1930, pp. 265–92.

OLDHAM, J. H., and GIBSON, B. D. *The Remaking of Man in Africa* (London: O.U.P., 1931).

—— 'Dr. Siegfried Knak on the Christian Task in Africa', *I.R.M.*, 1931, pp. 547–55.

—— 'Educational Work of Missionary Societies', *Africa*, 1934, pp. 47–59.

RAUM, OTTO. 'Dr. Gutmann's Work on Kilimanjaro: I. The Church and African Society', *I.R.M.*, 1937, pp. 500–7.

The Realignment of Native Life on a Christian Basis (being a Report of the Seventh General Missionary Conference of South Africa; Lovedale, 1930).

ROEHL, K. 'The Clan and the Gospel, being a review of Gutmann: *Das Dschaggaland und seine Christen* (Leipzig, 1925), and *Gemeindeaufbau aus dem Evangelium* (ibid.)', *I.R.M.*, 1926, pp. 599–602.

SCHAPERA, I. (ed.). *Western Civilization and the Natives of South Africa* (London: Routledge, 1934). Chap. III: 'Christianity and the Religious Life of the Bantu' by W. M. Eiselen.

SCHLUNK, MARTIN. 'The Relation of Missions to Native Society', *I.R.M.*, 1927, pp. 350–63.

SHAW, MABEL. *God's Candlelights* (New York: Friendship Press, 1935).

SHROPSHIRE, DENYS W. T. *The Church and Primitive Peoples* (The Religious Institutions and Beliefs of the Southern Bantu and Their Bearing on the Problems of the Christian Missionary) (London: S.P.C.K., 1938).

SMITH, EDWIN W. *African Beliefs and Christian Faith* (London: United Society for Christian Literature, 1936).

—— *The Golden Stool* (London: Holborn Publishing House, 1926).

—— 'Social Anthropology and Mission Work', *I.R.M.*, 1924, pp. 318–31.

STAUFFER, MILTON (ed.). *Thinking with Africa* (New York: Missionary Education Movement, 1927). Especially: III. 'Religion in Native Life' by A. W. Hoernlé.

SIGNIFICANCE OF THE SOCIAL STRUCTURE 79

TUCKER, J. T. 'Fifty Years in Angola', *I.R.M.*, 1930, pp. 256–65.

WAGNER, GÜNTER. Dr. Gutmann's Work II. 'An Anthropologist's Criticism', *I.R.M.*, 1937, pp. 508–13.

WESTERMANN, D. *Africa and Christianity* (London: O.U.P., 1937).

—— *The African Today* (London: International Institute of African Languages and Cultures, 1934).

WILLOUGHBY, W. C., and SPANTON, E. F. 'Building the African Church', *I.R.M.*, 1926, pp. 450–75.

—— *Race Problems in the New Africa* (Oxford: Clarendon Press, 1923).

—— *The Soul of the Bantu* (London: S.C.M., 1928).

WILSON, G. *An Essay on the Economics of Detribalization in Northern Rhodesia.* 2 parts (Rhodes-Livingstone Institute, N. Rhodesia, 1941, 1942).

WRONG, MARGARET. *The Land and Life of Africa* (London: Edinburgh House, 1935).

YOUNG, T. CULLEN. 'The Communal Bond in Bantu Africa', *I.R.M.*, 1933, pp. 105–14.

PART TWO

INDIVIDUAL DEVELOPMENT AND EDUCATION

The purpose of Part Two is (1) to describe the life-cycle or develop-
ment of the individual Ocimbundu from birth until adulthood, (2) to
analyse the Umbundu educational process, and (3) to indicate and
evaluate elements in this process that are or may be significant for the
educational work of Christian missions among the Ovimbundu.

Chapters V, VI, and VII describe the Umbundu life-cycle and
consist largely of Umbundu narrative given in direct translation.
The principal source is a composite manuscript compiled for classroom
use from the contributions of a number of Ovimbundu.[1] Comments and
other Umbundu material are interpolated from time to time into this
principal source.

In Chapter VIII there is an analysis of Umbundu development.
The evaluations are in Chapters IX, X, and XI.

CHAPTER V

THE UMBUNDU BABY

Birth

WHEN birth occurs in the house, it is supposed to take place on the
grinding-stone (*olumbambo*). That this was so is indicated by the
folk-tales and proverbs which refer to the place of birth as
polumbambo, or *kewe lioku cita* (on the stone of giving birth).[2] In
this case, and especially if a woman is giving birth for the first
time, she may be assisted by older women of the village. These, in
the case of widows, may be relatives of the husband, or in the case
of wives of householders, they will be his relatives by marriage.
A woman's own mother may assist, but when she lives in a different
village she is unlikely to attend. It would not be proper for the

---

[1] This source is given in quotation but without further reference. The chief
contributors were R. Kavita Evambi, of Ciyaka; Abrão Ngulu and A. Siku
Nunda, both of Bailundu; R. Kalupeteka of Ngalangi; I. Kayalo of Viye;
Ndondi students of the normal classes and several women there. It was compiled and edited (in Umbundu) by Pedro Paulo of the Currie Institute staff.

[2] Cf. the 'birth-stool' of the Hebrews (or Egyptians), *vide* Exod. i. 16.

G

82 UMBUNDU KINSHIP AND CHARACTER

husband's mother (whether uterine or classificatory) to attend the labour of her daughter-in-law. The husband does not attend. As Mr. Hambly's informant phrased it, 'The child would be ashamed to be born.'[1] It seems that the husband's non-attendance may be connected with the danger to him of the blood.[2] No other man will be present unless delayed labour entails the intervention of a medical practitioner, especially a diviner. Resort will not be had to outside aid until it seems impossible otherwise for the child to be born, and nowadays even where modern medical aid is available, often it will only be resorted to after the woman has been in labour for more than twenty-four hours[3]—sometimes much more, and then when it is already too late. Difficult delivery may be caused by:

(a) *Broken taboos*, as, for example, theft, either by the mother or the father. Only after confession can someone go out and steal something, after which the child 'consents' to be born.

(b) *Adultery* on the part of the mother, which must be confessed before the child will 'consent' to be born. The father's adultery may also cause trouble at this time, but this is more often believed to be the cause of a disease in his off-spring known as *onjamba*. Failing confession of the above faults, a diviner may be called, but his diagnosis may more often indicate

(c) *Sorcery*, to which difficult labour, along with many other ills of life, may be attributed.[4]

(d) It is also believed that in some cases a woman may herself refuse to give birth and may extend her pregnancy far beyond the nine months' period, the limits of which, and its method of reckoning, are not understood. Such cases as

[1] Hambly, op. cit., p. 185.

[2] Among church-members the husband often attends the birth and is sometimes the only attendant.

[3] A labour of twelve or fourteen hours is considered quite usual, and a shorter one as light.

[4] Sorcery, together with ill will and anger recognized as its principal roots, are great dangers to a woman giving birth. Anyone who dislikes the woman in labour, or even one who has ever shown ill will against her, will stay strictly away from the birth. While a woman is in labour all women of the village are expected to stay at home and refrain from ordinary activities—to commune with the spirits. As one of many proverbs has it: *Ukuene nda o cita, vu salela: oku cita kukuene, oku cita kuove*; 'Your fellow, if she gives birth, you stay in: childbirth of your fellow, is childbirth of yours.'

THE UMBUNDU BABY

have come to my notice finally turned out to be fibroid tumours, but it is held that there are women who have extended their periods of pregnancy to two years and then had normal deliveries. I failed to learn what was gained or intended by this procedure.

It is not to be inferred that difficult deliveries or prolonged labour are the rule, for while they do occur, they are rather the exception. In 1857 Magyar observed that 'women . . . are . . . very fecund and except in few cases bear happily the pains of child-birth'.[1] Such a statement would now have to be classed as a bit optimistic, but it has its point, speaking comparatively with our own society in mind. During labour the woman usually kneels, but in some regions she stands holding on to a post which the husband has put into the floor of the hut for this purpose.[2] 'With the breaking of the foetal bag the baby, which has been in the warmth, feels the air and begins to cry, *Ña, ña, ña.*'[3] From this cry is derived the word for baby, *oñaña*.

Hereupon I turn to the general narrative:

'When the mother recognizes that her time for giving birth has come, if this is her first,[4] she tells her husband to call the elder women who are skilled in causing to give birth. When the baby is born they arrange to cut (the cord of) the navel. First they tie it up with a piece of rag just picked up in the house or from the refuse heap, then they pick up a porridge-stick or a piece of fire-wood over which they stretch the cord and cut it with a knife[5] (which has not been boiled, for they do not arrange beforehand the cloths of the navel nor the knives for cutting as do Europeans). Everything they look for after the baby has already come. The knife and the porridge-stick they tie up to the roof of the house and

---

[1] Magyar, *Reisen in Süd-Afrika*, p. 283 (foot of page).

[2] e.g. in Civula. The Umbundu hut, whether round or rectangular, has no central pole. Does this custom indicate that in former times there was a central pole?

[3] From a statement of an old woman at Ndondi, other parts of which have been incorporated in the general narrative. She also stated that ordinarily a baby was not 'received', but was born on to the floor of the hut. From other informants and from the observations of my wife, I think this is the case only when a woman is alone and has no attendants (q.v. *infra*).

[4] Lit., if she is *onumua*, i.e. one who has not yet given birth.

[5] Hambly's note that a hoe is used to cut a girl's cord and an arrow to cut a boy's is 'theoretically' or symbolically correct, but nowadays people do not bother to follow the symbolism unless convenient (Hambly, op. cit., p. 185).

84 UMBUNDU KINSHIP AND CHARACTER

never use them again. The placenta they put in a broken gourd and bury it at the corner of the house or under the threshold: in the case of a boy outside the house, and in the case of a girl within.

'After this then they wash[1] the baby and anoint it with oil, and they tie a girdle of rag around its little loins. When all is ready, then some step outside and begin to shout for joy (*oku ulula*) saying, *Ulú! Ulú! Ulú!*[2] There has come a great big man here. Or if the baby is a girl they say, *Ulú! Ulú! Ulú!* There has come a girl here! A girl for the pounding-rock, *we-e-e! Ulú! Ulú! Ulú!* We are very grateful that she has increased our number.

'When the people hear the shouting, they hasten with joy to greet the parents and to congratulate them. Some seize the hand of the male parent and greet him saying, You have done well, you have begotten[3] for us a youth for the road, and a gatherer of firewood for the club-house. In the case of a girl, they say, A girl for the pounding-rock, the grinding stone is dirty.[4]

'In case the woman had already borne before, it is usual for her just to do it all alone by herself. She herself cuts the (cord of the) navel and buries the placenta. Many prefer to give birth in the field. Should a child have been born in the field (the cord of) his navel may be cut with a blade of corn in case there is no knife at hand. To tie up the cord she may just tear a bit of rag from her own cloth. When she comes to the village, the people will notice that she carries her basket on her head and the child in her hand, and straightway they greet her.'

It will be seen from this that childbirth is nothing if not simple among the Ovimbundu. Immediately after giving birth the mother purifies herself by washing in a running stream. She is accompanied only by her mentor. There is a lying-in period (until the cord falls from the navel) to be observed by the child *and* the mother, but it seems that in these days it is often observed in the breach. In the folk-tale of 'Baby and his Elder Sister' (*Ñana la Kota liaye*), the mother did not observe her part of the taboo but left the house to Elder Sister, and it was perhaps for that reason that Baby took vengeance by eating up the beans left cooking on

---

[1] The water is warmed by being taken into the mouth and then squirted on to the baby.

[2] The sound made by plucking at the lips while shouting.

[3] The verb *oku cita*, to bear or to beget, is used of males and of females without distinction.

[4] i.e. needs attention.

THE UMBUNDU BABY

the fire, while no one was looking. Before going on to that period, the narrative will tell a little about the birth of

Twins (Olonjamba).[1] 'If twins are born, when they have finished cutting (the cords of) the navels they bury their placentas out of doors at a cross-road. After washing and anointing them with oil, they shout saying, *Ulú! Ulú! Ulú!* There have come here a man and a woman. When the people come, they begin while yet outside (the hut), to curse[2] (and continue) until they enter, cursing the parents. It is called *Ongombo,* The Diviner's Basket. In that way such children are followed about by all, that none of them may die. And all the time that such children are growing, it is done month by month. The parent comes out and begins to curse the people who are in the village, and then all come from their houses and follow cursing her.'

In the case of triplets, when they are weaned, one is given to the king.[3]

As soon as the midwives have finished their task, the father may come in and take up the child, but men do not 'like' to hold a child which is still 'red' (i.e. not yet black) and whose 'neck is not yet strong'. Should a woman abort (*pulumuisa*), or should the child be stillborn or die at birth, the loss is accepted philosophically, quoting the proverb:

Cinene ombenje akolovi hacimueko.
The main thing (is) the gourd jug, the shavings (are) nothing.

Should the mother also die, then they quote:

Olũsĩ ka kuatele, ocinunga ca enda lovava.
A fish (he) did not catch, the bracelet went with water.

Should a young woman complain that her baby is too small, the others may remind her:

Esaila olio osanji.
The egg that (is) the chicken.

Should she complain that her baby does not grow properly, they will say:

Ka ci kuli omõlã ombia, omõlã omunu o kula
It does not grow the child of (a) pot, (the) child of (a) person grows.

---

[1] Lit., Elephants. The reference is to the names given to twins: *Njamba* (Elephant), *Hosi* (Lion), or *Ngeve* (Hippopotamus).

[2] *Tukãlã,* which literally means to call *hard* names.

[3] I knew of one such case in Ciyaka.

86 UMBUNDU KINSHIP AND CHARACTER

Naming (oku luka). The Ovimbundu name their children with great care. It is important to name a first-born (*uveli*) on the day of its birth, but if the child is evidently weak and not likely to live, they wait a few days. Names are in a sense family property and given over and over again. In naming the baby several factors may be taken into consideration:

1. The name (*onduko*) should have been borne by an ancestor, whether living or dead, whose character and state of well-being are satisfactory.

2. Ordinarily the baby is named by the father from his family unless there should be some reason for not doing so, in which case the name is given by the mother from her family, but if either family has a bad record for deaths or other misfortunes, that may prevent the parents following the custom, for

3. The name must not prejudice but rather assist the child's chance of survival. Thus a child born after the death of several siblings may be given an insignificant name, intended to cause the spirits to overlook it or to consider it as less than human, as, for example, *Katekãvã*, Little-black-thing; *Cĩvĩ*, Bad; *Mbili*, I-do-not-know-it; *Kacinyama*, Little animal; *Kalũsuẽ*, Nit; *Cilũlũ*, Ghost; *Vimbuandu*, Filth; or even *Kaniña*, Little excrement. A child may be given a name never used in the family if extreme measures to prevent its recognition by the spirits are thought necessary.

4. Events or persons prominent at the time of birth may influence the choice. A namesake, whether intentional or not, is known as *Sando* (from the Portuguese *santo* (saint), and the Roman Catholic custom of naming after the saints). Events of the time of birth or its calendric period may be summed up in a proverb or a sentence, a keyword of which is used as the name.[1]

5. While names remain in a family, some names may belong to several families. Certain names belong to families predominantly agricultural, others to trading or wealthy families, others to kings' families, &c. Kings' families were especially jealous of their names and commoners were not allowed to use them.

As already explained, parents take the name of their first-born. Should the child die young, the name will not be retained. During illness a person may change his name, taking one calcu-

[1] *Vide* E. L. Ennis, 'Women's names among the Ovimbundu', *African Studies* (Johannesburg), March 1945.

THE UMBUNDU BABY

lated either to cause the spirits to pass him by or to facilitate his cure. In adolescence young people discard the names with which they were born and name themselves (*oku lisapa*) according to their own choice. I have collected the explanations for about two hundred names.

The names of children are used, and that is one reason for choosing them with care, for the name will be heard often by the spirits. It is his superiors and those with whom he has respect-relationships whose names one may not pronounce. A child's name may be affected by whether there are recently deceased siblings, but he is not the reincarnation of such a one. Rather, he may reincarnate an ancestor. This is doubtless one reason for naming him after an ancestor. This, however, is a subject for treatment elsewhere.

The Period of Lying-in (Ocitete)[1]

'During lying-in the work of the mother is to cause the cord to fall from the navel of her child. On the navel she rubs castor-bean charcoal mixed with palm oil, or palm oil mixed with ashes, or with the soot from burning a sleeping-mat of reeds. A chicken feather is required from a wing or the tail, to dip it in the soot. That is done day by day until the navel is freed.' It must be noted that although a large percentage of the babies get infected navels, this does not seem to be as serious among the Ovimbundu as with us. 'For the bed of mother and baby are spread leaves that it may be soft, if possible leaves of the *ongonguila* tree. Over the leaves are spread a sleeping-mat (*esisa*) and some little cloths. During that time the mother does not sleep in the dark. The father must bring firewood and firelogs that it may be warm and light in the house, so that if the baby defecates in the night, it may be wiped properly.' No cloths or diapers are used for babies either at this period or later. An additional reason given for having a good fire in the hut is that the baby is supposed to be very much afraid of the dark.

'During those first days the women come to entertain[2] the mother and to hold the baby. Some bring meal and meat, some meal and beans, some porridge and relish, some sour beer and

---

[1] *Ocitete* seems to be derived from *oku teta*, to cut, in reference to the cutting of the cord.

[2] *Oku poka*, to provide for and entertain, as for a guest.

88 UMBUNDU KINSHIP AND CHARACTER

firewood. When they bring something, the mother thanks them saying, You have provided very well. She who brought supplies sits down and takes the baby and asks whether it is doing well. Conversing with the mother, she advises her how to attend to the baby, and then she returns the baby to its mother and bids her good-bye, saying, May you rest well. The mother replies *E-e-e*. Then she goes out and goes away. All who come do that. During all that time the mother cannot go out until the navel has healed. Then some day when another gives birth, she will do likewise, she will prepare food to go and greet the parent.'

The Baby's Food, Drink, and Medicine. 'From the time the baby is born they set its gruel (*ekela*) (on the fire), and when it is done they begin to feed (it to him). It is difficult to feed a baby because he struggles greatly, and so when they feed him they hold his little arms and legs and put the food in his mouth when he cries. The mother takes the gruel from the pot and first puts it in her own mouth to cool it with her saliva, then she takes it out and, with the crook of her finger, puts it into the baby's mouth. If the baby's mouth fills up and runs over, she wipes it up and throws it back again. When she sees that sleep has taken him away, she sucks the gruel from the child's mouth and spits it out on the floor. Then she wipes his face clean with a little water. This gruel is stirred up with unfermented beer (*ocisangua*) in place of water that it may be tasty.

'Likewise from the time of his birth they set aside for the baby a little gourd or pot of beer (*ocisangua*), which is tasty, very tasty. Into that beer they throw some sweet-smelling medicine, as for instance *ocisangu, olukata, ocilombo,* and *okakonga.* That medicine helps that the stomach may not ache and that worms may not come. *Olukata* is useful for stopping diarrhoea. Should he not eat well, they put in *okakonga.* In giving him to drink they use a little piece of gourd. As with feeding him likewise, although he struggles they hold his little arms and legs and make him drink.' The chief purpose of the beer and the sweet-smelling medicines is to tempt the baby to eat and drink, for it is believed that a baby is born with its senses of taste and smell fully developed. In case of more serious, or supposedly more serious, trouble, these simple remedies do not suffice and the diviner (*ocimbanda*) will be consulted.

'Should the baby be sick in the belly, making a noise *cõlõlõ,*

THE UMBUNDU BABY

cōlōlō, they will say, They have bewitched him with *oloseta*.[1] In going to the diviner they take a cock for the cure. They kill their cock, the diviner eats it, they (go) to the threshing-floor for the cure. That threshing-floor is holy and no one may pass over it unless in passing he spits out a little saliva and says, There may it stay, there. Only so may they pass on, even though they may be many, each person does just that.' The 'many' who go to the diviner are representatives of the family, for their presence is necessary not only for proper diagnosis but also to show their concern and good faith.

Babyhood Proper
(*From the second week until about the seventh month*)

The period of lying-in is terminated when the cord falls and the navel heals, but the second period only begins when the baby turns dark. This period begins with 'Breaking the pot' (*Oku ipaya ombia*). The reference is to the gourd or pot in which the beer and medicine have been kept. 'Breaking the pot', says one informant, 'means dividing the dark from the light.'

'When a child is first born he is perfectly pink and it is not possible to say whether he will be light or dark. When six or eight days have passed he begins to change and to get the skin with which he will grow. At that time they recognize whether the child will be light or dark. Then is the time when those who do not like to hold a pink baby will begin to take him up, for also it is then that his neck begins to be strong. Then too the baby begins to cause people to laugh. Should he be a boy, those who take him will say, Ah my husband are you well? Ha, how is the man? Then the parent will rejoice and say, Shucks, this man doesn't give any cloth at all. Should she be a girl, they will also say, How is my girl? The parent replies, She is quite well. The man then says, Where is a beer-jug for a man? The parent says, Shucks, your girl can't brew at all, she's no good, they've just put her out of her house; they've just divorced her because she can't keep house properly.'

This period from about the eighth day until about the end of the sixth month is the period of babyhood proper. At night the baby sleeps with his mother and by day he is carried in a cloth on her back (*oku velekua*). When it is not raining his head may be seen

[1] *Oloseta* (plural) are a wild fruit, hard and about the size of hazel-nuts, used for playing *ocela*.

UMBUNDU KINSHIP AND CHARACTER

protruding from the cloth and he seems to spend most of his time sleeping. Whenever he cries the mother will slide him around under her arm and give him the breast.[1] The only exception to absolute irregularity in suckling is that when the mother reaches the field for her morning work, she will offer the breast lest the baby may soon demand it and hinder her after she has begun her work. If she has no helper, she will do her field work with her baby on her back. Theoretically, the baby is almost never left alone.[2] There is a folk-tale telling how a woman put her baby down while cultivating and then accidentally beheaded him with her hoe.[3] If there is a young relative or if baby has an elder sibling, 'Then she (the mother) will give him to her to hold and to make him laugh under a tree where also has been placed his little jug of beer (non-alcoholic, *ocisangua*) and his little basket of gruel. There he will stay with his elder sibling while their mother does her work whether of cultivating or of breaking ground. Should he cry, the mother will sit down to nurse him and to feed him his gruel meanwhile looking to see whether there are lice in his head. She will say, Won't you nurse little father? Then shall we cultivate your little field?[4] A man doesn't cry, *he*? Then shan't we go to the village to stir up your gruel? Then the child will answer while nursing, *um, um, um*. When he finishes nursing she gives him back to his elder sibling and returns to her work. The elder sibling goes off with him in a hurry, lest being near his mother he may cry. She carries him on her back (*veleka*), and walking around the field she may talk to him saying, Ha! The ox is coming! *Haka*,[5] the hyena! Don't you see the bugaboo (*nono* or *nonono*) is coming to bite you if you cry again! Don't cry now. Shall we go to papa? Hasn't papa gone and caught a rat for you? When the mother lays off work, they go to the village. Passing through the woods on

[1] Hambly, op. cit., Plates L and LI for positions of nursing and carrying, respectively.

[2] Baby is sometimes left alone in the hut for a short time and then it may happen that he rolls into the fire. *Vide* also, reference to the folk-tale of 'Baby and his Elder Sister', *supra*, p. 84.

[3] One version of this tale may be found in the *Journal of the American Folk-lore Society*, 1922, vol. 35, p. 126.

[4] The reference is to the custom of cultivating a new field for each child at his birth. This field may become the child's own responsibility when he is able to assume it.

[5] *Haka*, an expletive which may express surprise, fear, disgust, pain, &c., according to context and tone.

THE UMBUNDU BABY 91

the way they gather firewood (*tiaña olõhuĩ*) and dig beer-root (*ombundi*) for the child's beer. When they come to the village they stir up his gruel and feed him.'

In the afternoon and evening the baby's father may hold him, but he is not likely to do so with any regularity until a little later. The European clothing worn by the men is harsh to the baby's tender skin as compared with the soft warmth of his mother's body. His elder sibling or cross-cousin holds and carries him, but whenever he cries his mother will take him up and nurse him. Indeed European or American mothers are considered very cruel to let their babies cry so endlessly. It goes almost without saying that feeding schedules would be considered as quite needless complications. It seems that feeding baby when he cries is more than a mere pacifier. He is credited with *knowing* when he wants to suckle, in spite of the fact that he will only take other food and drink if forced to.

'As to recognition of people, there are two sorts: first the child recognizes only the *smell* of his father and his mother since they sleep with him. But when six months have passed, then he begins to recognize his father and his mother "by heart".[1] He will very soon recognize his elder sibling (*huvaye*) or the cross-cousin (*epalume*), his young nurse (*naveleka*, lit. mother of carrying), and before long the others of the village will be known to him. But during this period only his mother is of real importance to him.' Only in case of her death would other women nurse him.[2] Even when there is a young nurse it is the mother who 'must care for him a great deal and since he has not as yet any sense, she must prevent him from doing everything which he wishes to do'.

At some time between six and twelve months, according to the child's development or the inclination of the parents, in order 'to accustom the child to sit, the parent digs a little hole in the ground just the size of his buttocks that he may not fall over. There they always place him and if he starts to fall over, they set him up again, until finally he sits up properly by himself and does not fall over. At that time he snatches at everything to play with it or to put it in his mouth.'

[1] *Utima*, the heart, is considered the seat of the intelligence.

[2] It is a curious fact that older women, although at the time without children themselves, may again produce liquid in the mammary glands if they take a baby to nurse. I do not believe that a test of such liquid has ever been made.

92 UMBUNDU KINSHIP AND CHARACTER

The Sitting Baby or Toddler (Ocisembe)

When a child can sit alone there begins a new period in his life. He is no longer a baby (*oñaña*) but an *ocisembe*. In comparison with the period just passed his development is now rapid, although in comparison with American children it seems slow, for an Ocimbundu child is held and carried so much that walking comes late, rarely or never before twenty-four months. In other respects, however, his physical development is not behind that of other children. His talking may come even *more* rapidly than with many.

Crawling (oku yaila). 'Crawling begins with reaching for what he sees: he moves little by little until he gets it. There are two kinds of crawling: some children in order to crawl hold the ground with their hands and doubling up one leg they drag themselves along. That sort of crawling is called *ocela*,[1] or crawling like a lion (*oku yaila ndohosi*). In the second, some children plant all their feet and hands on the ground while their buttocks go up and they move, but not like an animal. That crawling is described saying, He goes as an ox (*enda ngombe*).'[2]

Teething (Oku tunda ovayo). 'When a child has seven months then his teeth begin to come out. First when his gums swell the child has a little fever and diarrhoea and he squirts much saliva from the mouth. They call it the squirting of saliva (*oku pamba ovate*). Then a little tooth begins to show in the lower gum, then another, and so it goes on until in his mouth they come together.' The appearance of teeth in the upper gum first is a bad omen and is much feared.

Speech. 'When a child begins to speak, at first he only scolds and nothing is understood. Then he begins to say, *Ta-ta, ta-ta* until he calls, *Tate* (my father). Afterwards he will say, *Maĩ* (my mother). It is much more difficult for a child to say *Maĩ* than *Tate*. Thus they say that if a child begins with *Maĩ*, he will become a fool and be unable to speak any more. When he can say these names well, he begins to pronounce the names of the people

---

[1] From the game *ocela* in which the counters are moved from one hole to another.

[2] The reference is especially to the stiff walk of the unbending hind legs, but also to the deliberate gait of the ox. It is believed that the way in which a child crawls is some indication of what his character will be. The deliberation and openness of the ox are contrasted with the cunning and slyness of the lion.

THE UMBUNDU BABY 93

in the household and then the names of all kinds of little objects until his speech is perfected.'

Weaning (Oku sumũhã or *oku nyamũhã).* Every day the child goes to the fields with his mother. As he grows and gets fatter and heavier he becomes quite a burden for her or for his young nurse. Until he has passed twelve months, however, there is no alternative, and more often his daily excursions continue well past his second birthday. When he is able to walk a little, then his mother may begin to leave him in the village with his young nurse while she goes to her field-work. 'So in the morning at daybreak his mother will give him his food on a little dish and the toddler (*ocisembe*) will eat until he is full. Then his mother will speak to him saying, Suckle (*Nyama*) for I am going to the veld; so he will suckle and his mother will go.' He will not suckle again until she returns at from 2 to 4 in the afternoon. Thus he begins to be weaned quite unconsciously, but that does not mean that the process will be finished quickly; it may continue for even more than two years yet, unless a younger brother or sister intervenes.

'Some children, however, do not stop suckling quickly and if that is the case, his mother will frighten him when he wants to suckle, for she will say, Look out, here is a bugaboo; for perhaps she will have put an ugly worm on her breast, or perhaps she will have rubbed on pepper and the child nursing will burn his mouth and begin to cry. But some children are shrewd so that when they taste the bitterness they will fetch water and wash the breast and it is very hard to wean them. The parent will try many different things until the child is weaned. Some children are only weaned after they are four years old or even older, but that is not common.'

As the preceding paragraph suggests, children of this age may be tyrants to their mothers and all the more since the Ovimbundu punish their children with reluctance. But field-work presses inexorably and much more can be accomplished without a child to hinder one. His mother may promise that if he doesn't cry she will bring him a rat or a bird. Then if he still does not *consent* to stay she may, with reluctance, apply the sterner measures of a slap or a proverb said in exasperation:[1]

Ove oku ku pikila ku kuta.
You, making for you mush, you do not fill.

[1] The serious regard for the spoken word must be kept in mind.

94 UMBUNDU KINSHIP AND CHARACTER

Oku longa ku yevi, vumõlã hẽ?
Teaching you do not hear, are you child?

One who fails properly to absorb both mush and teaching can hardly be a proper human being. The implication of the question is that if he is not a child he may be some unearthly creature. There may be a similar implication in this other proverb which may also be used on similar occasions:

Ku ka ñavise ame konjembo si endi love.
Do not tire me I to hades shall not go with you.

U lonjila yaye, u lonjila yaye.
Each with path his (own), each with path his (own).

With the aid of elder sister mother usually wins out. Picking up her hoe and basket she gives the children their injunctions for the day. 'Stay then and I'll come right back, but don't play with the neighbour's chickens, don't beat each other, don't play with bows lest you put out the eye of another, and don't steal from the cooking pot, there now!'

With children of all ages left alone in the village, these injunctions are a minimum of necessity. The mother might also go on to detail the consequences of disobedience, how one who put out another's eye would be sold into slavery, nor was the mother exaggerating. If the Ovimbundu punish their children with reluctance, they have no reticence in instilling in them what they consider to be a healthy fear, whether of persons, animals, things, their own actions, or quite imaginary dangers. Older children likewise work on the younger. Nor are occasions for further instilling fear lacking. 'Always when they stay in the village, they go to the dancing-floor (*ocīlã*) to play with the other children. During that time should something come to frighten them and make them run away, those who haven't younger siblings to carry are glad to get away quickly. But those who have younger siblings to carry see much hardship. They tire themselves terribly trying to carry their heavy young siblings and being unable to continue, they drag them, both of them crying and crying.' Nowadays, in case of need or simply tiring of their play, children may start off for the fields in search of mother, but formerly children were not allowed to venture unaccompanied outside the safety of the village palisades. The danger of kidnappers and of raiding parties was very real. One of the most vivid memories of the Rev. Paulino Ngonga's early child-

THE UMBUNDU BABY

hood was a day when he and an elder brother set off for the fields and almost ran into a party of raiders. The scolding which they received was not forgotten.

The practice of leaving the *ocisembe* in the village by day makes his elder sibling responsible for much of his education. This is the beginning of a close bond which lasts through life. She herself may not be more than six or seven years old and consequently cannot be expected to 'educate' her little charge very thoroughly. She interests herself in his walking and talking and he will imitate her in many things, but the rest of 'conscious education' must be attended to by the parents.

Cleanliness. Instruction in cleanliness begins at this age, but I fear that it is lacking either in intensity or in persistence for its effect seems to be rather long-delayed. Small babies are not washed very often but their bodies and heads are anointed with palm-oil against infestation with the various parasites of the tropics. Anointing the body continues to be a part of the toilet of the Ocimbundu through life. When palm-oil is scarce, such afflictions as common itch are more prevalent. Nowadays, in the well-appointed household, the *ocisembe* has his hands and face washed before breakfast. If such a connexion between washing and eating were always and everywhere maintained, habits of personal cleanliness might be more widespread. Brushing the teeth may be begun in imitation of mother. Sphincter training is begun very early, for the mother feels every muscular movement made or attempted by the baby on her back. Hence she is apt to know when it is necessary to take him down for defecation. If and when this procedure is followed through with regularity and persistence early sphincter control may be established, but too often this is not the case. Establishment of bladder control is apt to come even more uncertainly as a favourite proverb concerning the weather indicates:

Ilu lia soka ndetako lioñaña.
The sky is like the bottom of a baby.

The Ovimbundu do not associate these bodily functions with shame to the extent which is the case in our culture, but euphemisms are used in place of the exact terminology.[1] If an

---

[1] There are prohibitions regarding these functions during visits to relatives-in-law with whom one has respect-relations, also to the bride during the wedding ceremonies. (See Folk-tales nos. 12 and 13 of the short collection in the *Journal*

96 UMBUNDU KINSHIP AND CHARACTER

ocisembe defecates on the bed he will be slapped that he may not repeat, but less flagrant breaches do not seem to call for punishment.

Language. The progress of toddlers in language mastery is rapid. Some mispronunciations are allowed. Some children pronounce correctly more rapidly than do others. Correct use of the language including mastery of the complicated grammatical structure, however, is mastered much earlier than is the case with English-speaking children. One could almost say as does Father Van Wing of the Kongo child: 'À quatre ans il parle mieux sa belle langue Kikongo, qu'un Européen de douze ans ne parle la sienne.'[1] The baby's earliest babblings, as well as his later evident imitations of his elders, are all recognized as his attempts at self-expression which as a matter of course will straighten themselves out in due time.[2] Parents speak to their children in a tone distinctly different from that employed in ordinary adult conversation, but they rarely if ever use the baby's own mispronunciations or 'baby-talk' as do Europeans and Americans. This, and the fact that young children have much more practice than have our children, owing to the constant companionship of their elders, seems to be the secret of their rapid progress. Whether the nature of the language itself has any effect would be an interesting subject for investigation.

Manners are also taken on quickly during this time. Toddlers are not expected to practise any very wide range of the social niceties, but what they do, they do correctly. They give and receive with both hands. They both give and answer greetings with proper terms of respect. An outsider, however, can rarely observe such behaviour naturally in the young child. He has been so

---

of the American Folk-Lore Society, vol. xxxv, pp. 129 ff.) The terms used are as follows:

Exact terms	Euphemisms
To urinate, *oku sũsã*	*oku talamẽlãko*, lit. 'to stand to something'.
(urine, *ovãsũ*)	*oku litapela*, lit. 'to water oneself' (said of a child when it wets itself or its bed).
To defecate, *oku nia*	*oku enda kusenge*, lit. 'to go to the bush'.
(feces, *eniña*)	*oku enda kofeka*, lit. 'to go to the country'.

The verb *oku nia* is used as a strong or profane expletive or interjectory phrase, especially in the first person with *etaili* (to-day), as *Etaili nda nia*. The verb is commonly left off.

[1] *Études Bakongo*, p. 262.

[2] Cf. the proverb: *Wa sema, wa imba: wa tumbuka, wa popia*, 'He mispronounces, he sings: he babbles, he speaks.'

THE UMBUNDU BABY

thoroughly drilled in fear of the stranger that he can rarely act naturally in the presence of one.

Physical development. From the time that the child is weaned his physical development proceeds more slowly on the whole than is the case with the children of European peoples. This slow development continues to be noticeable through childhood and adolescence. In early childhood there also seems to take place an increase in the rate of mortality. These facts may be due, at least in part, to specific deficiencies of diet. As has been noted, the customary diet of the Ovimbundu is lacking in fats, in calcium, and in certain vitamins, elements which are very necessary for the growing child, and which, before weaning, the mother's milk had supplied. The difference in physical well-being as between babies and children after weaning is marked among the Ovimbundu.

H

CHAPTER VI

CHILDHOOD

The Child (oneñe or omõlã[1])
(From the achievement of physical independence until about nine years)

'IF a toddling child (*omõlã ocisembe*) has finished learning to walk and expects a younger sibling, he is not carried any more and even though his mother should go to (visit) another village, he will stay behind perfectly well without crying. Now he has changed a great deal: that which he formerly did, he now no longer does.' This statement is perhaps a little optimistic, but it may be taken as sufficiently realistic and representative for practical purposes.

The child continues to see the same adults and to play with the same children as before, i.e. those of his own home village, but with two differences which the narratives will bring out. *First*, he is not now dependent to such an extent upon the elder sibling or cousin, and this independence brings the beginning of his life-long association with his age-mates. *Second*, the sex division of society begins for him at this time. From about eight years of age boys and girls will play in sex groups, and boys will begin to eat in the *onjango* with their fathers, girls continuing in the kitchen with mother and the younger siblings. The child does not go beyond the sheltering friendliness of the village except in the company of adults until toward the middle of this period of childhood. With mother or father he may often go to the fields or on excursions to neighbouring villages or to the chief's village.

The conscious education of the child is very much intensified from the time he achieves independence, but parents rarely realize the importance of the years from about four until about eight when little boys begin eating in the *onjango*. Theoretically the balance between the male and female sides of the house, characteristic of Umbundu social structure, is maintained in the training and education of the children. Actually what generally happens is that, until about eight, the mother and the older sibling or cross-cousin are very largely responsible for whatever is given and after that the father becomes responsible for the boys while the mother continues with the girls. This arrangement is modified somewhat by

[1] *Omõlã* is the term generally used but its primary meaning is *son* or *daughter*.

CHILDHOOD 99

the father's taking children of either sex with him on trips and by their being sent to stay for periods with the mother's family (*oluina*).

During this early period the child's education is comprised largely under three heads: (1) psychological, chiefly fear of real and imaginary dangers; (2) social, chiefly usages of etiquette and acquaintance with the kinship structure and its requirements; and (3) practical, or the beginning of skills. The first is imparted by mother, elder siblings, and perhaps by a grandmother. The second is taught both consciously and unconsciously by every older relative with whom the child comes into contact. The third is undertaken by elder siblings or cousins of the same sex. After illustrating the process of each of these three, I shall try to summarize the Umbundu theory of personality and then pass on to the activities of later childhood.

1. *Psychological.* 'Children have no fear of ghosts unless there is someone who has told them of ghosts, or tried to imitate their cries or to make them see one. If after dark a child teases and cries, his mother may say, If you cry like that a ghost (*ocilūlū*) will come and eat you. Since it is dark the child is startled, thinking there are ghosts, and he becomes quiet. Sometimes she tells him, Look out for the oxen, *mu, mu*, or perhaps it will be a leopard. Since the child does not see it, he may disbelieve his mother and think that what she says is untrue. Then again she may name a person, but since the child knows what a person is, but sees none, he will not stop (crying). Often if a child does not go to sleep quickly, his mother may say, Look out, the little old woman will come and pour live coals on your head and you will burn up. Hurry up and go to sleep. Then the child may leave the fireplace in a hurry and fall right into bed trembling. Sometimes a mother may send an elder sibling outside to the threshing-floor, to cry like a hyena, *ĩ . . . . ĩ . . . . ĩ*, while she herself stays in to mock the child, saying, He is crying and coming to eat you up. In the house the child hears the noise and shrieks, Don't come, don't come, I shan't cry any more, I'm going to sleep. It is from such things as these that children's fears come, from long ago until to-day. Children hear these things in their own houses from their parents, from their cross-cousins (*apalume*), from their elder siblings, or from their grandmothers. These same children, however, when they become adults, again begin to emphasize belief in ghosts with their little

UMBUNDU KINSHIP AND CHARACTER

children, even though they may not have seen them themselves. Sometimes at night when it is desired to send a child saying, Go and fetch such-and-such a thing (*ongandi*), then he will begin to tremble, for since it is as black as sin . . . he thinks to himself saying, Everything is full of ghosts, maybe they'll catch me if I go outside. . . . The male parent does not like to teach the children such great fear of ghosts, and he may say, He has great fear of ghosts, and that is a sorcerer which also kills people. There, there, my child, go and get what they've sent you for; fear is not good, go on, my child.'

There is a good deal of realism in ascribing most of the teaching of fear to the 'side of the basket', but it should be remembered, however, that the narrative was composed by men. Fear is also instilled through folk-tales telling of punishments inflicted by the spirits and by various mythical monsters. The fact of their being told at night also adds to their effectiveness.

2. *Social Usage.* 'Children are generally ignorant until they have been taught by their relatives with whom they live. First the parents, or an elder sibling, may ask the child saying, Who is this? He answers, Mother (*Maĩ*) or Father (*Tate*) (as the case may be). If the child is the first-born, his cross-cousins (*apalume*) may try him out, saying, Revile your Mother, and (if) he reviles her, they will remember that he has no fear of his mother or his father and they will say, *Avoyo*,[1] the child has no sense (*olondunge*) yet.

'When the child has grown a little so that he appears as one who should distinguish those who are worthy of respect, they try him again, saying, Revile[2] your elder sibling (*huvove*), and he reviles him; Revile your mother (*nyõhõ*), and he does, Revile your father (*so*), but he refuses. Then they recognize that the child now has sense (*olondunge*) and so they switch him with switches. From that time the child ceases (to revile) and begins to respect all people. He does not again err in thinking that only Father is worthy of respect, but rather all people whoever they may be.[3] Children are verbally

---

[1] *Avoyo*, an expletive expressive of surprise, disgust, &c., according to context and tone used.

[2] *Tuka*, to revile, to speak evil. The child may say, so-and-so is bad (*huka*), or so-and-so stinks (*lẽhã*), or so-and-so is 'crazy' (*topa*), or he may simply say I revile him (*Ndu tuka*). *Tuka* comes from the same root as *tukula*, to call by name.

[3] i.e. those older than the child. Only those of one's age set or older may merit respect.

CHILDHOOD

warned against that which is taboo (*eci ci kola*)—anger, theft, and doing evil to people. Should a child hear bad words from children with whom he stays when his parents go to the fields, he will imitate them and if elders hear him they will report. When parents go off to the fields they warn their child saying, When you stay here in the village, do not wound your playmate or put out his eye, lest it bring trouble (*ovimbu*, lit. 'fines') on your family. Or again, As to stealing eggs or snatching from the pot cooking on the fire, don't do it. Should your playmate say, Let's go and steal such-and-such a thing, you run away; and don't greet a person you don't know lest you may find trouble (*ovimbu*). Then the child will remain with that fear.

'From his infancy a child is bashful about coming in where elders are, but a little later he likes to be among them to hear what they are saying and to become accustomed to the points of their talk. In order to catch them (the points), he is quiet. He notices how they greet people, whether in the morning or during the day, or again how they greet guests coming from afar; for there are great differences between the various greetings. Even a small child may be taught to greet people until he is accustomed to it and remembers that people are to be greeted. But if a child grows up without learning to greet people (i.e. properly), they will say of him, His parents taught him badly, the child is a fool for when he meets people he does not greet them, not even guests. His parents will hear it said that their child has not been taught, that he is an indecent fellow, and that even among those who make shame, he does even that which ties up with shame. Among people he speaks standing up instead of bowing over or kneeling and snapping his fingers (i.e. for permission to speak).

'His parents must teach him to direct his glance properly that his eyes remain properly in his head.[1] Likewise his mouth, if while he is speaking he should twist it to one side, then if his parents or his grandmother should see it, they will warn him saying, Your mouth, you must not twist it to the side while you speak, lest people should think, He ridicules (us). The child is taught that while speaking with a person he must neither eat, nor

---

[1] i.e. he must not look his interlocutor in the eye. It is proper to remain with downcast look or to look away at something else. Europeans not understanding this demeanour take it to indicate inattention. One of our pupils failed in his official school examination for this reason, in January 1938.

UMBUNDU KINSHIP AND CHARACTER

spit, nor toy with anything in his hand. Should his knees knock together, *puaki puaki*,[1] when he runs, they will warn him (against it), saying, Lest when you are grown you may retain the habit and may not be able to walk properly as everyone walks. When a visitor comes into the hut to visit with his parents, while they talk, the well-taught child does not interrupt but is strictly silent, for it is taboo. Otherwise, it would be said, Their child has been taught as by a widow,[2] interrupting when people converse. But if he is spoken to, he must reply with care and with respect to the person speaking, saying, Yes sir (*nã oco*); Yes, thank you (*ã kuku*, lit. yes, great-grandfather!); Yes indeed, thank you (*oco muēlē a kuku*); Sir Lion (*nã Hosi*); Ah, Sir Lord (*Nã a Ñalã*); Ah, Master of the Paws (*nã a Cime-cakasa*).[3]

'Should the elders send him (somewhere), he will obey quickly. He will also imitate the elders in everything. Then they may say of him, This boy now begins to have the habits of adults. They may begin to liken him to someone who died a long time ago. Those who have known his family may say, This child completes so-and-so (*Ngandi*), surely he is likely to be the inheritor of so-and-so (*Kapiñalã ka Ngandi*), perhaps it is his great-grandfather.[4]

'These then are the habits which belong to being grown-up and should a person omit them, people's words will have no meaning for him, and he will have lost his chance.'

From the foregoing it will be seen that a child of about eight is supposed to know his social status and all the etiquette which pertains to it. Where the *onjango* (men's club) still functions as an institution, there the boys learn much of the Umbundu way of life, for there they eat daily in company with all the men and boys of the village. Children are supposed to learn 'table-manners' by watching and imitating their elders. In the *onjango* the hierarchy of age is observed, honoured guests and old men being served first, and so on down the line. Guests are provided with individual servings, but it is hardly proper for one to finish up everything. Any one of the boys will count it a privilege to do that for him. The greater the guest, the greater the honour to finish his plate. A guest of special category, as, for example, the king, who is unable

---

[1] *Puaki, puaki*, imitation of the sound made by knees knocking together.

[2] It is proverbial that a widow (alone) is unable to bring up her child. Cf. the proverb: *Ocimbumba ka ci longi omõlã*. 'A widow does not educate a child.'

[3] The last three are addressed only to a king or a chief; the others to any older person of either sex.   [4] The reference is to reincarnation.

CHILDHOOD

to eat in public, will be served by himself in the *etambo* (spirit-hut). With the decline of the *onjango* as an institution, there has been a great decline in the teaching of etiquette and social usage. As might be expected, this has affected boys more directly than girls. Girls and young women of the present generation and of the generation now coming on are, on the whole, more given to customary usage and forms of civility than are boys and young men. It is probable that contacts with Europeans, which have been going on for more than 150 years, have produced a number of individuals and families who have paid less heed to correct usage and have neglected to teach children properly, but never has there been the wholesale disregard which is now encountered. If the analogy of the South African Bantu peoples is any criterion, a reaction back to things Umbundu may soon be expected. Some observers feel that it is already under way.

Little direct sex teaching is attempted, but the very fact of the sex division of society is a considerable factor.

'A mother will teach her daughter saying, A girl does not play with boys, for boys are sharp ones.[1] Don't play with them. This advice is because of sex, although the child may not understand it at the time. But when the boys call her, she will remember the advice of her mother and may quickly reply, saying, My mother says, Don't play with boys: they'll hurt you. Thus she has taken to heart what her mother has told her and may go ahead in the same way. But as she grows up and separates from her parents,[2] then she may separate herself from their teaching.' Young children acquire incidentally a good deal of knowledge about sex both from other children and from adults. Although adults observe considerable reticence in speaking of sexual matters in the presence of children, living as they do with their parents in one-room homes, it is inevitable that sexual intercourse should sometimes be observed by children.[3] Although euphemisms of speech are employed in the presence of children, all the true terms are known by them. Hetero-sexual play is not in vogue.

---

[1] *Imelẽlẽ*, lit. sharpened stakes such as those used at the bottom of a pit-fall to trap game.

[2] i.e. at adolescence, when she leaves her mother to stay with other girls of her age.

[3] Cf. Father Van Wing on the Congo child: 'A six ans . . . il en emporte une connaissance de la vie qui ferait rougir de bons jeunes gens d'Europe' (op. cit., p. 262).

104 UMBUNDU KINSHIP AND CHARACTER

The practice and teaching of modesty seem to have been changing considerably for a long time. The influence of Europeans has doubtless had its effect, but more fundamental, it seems, has been the effect of increasingly generalized use of clothing, a process which began perhaps 200 years ago, but is yet far from complete. The time when boy or girl may begin to wear clothing is determined less by age than by the economic status of his family. There seems to be no shame (on the part of the child) connected with late wearing of clothes, but once a child has begun to wear a cloth, he or she is taught that it is shameful to take it off in the presence of those who are older. That this attitude is not of recent origin is attested by its appearance in a biographical narrative which goes back sixty years or more.[1] A large proportion of the women have only enough cloth for workaday wear for a short skirt, so that they leave the torso bare, but once one becomes accustomed to covering the torso always, she would be ashamed not to. This feeling belongs more to the field of economic status than to that of modesty. This shows up clearly in the strong objection to being ragged (*epēlē*), which has nothing to do with modesty but rather with economic status. The narrative concludes the teaching of social usage with this observation: 'From the time that children first enter into the school of understanding (*olondunge*), parents recognize that it is proper to respect them, rather than to revile them or tell them that which is evil.'

3. *Training in skills.* Before the age of eight or nine, children acquire few definite skills. Many of their games, however, are in imitation of adult activities, and adults recognize their preparatory nature and value. The little girl in caring for her younger sibling acquires certain skills, but with little or no definite adult guidance. Little boys begin early to make and set traps and snares under the tuition of an elder sibling or cousin. The first rat or bird caught belongs to the tutor. Games of many sorts are played: games with sides, round games, games with an 'It', imaginative games, and competitive games; games demanding skill, especially with dances of some intricacy. Games in imitation of animals are favourites, including 'birdcalls', in which very ingenious words are set to the bird songs.

4. The Ovimbundu have a custom somewhat comparable to what Vedder calls '*child insurance*' among the Herero,[2] i.e., the

---

[1] From a manuscript by Daniel Kalei of Bailundu.
[2] In Hahn *et al.*, op. cit., p. 177.

CHILDHOOD 105

sending of children to stay with relatives or friends. The Ovimbundu consider it definitely an educational device. From the age of six or seven years children are sent singly or in pairs to spend as much as one or two years in the home of the mother's brother. If conditions are favourable they may also be sent to stay with the father's sister or brother, and girls (other than the first-born) may be sent to the mother's mother. Formerly, prominent families arranged for their sons to stay in the king's capital. These periods spent away from home may continue well into adolescence. Not only relatives but also friends, blood-brothers, and *vakuacisoko* (members of a certain communal order)[1] exchange children for certain periods in this way. This custom is by no means dead. It is now being carried on even within the Christian community. Its educational purpose is obvious.

Later Childhood
(*From about nine years until puberty*)

There is no definite time which marks the transition from early to later childhood, but there are marked differences between the two periods. The chief criterion is one of physical development for as soon as the child is physically able, he will begin to assume a definite role in the work of the adult community. This rarely comes before nine years of age and may be somewhat delayed. Soon after a child gets the permanent teeth, a notch in the form of an inverted V (Λ) is chipped between the two upper front incisors.[2] This is a sort of national mark which many people omit to give their children at present. The line of observance is not sharply drawn as between Christians and non-Christians, as with the Herero.[3]

Formerly, the beginning of the period was well marked for the boy by his first trip with a trading caravan. Most of the present older generation have had this experience and nearly every man of the present middle-aged generation as well. Nowadays the boy of this age may begin to work in the fields with his father, he may begin to learn a trade, or he may be sent to school. Few Ovimbundu put their children in school before this age, and they evidently do not believe that younger children would profit by the instruction

[1] See *infra*, p. 114 f.
[2] See Hambly, op. cit., Plates XLIX and LIV.
[3] Vedder in Hahn *et al.*, op. cit., p. 177 f.

106   UMBUNDU KINSHIP AND CHARACTER

offered.[1] Boys may also help with younger siblings and fetch wood and water especially if there is no girl in the family, but it is my impression that at this age boys find much more time for play than do girls.

The girl of this age has already been performing useful tasks for several years in helping to care for the younger siblings or younger cousins, but the eagerness with which a girl takes up the care of a younger child makes it evident that she considers that activity rather in the nature of play. If there is no baby for whom she is expected to be responsible, she may borrow one from a neighbour. It seems almost more natural for her to carry a baby than to carry a doll (made of an ear of maize). This she will do only if she lacks a baby. Field-work and housework, chiefly the cultivation and preparation of food, are the adult activities which she must learn and which she regards as work.

The Ovimbundu consider that a child's socio-psychological education should be completed during early childhood. It is felt that after this time direct instruction should not be necessary, but reproof may be given should a child omit a usage or commit a fault. Should a child have plainly failed to attain the customary standards, a fatalistic attitude is often assumed as illustrated by this proverb:

> *Omõlã wa linga Cipupulungunju;*
> The child has become a worthless thing.
> *Nda longele, Nda kava.*
> I have done with educating, I am tired.

Acquiring skills. Later childhood is the time *par excellence* for technical education. That is the time recognized for beginning to learn a profession (*ocipinduko*), and a boy is expected to try that in which either his father or his mother's brother is expert. After that, should he wish to learn some other profession and can find a master, he may apprentice himself. All children, both boys and girls, are expected to learn to cultivate, but that is not counted as a profession as the following clearly shows:

'As to cultivating (*oku lima*), formerly the purpose was only for food, that one may not be hungry, whether during the dry season (*okuenye*), or during the rains (*ondombo*), that a person and his

---

[1] Considering the type of formal education available, the Ovimbundu are probably right: young children need far more activity than the formal school offers or allows.

CHILDHOOD 107

children may have enough food. Therefore while parents have their children with them, they teach them, saying, Let us work that we may have much food, for if a person lacks food he will die of hunger, or perhaps he may steal from another's field and get into trouble. Children must be diligent in working.

'But should a parent have a child who does not want to work, the parent may beat that child to teach him sense lest he may be a sluggard (*ocisiãi*).' Parents have a proverb saying,

> *U wa ku vetela*[1] *kepia,*
> He who you beat in the field
> *ka ku vetele,*
> did not you punish
> *wa ku longisa olondunge.*
> he you taught sense.

'Before beginning, parents always encourage their children to work. Cultivation, however, is not counted as a profession (*ocipinduko*). Should a person cultivate a great deal so that from his field he has very much food, then people will take notice and say, So-and-so has enslaved a spirit[2] to the seeds, he has spirits (*ilũlũ*) and they are helping him. That causes great fear, for people fear (those who) have spirits.[3] Thus, even though a person should purpose to teach another how to cultivate in order to have much food, the other will only apparently agree[4] because of his fear. Therefore the work of cultivation is not sought after as a profession by children, for they say, Being a farmer (*ongunja*)[5] is the work of sorcerers (*olonganga*) and not of ordinary people.'[6]

[1] *Vetela* is the relative mood (or form) of the verb *oku veta*. There is a pun in its use here since it is also used with *epia* in the sense of breaking ground for a new field.

[2] The verb used here—*oku andeka, andekela*—means securing the services of a person's spirit by killing the person (whether by witchcraft or by actual violence). The person is often a child and often of one's own family. In some cases parts of the body are said to have been kept for subsequent ritual use, e.g. bones and flesh dried and ground for 'fertilizer', or the skull for a drinking-cup. It will be seen that this is sorcery. The reflexive form of this verb, *oku liandeka*, means to form a blood-brotherhood, but it is a sorcerer's pact involving the sacrifice of a third person.

[3] The expression used means either to have or to have the reputation for having.

[4] He agrees with *ocenyo*, a term commonly translated as 'irony' or 'contempt'.

[5] This is the term which we commonly use for 'farmer'. Its connotation should be understood.

[6] This section is translated from a manuscript by Raul Kavita Evambi of Ciyaka.

108 UMBUNDU KINSHIP AND CHARACTER

The attitude toward success in agriculture indicated by the foregoing is held in some measure toward marked success in other professions, but in lesser degree, except perhaps where trading is taken up individually or by two persons in partnership. One of the earliest observers, Pinheiro de Lacerda (*c.* 1790), noted that accusations of witchcraft were most often levelled at the wealthier members of the community.[1] This fear of success has continued down to the present day, but while trading was an open group enterprise in which many individuals acquired wealth, success in that field came to be accepted more quickly than in the more individualistic work of farming. At the present time, commercial activities are carried on largely by individuals alone or in a limited partnership, and the practice, or at least the suspicion, of witchcraft in connexion with them seems to be on the increase. Some may feel that similar attitudes with regard to successful results from cultivation of the soil are now held less strongly than formerly, but I know of no evidence to support such a feeling. One of the commonest traditional patterns for witchcraft is that of a partnership of a senior and a junior member—of parent and child, or of mother's brother and sister's son. That is one reason why urgent suggestions by an older person concerning choice of a profession by a younger are looked upon with disfavour among the Ovimbundu.

A child should be taught enough diligence and application in cultivating that he or she may not lack the necessities in later adult life. Every boy will take to trading and bargaining almost as naturally as eating, drinking, breathing, and sleeping. Commerce still retains so much of its former glamour that every boy will take it up if and when opportunity offers. The care of younger children comes even more naturally to the girl, and she must also learn the housekeeper's art. Many folk-tales and songs indicate a reluctance on the part of girls to dedicate themselves with diligence to cultivation. In the days of the rubber trade, when girls could also join caravans for the coast and to the interior as porters, there may have been some real basis for this, but at the present time girls are convinced and enthusiastic cultivators, almost 100 per cent.[2] The

---

[1] *Annaes Maritimos e Coloniaes*, 5a Ser., p. 489 f.

[2] Women coming to live in the coast towns or in other European settlements where they have no fields or gardens find adjustment to life without agricultural labours very difficult.

CHILDHOOD

heavy tasks and the close and constant routine of housework, on the other hand, sometimes require more than casual urging by the mother. Biographical evidence agrees with observation on this point, but nevertheless few girls reach puberty without attaining proficiency in the various household tasks. The decline of poly-gyny has probably hastened the girl's education in the household arts. When there is only one wife in the household, not only must she have more regular help from her daughters, but also it is more likely that the daughters will have to take on full responsibility at those times when the mother is unable for ritual reasons to take part in the preparation of her husband's food.[1] Biographical sources indicate that this tendency was already operating at least fifty or sixty years ago.

Every Ocimbundu assumes that his sustenance will come from cultivation of the soil. The 'professions' which a child may learn are therefore in the nature of side-lines. Although the Ovimbundu are not a true cattle-rearing people, they possess many domestic animals, especially dogs, pigs, sheep, goats, and chickens. Chickens are owned and looked after by both men and women, but the other animals only by the men. Boys may have small stock of their own, and a boy's economic independence most frequently begins with owning a chicken. Herding has been a function of the sister's son and even now there is reluctance on the part of boys to herd for their fathers. Animal husbandry is largely a commercial enterprise, save in the extreme southern tribes of Kalukembe, Ngalangi, &c.

The principal side-line 'professions' (*ovipinduko*) may be listed as follows:

FOR GIRLS

> *Basket-making*, which is practised by all to a limited extent, but ex-celled in by relatively few.
> *Pottery-making.*
> *Medical-practice and Divination* (for conditions, see *infra*).

FOR BOYS

> *Mat-making*, which includes the making of four distinct types of mats each of which has its specialist; the making of trays and large baskets for granaries.

---

[1] i.e. at the times of her menstrual periods, after the birth of a child, &c.

UMBUNDU KINSHIP AND CHARACTER

Wood-working, including the following specializations:
Doors, windows, and their frames; coffins.
Beds, tables, chairs, &c.
Mortars, pestles, grinding-handles, and handles for various iron implements.
Stools, household utensils, carved images, staves, knobkerries, &c.
Drums and other musical instruments.
Canoes (dug-outs and coracles).
Rope-making, nets, and rudimentary weaving.
Thatching has its specialists although all men can thatch.
Fishing.
Bee-hunting, including the making of hives.
Hunting.
Iron-smelting and smithing.
Medical-practice and Divination.

The last three professions of the list are sacred and are entered under special conditions. They are often passed on by inheritance, but not always. All of them require sacrifice at certain stages, and when the enslavement of a spirit (*oku andeka*) is required, it is socially allowable. This seems to be the case with these offices as with those of the king and his ministers, both because of benefits accruing to the community in their exercise and also because of inherent danger to the individuals who exercise these functions.

The advent of European commerce, industry, and government has created a number of types of employment for boys and young men, some of which entail prolonged absence from the village and a loosening or severing of kinship ties. Church and mission have also offered employment and have opened new opportunities for advance in place and in position.

Later childhood, then, is the period of technical training during which it is expected that a large amount of economic responsibility will be assumed. A child begins to own property even before this, and from the beginning of later childhood will be accounted legally responsible for his actions. It is recognized, however, that he should not be set tasks beyond the experience or ability of his age and that the full responsibility of adulthood will only come with marriage.

> *Umãlêhẽ ka tonyõlã ongulu yuvala;*
> A youth does not scrape the pig for the wedding feast;
> *pekonjo pa siala (ovonya).*
> on the hoof there remain (bristles).

CHAPTER VII
ADOLESCENCE

From Puberty until Marriage
The Youth (*Ukuenje* or *umãlẽhẽ*); The Girl (*Ufeko*)

THE onset of puberty is generally late among the Ovimbundu both for boys and for girls.[1] The number of individuals who have exact records of their birth is not yet large, and for other reasons it is difficult to collect a large mass of exact data on this subject. From exact data in a few cases, biographical and genealogical data in more, and observation of a great many, I have concluded that, in general, puberty comes for girls at about fourteen to sixteen and for boys at about fifteen to seventeen. I have the impression that this may be due to faulty diet and other poor conditions of living. A careful study of this problem might yield interesting and significant results.

Soon after puberty young people generally stop sleeping in the parents' house. The girls congregate in kitchens and each boy builds himself a house. 'When he builds he does not wait for anyone to act as his teacher at all: he just goes ahead. A boy's father will show him saying, Begin there your house; stand a pole here, another there, and in the ground between, run a trench straight through. Then he will begin to cut poles and after that to build (the house) and thatch it. On the day of plastering it, they will show him how to mix the mud and throw it on, right up to the eaves.'[2] This is the boy's own house in which he will live through adolescence and young manhood, and to which he will bring his bride.

Before his marriage can take place, there must be a great deal of preparation, most of which must be undertaken by the young man himself, just as he has himself built the house. Umbundu adolescent development involves growth and progress on those lines already begun in childhood, but it takes on a conscious urge and direction, for it is now preparation for the responsibilities of adult life,

---

[1] This is in contradiction to the opinion given by Magyar (op. cit., p. 283). Might it be that dietary and other conditions of life have changed enough in eighty years to produce this result? I think it more likely that Magyar's observations were faulty.

[2] R. Kavita Evambi: manuscript cited.

112 UMBUNDU KINSHIP AND CHARACTER

chiefly for marriage. Indeed, marriage is the beginning of adulthood; no Ocimbundu is considered fully an adult until married.

Where the initiation camps have not taken hold, i.e. among the great majority of the people, it is the father's sister (*apahãi*) whose duty it is, at least in theory, to tell her brother's daughter how she should take care of herself during the times of menstrual flow. Actually a girl generally learns such things from observation and from girls of the immediately superior age-group, her sisters and cousins. She will not need to be told that during those times a girl or woman must not even touch anything belonging to a man and especially she must have nothing to do with preparing his food. This period is known as 'sitting on the ground' (*oku tumãlã posi*) since that is what a woman is supposed to do at that time. Modern usage has also taken that phrase to mean 'unemployment'.[1]

In the house which the boy or young man has built for himself, one of the most characteristic customs of adolescence among the Ovimbundu takes place: the trial marriage. There are several Umbundu names for this custom, as *oku tumisa* (lit. to cause to send), referring to the fact that the young man sends a male friend or relative both to ask permission of the girl's mother and also to bring the girl each night to his hut. Names for the correlative but all-inclusive custom are *uponji*, the girl being called *eponji*; and *uvaisi*, the girl being called *ombaisi*. A young man may first *tumisa* at about seventeen to eighteen years of age, but he must have acquired enough to make small presents to the girl and to her parents and he must have or have in prospect money or goods sufficient to make the betrothal payment.[2] This payment is known as *itambelo*, 'enticements', or *oku lupula ikuelume*, 'chasing away jealousies'. This indicates that the custom of *uvaisi* is definitely regarded as a prelude to marriage. For this reason, the term 'trial marriage' is preferred to that of 'premarital sexual intercourse'. The nature of the intercourse, moreover, is carefully circumscribed. 'When the respective parents have agreed, then those of the girl will warn her saying, Should that boy be bad, and want to play with your cloth, even though it be late at night, run away.'[3] In such a case the boy's parents would take him to task and require that for the time being he sleep in their kitchen and so under

---

[1] For early notice of this cf. Magyar, op. cit., p. 284.

[2] From 10,00 to 50,00 *Angolares* according to locality, family, status, &c.

[3] From a manuscript dictated by R. Kalupeteka of Ngalangi.

ADOLESCENCE

observation, and not in his own house. During that time he will not be allowed to *tumisa*. Or again, 'the girl's parents may warn her saying, Should the boy try *to sting*[1] you, do not let him: do not stay, but run away.'[2] All informants stress the point that the chief purpose of the custom is that the two young people may come to know each other as well as possible with marriage in view. There are severe sanctions against premarital pregnancy; fines to be paid by the young man or his family, lessened desirability for the girl in marriage, and a distinction in the ceremony between brides who are virgin and those who are not. Proofs of virginity are required on the marriage morning. Those families and regions which have girls' initiation camps include in the procedure a test of virginity.[3] There are not the periodic tests of virginity which are found among the Zulus, Mpondos, &c.,[4] but the Ovimbundu do not expect that the contact will be as close as these other tribes evidently do.[5] The closest parallel which I know is with the (American) colonial custom of 'bundling'.

It is said that the custom of *uponji* has been in a decadent state for a long time. This is not only because of its having been misunderstood and forbidden by the church or the missions.[6] Although this is partly the case, the chief difficulty came from the time of the rubber trade (1874–1900) when young men began without ceremony to go to the kitchens to sleep with girls instead of properly arranging matters. Whether their affluence made them reckless (i.e. of expected fines, &c.), or whether they were apeing Europeans or the customs of other tribes, is not known. At any rate, it is said that for large numbers of people this put an end to propriety. Numbers of Europeans began to settle in the country from 1891 (Viye) and 1903 (Bailundu and elsewhere), and from then until now casual relations have very greatly increased year by year.[7] That the Ovimbundu have held to their traditional forms

---

[1] *Lumana*, euphemism for immission.

[2] From a statement by R. Kavita Evambi of Ciyaka.

[3] A pullet's egg is used for the test (manuscript by R. Kavita Evambi).

[4] Krige in Schapera, 1937, op. cit., p. 110 f.

[5] Among the songs which I have collected are two sung by girls to tease the young men and with references to nights spent in *uponji*.

[6] *Uvaisi* has been used in translations for 'fornication' or 'adultery' and used so persistently that it has now nearly come to have those meanings. The *Umbundu–English Vocabulary* (1911) gave a correct definition for *eponji* but not for *uponji*; its references to *ombaisi* and *uvaisi* are likewise in error, while *tumisa* is not listed.   [7] Information from R. Kalupeteka and others.

I

UMBUNDU KINSHIP AND CHARACTER

of marriage through all these changes, whether with or without the trial marriage, is a testimony to the vitality of their culture.

Young people of the same age-groups are thrown constantly more closely together during adolescence in all their activities and in all aspects of their life. Strengthening of the age-groups is therefore to be expected. New names are taken at this time and the names received at birth discarded so far as possible. Boys used to go off together on hunts, on trading expeditions, &c. The girls work more individually in the fields, but are together in such communal labours as harvests. The preparation of food allows them more sociability and they have the additional advantage of congregating in kitchens not only for meals, but for the night as well. Ceremonial and social occasions are always opportunities for those of the same age-groups to get together. There is a limited amount of fagging of the immediately inferior age-group, but it is not institutionalized save where initiation camps have entered the picture.

Folk-lore, music, and the dance have very important roles in the education of the young. The Bantu are probably among the most naturally musical of all peoples and the Ovimbundu are perhaps excelled by few other Bantu. Their vocal ability is certainly superior to that of several of their immediate neighbours. Many of their songs are sung in connexion with dances. Other musical forms are road and work songs. Dancing is much enjoyed during adolescence but by no means only at that time, for it is learned in early childhood, very soon after walking, and continued on through life as long as the man or woman can get about unaided. It is a great sight to see toddlers, hardly more than able to walk, climb down off their mothers' backs and try a few steps at dancing; or again, to see a wizened and white-haired old man or woman step out and execute a *pas seul* on some ceremonial occasion. The adolescents, however, enjoy their dancing most, and they are the originators of most of the new steps and new dances which appear from time to time. The dance is of great importance to Umbundu life: social, educational, and ceremonial.

It remains to speak briefly of two institutions, neither of which is practised extensively throughout the country, nor does either seem to be a typical or integral part of Umbundu culture. These are the institutions of initiation at puberty, and the communistic order of the *vakuacisoko* (lit. 'those of the set').

ADOLESCENCE

The extent to which the order of the *vakuacisoko* exists at present or has existed among the Ovimbundu would be a very interesting subject of inquiry. It is certain that the institution does not exist throughout the territory but only in certain families which belong to the order and pass on membership in it by heredity. Whether there are certain regions where it is or was in the past more strongly held to is not known. It seems to be or to have been more strongly entrenched among the cattle-rearing people to the south, but it is also said to have been practised in Lupolo (Libolo) and even in the region of Luanda.[1] Among the Ovimbundu it seems to have been stronger in the past than at present. Few if any practising members of the set are now known. All 'coevals' or members of the set were in duty bound to render mutual assistance. All had mutual rights to the property of the others without complaint or remedy. These mutual rights seem to have been extended to the extreme limit of having intercourse with each other's wives, nor did the injury or even the death of one brought about by another allow the injured family to seek revenge or legal redress. It was the duty of *vakuacisoko* to bury their fellows, themselves digging the grave and attending to all expenses not already supplied by the family. Theirs was also the duty of burying strangers without family who would not be buried by others fearing defilement or responsibility for their debts. Bastos gives a tradition ascribing the origin of this institution to a wager laid between two chiefs.[2] It seems more probable, however, that it is connected with circumcision and tribal initiation. An analogous set of rights and duties is said to have existed among the Herero between 'coevals' circumcised at the same time.[3]

Tribal initiation for both boys (*oku lisevisa evamba*) and girls (*uso wakãi*) is carried on in camps or 'schools' in the southern and south-eastern tribes of the Ovimbundu. These camps are regularly held in Kalukembe, Kakonda, and Ngalangi. Sporadic instances of individual camps have also occurred recently in Viye, Bailundu, Sambu, Wambu, Cingolo, and Cikuma. Even in those regions where camps are regularly held, only the children of certain families enter. It seems that there has been some passing on of the custom by heredity and, in general, there is intermarriage only between families and individuals who adhere to the initiation

---

[1] Bastos, 1909, op. cit., pp. 67–70.   [2] Ibid., p. 69 f.

[3] Vedder in Hahn *et al.*, op. cit., p. 178.

116 UMBUNDU KINSHIP AND CHARACTER

rites. It seems, however, that it is largely by imitation that the camps have spread from Kalukembe, Kakonda, and Ngalangi into adjoining regions. The girls' camps have been less often imitated in these other regions than have those for boys. Whether these rites may have been taken over by the Ovimbundu from the practice of neighbouring peoples, or whether they may have survived from the customs of a culture previously prevalent in the region, is a question. In favour of the latter hypothesis is the fact that nearly all the neighbouring peoples seem to have or to have had these rites in one form or another and also that certain of the Umbundu kings are required to be circumcised before they can assume office. On the other hand, if the camps were held at all in former times, they must have been exceedingly inconspicuous to have escaped the notice of all the older writers. Bastos (1909) stated 'The Ovimbundu proper do not practise it (circumcision).'[1] Neither Silva Porto (1840–90), nor Magyar (1849–57), nor Pinheiro de Lacerda (c. 1790) makes any reference to initiation rites. The missionaries who came to the country in 1880 seem first to have encountered these camps on the Luimbi borders about 1900 but elsewhere hardly before 1915. The conclusion seems to be that it was toward the end of the rubber trade (1911) that the initiation camps were either revived or taken over from the neighbouring cultures to the south and east.[2] Whether initiation rites may spread further among the Ovimbundu or not remains to be seen. Their main emphasis seems to be quite contrary to the more typical trend of Umbundu education. The initiation camps of Ngalangi and Kakonda with their definite break from, and contrast to, the routine of life not only differ from the regular method of instruction but are quite contrary to it. In their methods of educating the young, the Ovimbundu certainly may be characterized as casual. The special times and occasions of education are the regular cycles of the social and economic life and special discipline to enforce specific teaching is used but rarely. The

---

[1] Bastos, op. cit., p. 50.

[2] Differences in these rites as practised by the various neighbouring tribes would form an interesting study. The majority initiate both boys and girls at or near puberty but some practise infant circumcision or circumcision at weaning or at the appearance of the permanent teeth. The Ambo are said to have let boys' initiation lapse but to attach much importance to rites for girls (Hahn et al., op. cit., pp. 27–31). I do not know of any nearby tribes which have for girls either any excision or elongation of the labia. Various tests of virginity are used.

ADOLESCENCE

hardship and the cruelty of the initiation camps have their parallel in the trading and slave-raiding expeditions of the past, but this is practically the only recognizable likeness. May it not be that initiation camps were adopted or revived to fill the lacuna that came about when trading expeditions ceased? As an 'educational institution' they do not seem to fit into the culture.

Whether with or without initiation rites, adolescence is largely preparation for marriage and full adult life. Traditionally, adolescence is not a time of conflict or of stress. Young people who as children had already assumed in considerable degree the responsibilities of life met the onset of puberty and made the transition to adult life without fuss or flourish. On the whole there was relatively small chance for conflict between the generations, since the place of each is recognized as mutually complementary. Nor was there competition between the sexes. This ordered and well-balanced society began to change with the rubber trade, and with the beginning of the present century changes have come rapidly. Contract and *corvée* labour have brought profound changes, especially for the young men. As for the girls, a few have gone to the towns; relatively few however, other than those who attend a boarding-school, lead a life essentially different from that which has been traditionally theirs. Conflict between the generations, adolescence as a period of stress, delinquence, hysteria, and other problems, some of them characteristic of our own culture, are beginning to appear among the young people of the mission schools. I feel that these manifestations are quite uncharacteristic of Umbundu culture.

As for adult life, there are no recognized divisions or separate periods. Adulthood comes with marriage and marriage is only recognized as fully complete with the birth of a child. The early years of marriage and family rearing are years of much hard work with less time for leisure or enjoyment than either before or after. It is not postponed, however, on that account. If the young man marries relatively late, it is largely because of the very considerable economic burdens involved. Singleness is coveted by no one. The Umbundu ideal is mature life when one may have acquired competence, but at any rate is assured of descendants and care in old age. There is not, however, any ceremonial status such as the fixing of the wax ring among the Thonga,[1] nor does the mature Ocimbundu cease to do manual labour. There may be some

[1] Junod, op. cit., 1927, vol. i, p. 129 f.

UMBUNDU KINSHIP AND CHARACTER

preference for a polygynous household at this age, but no definite tradition which urges one 'to become lord and master of a complete circular village'.[1] Women are happiest while carrying a baby on the back.

> *Onyima yiwa ka yi mōlī omōlã,*
> Back good (yet) it does not see a child,

wails a childless woman. No grandmother is satisfied without herself caring for at least one grandchild. Old age is subject to its own burden of the years but among the Ovimbundu the aged are treated with much respect and deference.

SUMMARY OF CHAPTERS V–VII

THE periods in the life of an Ocimbundu may be summarized as follows:

1. The 'Marginal' Period of the First Week (*ocitete*) until the funicle drops.
2. The Baby Proper (second week until about seventh month) (*oñaña*) (from turning black until sitting alone).
3. The Sitting-baby or Toddler (*ocisembe*) (from sitting alone until mastery of walking and completion of weaning).
4. Early Childhood (from weaning until about 9 years) (*oneñe*). Period of socio-psychological education.
5. Later Childhood (from about 9 until puberty) (*omōlã*). Period of technical training and assumption of economic responsibility.
6. Adolescence (from puberty until marriage). Period of preparation for marriage and full adulthood.
7. First Year of Marriage, during which the bride completes her training under her mother-in-law's guidance.
8. Full Adulthood (from birth of first child).

[1] Junod, op. cit., 1927, vol. i, p. 127.

CHAPTER VIII
ANALYSIS OF UMBUNDU DEVELOPMENT

THE question as to whether there is a Native African education is discussed by Mr. H. S. Scott in the *Year Book of Education 1938*.[1] He notes that anthropologists have insufficiently described the educational processes of the various African peoples and that educationists have been at fault in disregarding indigenous methods. It is to be hoped that the foregoing description of individual development has shown clearly that there is an Umbundu education, the function of which is the integration of the individual in the on-going process of society—the 'moulding of individuals to the social norm'.[2]

In order better to understand this process and to determine in what way it may be adapted to meet present needs, it is now necessary to analyse Umbundu educational concepts and methods.

The theory of personality upon which the Ovimbundu act does not seem to be entirely consistent. First, they act as though they believed that the child is born quite without character and that desirable traits have to be consciously formed. 'Children are generally ignorant until they have been taught by their relatives with whom they live.'[3] On this premiss, they proceed to instil psychological attitudes in the young child and to teach him social usages. With the social psychologist they seem to 'regard childhood . . . as an opportunity which must be used in *learning* useful behaviour through social contact'.[4] It is abundantly evident that they regard education as clearly a *social* process.

A baby is born pink and it is only when he turns dark at the sixth or eighth day that he shows the first indication of becoming a person (*omunu*). He shows further promise in that direction with his first show of sense, but all through childhood he is, in a

---

[1] *The Year Book of Education 1938* (Univ. of London, Inst. of Education, London: Evans Bros.), part x, pp. 639 ff.

[2] A. W. Hoernlé, 'An Outline of the Native Conception of Education in Africa', *Africa*, 1931, p. 147. This is quite close to Dewey's conception of education as 'transmission through communication'; cf. *Democracy and Education* (New York: Macmillan, 1916), chap. i.

[3] *Supra*, p. 100.

[4] F. H. Allport, *Social Psychology* (Boston and New York: Houghton Mifflin, 1924), p. 80.

120 UMBUNDU KINSHIP AND CHARACTER

sense, only a *potential* person. The permanency or stability of his personality (*unu*)[1] is only proven when he enters the state of adulthood at marriage. Then it is that he achieves true integration with society. Thus personality appears as a natural process of social integration.

On the other hand, the Umbundu belief in reincarnation[2] throws responsibility for determination of personality back upon the ancestral spirits (*olosuku, olosande*) or upon the Spirit World or Fate (*Kalunga*). Clearly this belief cuts across the assumption that children are born without definite character whereby the responsibility belongs to the parents. Practically the seeming contradiction seems to be resolved as follows: *potentially* a child's character may be pre-determined by the spirits, but actually or at least until the potentialities become manifest, education may play an important role by providing the spiritual forces with suitable vessels. At about eight or nine years of age the character of the reincarnation, if any, becomes manifest, but the social and psychological education is supposed to be well along by that time. Provision of the vessels and their moulding is, therefore, at the same time an active and a passive function.

The psychological and social education of early childhood and also the imparting of skills all have to do with this active moulding function as the manuscripts quoted have shown. Many folk-tales and proverbs could also be quoted to show the Umbundu ideas with regard to personality.[3]

The more passive function of providing suitable vessels for the indwelling of the spiritual forces is no less important. Even among those who have discarded or are seeking to discard the beliefs of their fathers, this side of educational theory is still important. It has greatly conditioned the outlook of the people. All observers have remarked on the considerate treatment of children by the Ovimbundu, on their recognition of personality in children and respect for it. In the narrative quoted this was seen in the mother's addressing her baby boy as 'little father'[4] and in the first visitors

---

[1] *Unu* lit. the quality of being a person (*omunu*). The word is used for one's dominant bent, or his character.

[2] See *supra*, p. 102, n. 4.

[3] I have identified about 100 Umbundu proverbs used in or having reference to education. About two-thirds of them deal with the period of early childhood. Their interest is about equally divided between the practical and the more philosophical aspects of life and education.   [4] See *supra*, p. 90.

ANALYSIS OF UMBUNDU DEVELOPMENT 121

giving the baby the respectful terms of 'my wife' or 'my husband';[1] also in the comment of the narrator that 'parents recognize that it is proper to respect them (children)'[2] and in parents' reluctance to punish. It seems that this respectful treatment of children stems from belief in reincarnation, whereby a child is potentially an ancestor to be respected, deferred to, and even worshipped.

It is doubtful whether at present many children could be found who have really gone through the ceremonial for becoming media for guardian spirits of the family (*olosande*). The drift away from those observances has become a flood. Nevertheless respectful treatment of children remains, perhaps even undiminished, for it still has the force of customary behaviour if not the supernatural sanction. Indulgence on the part of the parents rarely if ever goes to the length of pampering. Belief that the child's character ultimately, or to a large extent, depends upon spiritual forces may lead parents to adopt a sort of fatalism, but that is hardly more serious than the effects of belief in the influence of heredity popularly held in the West. The Ovimbundu do not believe, as do the Zulus, for example, that a child is tainted at birth, needing radical treatment against the subsequent appearance of the taint.[3] With the Ovimbundu the development of personality is a process which *may* involve spiritual forces, but at all events requires careful human attention.

Education and Society

What then are the means by which the Ovimbundu develop the personalities of their children or mould them to the social norm? Their success indicates that they along with other 'so-called backward races have proved to be educationists . . . of no mean order'.[4] What, then, are their methods?

The educational process is the whole process of life and culture. School is society and society is school; there is no division between adult and child life. Education and life are one. This has been recognized as true for many African and other primitive societies.[5]

[1] *Supra*, p. 89.

[2] *Supra*, p. 104.

[3] See Krige, op. cit., p. 67.

[4] W. D. Hambly, *Origins of Education among Primitive Peoples* (London: Macmillan, 1926), p. 401.

[5] See the interesting analysis of M. Fortes, *Social and Psychological Aspects of Education in Taleland*, p. 8 f. (Supplement to *Africa*, Oct. 1938); Margaret

122 UMBUNDU KINSHIP AND CHARACTER

This unity of 'the social sphere of adult and child' is a striking feature of the Umbundu educational process. A child learns by actual participation in adult activities. He participates as soon as he is able and in so far as he is able in all phases of adult life. A child begins early to assume responsibility both for himself and for as much regular 'adult activity' as his knowledge and ability may allow him to take on. This being the case, it is to be expected that all factors—physiological, psychological, social, and cultural— are so closely interrelated in the process of Umbundu education that their unity is almost organic.

Given this unitary social sphere, it is easy to understand that children always want to grow up. They are anxious to undertake full responsibility and full participation as early as they may. It has been pointed out that adults do not, or are expected not to, force the pace: they must not set tasks beyond the ability of the children in the actual stage of their development.[1] Normal development and normal behaviour are expected of children as a matter of course.[2] The possibility of aberrant behaviour[3] does not seem regularly to enter parents' minds, much less their utterances, as is too often the case with us. Adult expectation of normal development in children is perhaps best seen in the Umbundu concept of sense or intelligence (*olondunge*), something which every normal person is expected to have in some measure from the time of weaning. It is a relative term when applied to children and the young.[4] Some adults have it in greater measure than others. But every *person* will have it according to the proverb:

> *Omuku lovonya, omunu lolondunge.*
> A rat with fur, a person with sense.

As every rat has fur, every person has sense.

Learning, as he does, in the real social and cultural situation of Umbundu life, the child develops genetically the behaviour

Mead, *Coming of Age in Samoa* (New York: Morrow, 1928). Some writers have claimed this to be true of all the simpler cultures, e.g. Dewey, op. cit., p. 8 f., but cf. Margaret Mead, *Growing up in New Guinea* (New York: Morrow, 1930). Many of the African initiation rites seem to have been introduced from the outside and hence involve a distinct dichotomy, *vide* Stayt, op. cit.

[1] See *supra*, p. 110.

[2] See Fortes' discussion of a similar attitude among the Tallensi, op. cit., pp. 25–8.

[3] For the fatalistic attitude taken on failure to conform, see *supra*, p. 106.

[4] See *supra*, p. 100.

ANALYSIS OF UMBUNDU DEVELOPMENT 123

pattern 'singled out in the institutions of his culture'.[1] I agree with Fortes on the Tallensi that 'The total pattern is not built up brick by brick like a house, but evolves'.[2] I am not convinced, however, of the necessity for postulating 'embryonic forms' or *schemas* of the total patterns supposed to be present in the child from the beginning.[3] Whether the *schemas* are supposed to be a part of the child's innate equipment, Fortes does not make clear, but I see no necessity for any such hypothesis. The method by which and the situation in which the Ocimbundu child learns, are ample explanation for the early and thorough development of the pattern of his culture.

Neither is it necessary to postulate either 'faculties' or 'instinctive drives' to explain Umbundu education.[4] Rather this study takes a view of 'human nature . . . as consisting essentially of specific situations'.[5] Instances in support of this view could be cited from the descriptive part of this chapter but that would be outside the scope of this study. The most important fact with regard to Umbundu education is its identification with life: the absence of cleavage as between 'school' and society, as between the social sphere of the child and the adult. The most important educational method in use is actual participation in the social and cultural or 'real life' situation. The educational 'content' is the whole Umbundu culture, consisting of attitudes (psychological and social), social usages, skills, observances, and traditional 'literature'. By far the most important are the social attitudes and usages. I turn therefore to the problems of

Social Adjustment

The education of the Ocimbundu child in the traditional social setting is far more social than is the case with us. The child learns

[1] Ruth Benedict, *Patterns of Culture* (Boston and New York: Houghton Mifflin, 1934), p. 254. [2] M. Fortes, op. cit., p. 42.

[3] Ibid., pp. 42 ff. Fortes attributes the concept of *schemas* to F. C. Bartlett (*Remembering*).

[4] In his discussion of education among the Tallensi, quoted above, Fortes does not specifically mention either of these hypotheses and he rightly remarks that some writers have 'attributed an almost mystical significance to imitation' as the principal method by which a child learns. He then proceeds, however, to classify the learning processes under *Mimesis, Identification, Co-operation*, and *Play*. Except for the first, these activities are of much importance in Umbundu education.

[5] Hugh Hartshorne, *Character in Human Relations*, p. 195 (New York: Scribner's, 1932); see also Allport, op. cit., p. 81.

124 UMBUNDU KINSHIP AND CHARACTER

the correct adjustments early, naturally grows into a comparatively well-adjusted life, and so avoids the major conflicts to a much greater degree than is the case in our society. A very large proportion of those in conflict in present-day Umbundu society are de-tribalized or partially de-tribalized individuals, especially those who as children were brought up outside or largely outside the kinship groups. The large proportion of those brought up on the mission stations who are out of adjustment, and often in overt conflict, has been noticed by many observers. The biographies and autobiographies which I have collected witness clearly to the same fact, that most of the ill-adjusted individuals and those in overt conflict were products of an extra-tribal, de-tribalized, or non-traditional situation; while practically all of the well-adjusted persons were educated within the kinship system.

The three major conflicts which have been recognized in our society, that is, 'struggle', sex, and 'inferiority',[1] are all present in some form among the Ovimbundu. The adjustments by which they resolve these conflicts are distinctive.

Adjustments in anger by which the 'struggle conflict' is resolved are interesting and important educationally. The child is taught when quite young that the expression of anger is taboo.[2] Tantrums are rare among Ovimbundu children. Anger and ill-will are named by thoughtful Ovimbundu as the chief root-cause of sorcery. The more thoughtful ones also recognize these as an important cause of accusations of sorcery. Expression of anger is traditionally much feared. It is not desired in the character of the king.[3] Nowadays there are more who give free vent to expressions of anger, but they are for the most part either individuals who imitate Europeans and who seek to discard Umbundu cultural habits and values; or they are those who are considered sorcerers, either by themselves or others. An Ocimbundu who as a child has learned traditional adjustments in anger will rarely allow his anger to break through the resistance and become 'extroverted' except in recognized outlets. These outlets are somewhat analogous to our own rationalizations of anger.[4]

The chief 'introverted' reaction of anger which I have noted

[1] The psychological analysis follows Allport, op. cit., chap. xiv.

[2] See *supra*, p. 101.

[3] See *supra*, p. 21.

[4] Cf. Allport, op. cit., p. 344. The Ovimbundu have not thought up such a high-sounding term as 'moral indignation' as a euphemism for anger.

ANALYSIS OF UMBUNDU DEVELOPMENT 125

among the Ovimbundu is 'grudge-building'. This is probably fairly common and often eventuates either in sorcery or in suspicion of sorcery. There is special danger of this type of reaction between men and women who have an in-law relation to each other. This is probably a principal reason for the avoidance with which these relations are so carefully hedged and the respectful treatment mutually enjoined.[1] Grudges are sometimes inherited through several generations. According to folk-tales, children sometimes bear grudges against their parents for real or fancied ill treatment.[2]

Recognized outlets for anger in frankly 'extroverted' form are found in war and raiding parties, in the hunt, and in lawsuits. War is no longer resorted to but up to the present day anger still finds a recognized expression in actions at law. One of the commonest of such actions is the accusation of sorcery (*oku sunga owanga*) already touched upon above. Church councils and meetings have taken over some functions of the traditional courts of law and this is probably one reason for the decidedly stormy sessions which sometimes occur.

The importance of wit and humour as an outlet for anger has been recognized. 'The ability to turn one's anger into a jest goes with the trait of insight . . . and is sometimes appropriately called "the saving sense of humour".'[3] That the Ovimbundu have this ability and use it often and to good advantage is very much in their favour. May not this be one indication of a considerable degree of insight which many observers have noted in the Umbundu character?[4] I would not claim that the Ovimbundu have made any very remarkable attainments in the social control of anger: their achievements in that direction may be slight when compared to some of the more advanced peoples, as, for example, the Scandinavians, the Hollanders, or the English. What is remarkable, however, is that they have frankly recognized the necessity for such control more clearly than have some supposedly more advanced peoples.

Adjustments in family life are held to be resolutions of what are ultimately sex conflicts.[5] Marital adjustments are of prime

[1] See *supra*, pp. 57 ff.

[2] Cf. *Journal of American Folk-Lore Society*, 1922, vol. 35, no. 6, p. 123 f.

[3] Allport, op. cit., p. 344.

[4] Some writers have attributed to negroes a quality of 'insight' superior to that possessed by whites, cf. article 'Insight, &c.' in the *Atlantic Monthly*, Sept. 1938.　　　　[5] Allport, op. cit., pp. 345–53.

126 UMBUNDU KINSHIP AND CHARACTER

importance, but treatment of that subject must be reserved for another time. The balance maintained in the Umbundu social system, which has already been noted,[1] together with woman's important position in the economic sphere, give to the women and girls a relatively satisfactory place in Umbundu society. It has also been noted that woman's sphere has suffered less disintegration than has man's. Although the girl may have somewhat less freedom than the boy, her personal prospects are more stable, and in the long run more satisfactory.

Adjustments between parents and children among the Ovimbundu are relatively satisfactory. The fact that there are no specific father–daughter or mother–son avoidances or taboos, beyond the general laws of incest which nearly all cultures maintain, indicates an absence of strain in these relationships. In our own society adult–child fixations, and particularly the parent–child fixations, with the consequent repressions, are very common and are held to be responsible, at least in part, for much trouble including difficulties of adjustment at pubescence.[2] In traditional Umbundu society such fixations occur very infrequently, if at all.[3] In this context we should be reminded of the following factors:

1. The early and continued close association of the child largely (although not exclusively) with the parent of the same sex.[4]
2. The association of the child with many (classificatory) 'fathers' and 'mothers' which may result in a partial transfer of affection.[2]
3. The absence of fondling, kissing, and other close bodily contact in display of affection.[5]

The picture in these respects is not unlike that of the Samoans given by Margaret Mead.[6] In some other respects it is quite different but it is similar in the apparent absence of a period of adolescent *Sturm und Drang*. What actual correlations there may be between parent–child fixations and a period of adolescent stress I do not know. The absence of any such period has been reported

[1] *Vide supra*, p. 43.
[2] Cf. Allport, op. cit., pp. 355 ff.
[3] The proverbial inability of a widow properly to rear a child (*vide supra*, p. 102) may indicate difficulties of this sort.
[4] *Vide supra*, p. 98.
[5] No display of affection whatever is congenial to the Ovimbundu, except to babies and between adolescent age-mates of the same sex.
[6] Op. cit., chap. x.

ANALYSIS OF UMBUNDU DEVELOPMENT 127

from several primitive cultures,[1] and some experimental studies seem to indicate that it is less general in the United States than had previously been supposed.[2] It is recognized that in this country parent–child fixations have produced many pathological cases.[3] With the practical absence of such fixations among the Ovimbundu, no such group of pathological cases exists. This is a clear gain, but there is also probably a loss, in that there seems to be a corresponding scarcity of the more or less introverted idealistic persons, 'the tender-minded class described by William James'.[4]

Ovimbundu parents proverbially love their eldest child (*nuñulũ*) in a special way,[5] but there is not in their family situation as much invidious distinction as that which in ours often produces the domineering eldest child, the inadequate youngest, and others in the sequence with feelings of neglect or 'rejection'. The Umbundu family situation almost inevitably involves less sharpness of distinction, for although the eldest child may be loved in a special way he deals not only with his parents but with other relatives of their generation and with elder (classificatory) siblings and cross-cousins of his own generation. So, also, the last or youngest child of a sequence would hardly sense himself the youngest since there will almost certainly be younger (classificatory) siblings and cross-cousins toward whom he in turn will act as his elders acted toward him.[6] In a normal Umbundu family situation the problem of the 'only child', so acute in America, is almost inconceivable.

Some Ovimbundu, not only as children but also as younger siblings and as secondary wives, do suffer from feelings of neglect and rejection. I have not noted this from biographical or other direct evidence, except from observation of resentment on the part of younger siblings of fagging by their elders. Evidence exists, however, in the frequency of the Cinderella motif in Umbundu folk-tales. Many are the fables in which Little Hare (*Kandimba*), Little Tortoise (*Kambeu*), or Little Weasel (*Kavili*) gets the better of his stupid elders, represented by almost any and all of the larger

---

[1] Cf. Mead, loc. cit., Fortes, op. cit., p. 9.

[2] Gardner and Lois B. Murphy, *Experimental Social Psychology* (New York: Harpers, 1931), pp. 429–32.

[3] Allport, op. cit., p. 362.

[4] Quoted from Allport, op. cit., p. 362.

[5] Cf. the proverb: *Epungu liwa konendela; omōlā sole kunuñulũ,* '(Of) corn best the first fruits; (of) children (you) love the first born'.

[6] This seems to be the state of affairs quite generally in societies having a classificatory kinship system. Cf. M. Mead, op. cit., chaps. iii, iv.

128 UMBUNDU KINSHIP AND CHARACTER

animals.[1] Other tales with frankly human protagonists portray the same theme,[2] and there are a number of Umbundu adaptations and variations of such European versions of this theme as Cinderella, Snow White, &c. In some tales, such as 'Kalitangi', the hero escaped as an infant from an agreement made by his mother before his birth with another expectant mother that they would both destroy their offspring. Does this indicate a resentment of, or a protest against, child-sacrifice in certain Umbundu rites? I mention this as one possible source for the feeling of neglect and 'rejection' which, however, does not seem to be as acute or as widespread as in our own society.[3] The exact situation could only be determined by careful and extensive investigation.

Adjustments between siblings among the Ovimbundu on the whole are relatively satisfactory. Resentment on the part of the younger does sometimes occur as indicated above. Overt sibling conflict has also arisen quite frequently in the royal families because of disputes over the succession. Instances of this latter type of conflict may be found in narratives of the early missionaries,[4] in diaries of Silva Porto,[5] and in other early sources. Conflict from jealousy arising out of the parent–child relationship, however, seems to be relatively rare. In a kinship society regulated by the hierarchy of age, jealousy between siblings does not quite fit into the picture. The two most common terms for jealousy over personal relations refer strictly to sexual jealousy: *esepa*, woman's jealousy; and *ukuelume*, jealousy on the part of a man. The other terms are somewhat more applicable but they belong less to household affairs. The meaning of *onya* is jealousy and envy, while *ocipululu* is covetousness and so belongs to the economic sphere.

Friendship, especially between age-mates or 'coevals', has played and continues to play an important role in Umbundu social adjustments. Such differences as social station, family, distance of habitation, and even diversity of language and culture are easily bridged by friendship. Many friendships were formed on trading

[1] Cf. *Journal of the American Folk-Lore Society*, 1922, vol. 35, nos. 1 and 18, pp. 116 f., 140 ff.
[2] The tale of *Ñaña la kota liaye* (Baby and his elder sister) referred to *supra*, p. 84.
[3] Investigations of the 'foster-child phantasy', feelings of neglect ,'rejection', &c., reported by Murphy, op. cit., p. 415 f.; and by Allport, op. cit., p. 364 f.
[4] *Missionary Herald*, 1888, p. 242 f.
[5] In *Boletim da Sociedade de Geografia de Lisboa*, 1885, 1886.

PLATE IX

Photo. M. W. Ennis

b. Fetish charms and diviner's rattle

a. A potter at work (Dondi)

PLATE X

Photo. M. W. Ennis

a. Wounded bull eland (Malolo)

Photo. R. S. Webb

b. Head of wart hog (Bailundu)

ANALYSIS OF UMBUNDU DEVELOPMENT 129

expeditions. Many blood-brotherhoods were doubtless undertaken purely from motives of friendship.[1] The *vakuacisoko* is a friendly institution. The Ovimbundu are a friendly people.

Identification is a strikingly important feature of Umbundu social adjustments and of the whole learning process. Children overtly identify themselves with older siblings, with parents, with other older relatives both living and dead, with friends of their parents, with the village headman, or even the king.[2] This perhaps is the process involved in that which the Ovimbundu name reincarnation. It is largely through identification that character appears to run in families. This is why boys are so keen to learn the professions of their fathers or their mother's brothers. Identification with their seniors in social position and economic activity more closely cements the unity of the child–adult sphere and gives the children yet another urge to enter into adult life and assume complete responsibility as quickly as possible.

'Inferiority Conflict' has probably been present in Umbundu life for a long time, perhaps since the rubber trade (1874), perhaps even longer. When a people's activity is keyed to so high a pitch there will be some individuals who find themselves inadequate. There are a number of proverbs which ridicule the stay-at-homes or those 'too lazy' to undertake the exceedingly arduous trading expeditions. European domination has set new paces and created new frustrations, with one result, that 'inferiority conflicts' are probably on the increase. Many individual instances could be cited. A particularly striking one of my observation is of a man whose suffering from epileptic seizures had induced attitudes of inferiority. The conflict was exacerbated by his selection as a hospital assistant, in which position the responsibility required was plainly beyond his ability.[3] Individuals suffering from any physical disability find life difficult among such an aggressive people.

If the disability is great the handicapped individual generally finds the adjustment beyond his powers. I have observed a number of severely crippled individuals brought up in traditional kinship groups, and all of them were suffering from overt inferiority conflicts. All of these individuals had adopted compensatory

[1] Although the rite seems to have connotations of sorcery.
[2] Among the Tallensi, according to Fortes, identification is only with older siblings, with parents, and with 'the clan' (op. cit., pp. 46 ff.).
[3] Epilepsy (*ocinonya*) is considered by the Ovimbundu as a visitation of the spirits and is much feared.

K

130 UMBUNDU KINSHIP AND CHARACTER

behaviour of an anti-social nature.[1] The foregoing analysis refers chiefly to those of the Ovimbundu who now live or were reared within their traditional social structure, with but slight reference to other individuals.

The Umbundu Estimate of Character

The Umbundu concept of personality as being achieved by a process of social integration is of fundamental importance, bearing in mind that society consists of the whole kinship group—including the living and the dead, men and spirits. The process of achieving integration together with reactions to various cultural elements interestingly reveal the types of character appreciated and those disliked by the Ovimbundu.

Almost everything in Umbundu life and culture reveals them to be a strong and aggressive people. Their history, whether of raiding or of trading, is eloquent testimony to this. The early age at which children participate and assume responsibility in social and economic life has doubtless contributed toward the development of aggressive attitudes. The system of marriage which places the balance of responsibility in all particulars upon the bridegroom and not on his elders, but at the same time requires the willing consent of the bride, is evidently a development of a strongly aggressive people. Their economic life witnesses to the same fact, whether one considers their trade or their agriculture. None but an aggressive (or a very stubborn) people could succeed at farming in a region of such poor soil. Basing his observations only on their pillage and robbery of all their neighbours, and on the submission of the latter, Magyar remarked that the Ovimbundu were the greatest people of South Africa.[2]

In view of these facts it is not difficult to understand that the Ovimbundu appreciate character integration which includes a high degree of self-expression. Such 'traits'[3] as drive, extroversion, insight, ascendance, and expansion[4] are desired and appreciated by the Ovimbundu. Introversion and reclusion, on the other hand, are disliked. In the more extreme forms they are feared and

[1] Stealing is one of the commonest types of behaviour in such cases.

[2] L. Magyar, *Reisen in Süd-Afrika*, p. 265.

[3] The term is used merely for convenience to cover types of behaviour. The specificity of the responses which make up character is assumed; cf. Hugh Hartshorne and Mark May, *Studies in the Nature of Character*, 3 vols. (New York: Macmillan, 1928–30).   [4] After Allport, op. cit., chap. v.

ANALYSIS OF UMBUNDU DEVELOPMENT

suspected as indications of sorcery. It would of course be impossible to indicate what proportion achieve the ideal. It would seem that their respective manners of life have favoured its development in the men more largely than in the women. May this perhaps be one reason why women seem to be caught more often in the vicious circle of suspicion of sorcery?

Fearing anger and ill will as a root-cause of sorcery, yet developing a very aggressive type of character, and achieving in their villages and other social groupings such a large measure of socialized life, the adjustments in anger achieved have been, perhaps, a necessary prerequisite. That does not make the achievement any less important. Note has already been made of the ability to use humour as an outlet for anger, which is held to be an indication of true insight.[1]

Statesmanlike ability, good judgement, and dignity were often noted by the early missionaries as qualities of some of the old kings, councillors, and headmen.[2] After 1900 these qualities were less often observed, owing perhaps to the demoralizing effects of the rum trade. These qualities have, however, survived to the present day and may be observed in pastors, elders, teachers, and other leaders of the church. That shrewd behaviour (*oku lunguka*) is appreciated by this great trading people is easily understood, but it is not as universally or unreservedly admired as are some other types.

There is also a tender side to Umbundu character. It might conceivably be supposed that long-continued and intimate participation in such inhumane occupations as the slave-trade might leave a stamp of callous brutality on the character of the Ovimbundu generally.[3] On second thought a similar question might be raised with regard to Americans because of their participation in the same slave-traffic, or their more recent participation in equally ruthless practices under the banner of modern capitalism.

The rarity or absence among kings of the Ovimbundu of resort to 'revolting and wholesale punishments—so common at African courts' has been noted.[4] On the positive side, a most admirable

---

[1] Cf. Allport, op. cit., pp. 118, 344.

[2] Cf. *Missionary Herald*, 1883, p. 229; 1886, p. 143; 1887, pp. 26, 530, &c.

[3] H. W. Nevinson alleged some such effect. Cf. *A Modern Slavery*, chap. ii. The references are to people of Viye. The effects noted were more probably due to long association with Europeans.

[4] *Supra*, p. 21 f.

UMBUNDU KINSHIP AND CHARACTER

tenderness towards and consideration for those weaker than one-self, for women, for children, and for the aged may be seen among Ovimbundu who are quite untouched by Christianity or Christian teachings in any form. This was often noticed and remarked upon by the early missionaries.[1] Umbundu treatment of children, the habitually respectful form of address used in speaking to them, and respect for their personalities[2] is further evidence of this tender side of Umbundu character, as is also their banning of angry behaviour from the relations of the home.[3]

Such a combination of aggressive, dignified, and tender behaviour makes for character worthy of admiration. It is a heritage worth conserving and passing on to succeeding generations.

Description and analysis now hands the problem to education. I cannot find a more fitting close for this chapter than the following statement of the problem:

From the obscurities that for us still hang about African childhood, the fact emerges that Africans do educate their children. It is a genuine education. . . . What the African sets out to do, namely, to prepare the new generation to take its place in the community and carry on the tribal tradition, he accomplishes with a very considerable measure of success. . . . What Mr. Bryant has said of the Zulus may be said of some other African tribes: 'Through the ages, this admirable system of forming character and imparting knowledge continued, until at length was evolved a Zulu race noble of heart, dignified of bearing, refined of manners, and learned in natural science—qualities, alas! rapidly dying out before the destructive and demoralizing advance of European civilization!' The concluding sentence applies to many a tribe. No small part of the demoralization is caused by the disturbance of family life through the prolonged absence of the senior males at work on European mines and plantations and through the flocking of boys to European towns; it is in the family life, as we have seen, that the most

---

[1] 'We saw a party crossing the Kulili (*Kulēlē*) River on a bridge of the frailest construction. The young men went first, deposited their loads on the bank, and returned for the loads of the old men, who carefully crept over unburdened. Then some of the young men recrossed and took their baskets from the women, and their babies as well. Last of all, two strong youths assisted the women themselves to cross. Nothing could be more tenderly considerate.

'Whatever customs may prevail in other parts of Africa, here it is entirely false to say that women are ill-treated. No one of either sex does any great amount of work, but such as it is is fairly divided. . . . They are certainly as well-treated as the wives of the poorer classes at home, and do infinitely less drudgery.' From a letter of Dr. Nichols in the *Missionary Herald* for 1883, p. 229.

[2] See *supra*, p. 120 f.

[3] See *supra*, p. 124 f.

ANALYSIS OF UMBUNDU DEVELOPMENT 133

vital discipline and instruction are given. It becomes a problem of urgent importance, how, while introducing the European system of schools, to conserve the very real values of the indigenous African system. The problem awaits solution.[1]

[1] Edwin W. Smith, 'Indigenous Education in Africa', p. 333 f. (in *Essays Presented to C. G. Seligman*, London: Kegan Paul, 1934). The sentence quoted is from A. T. Bryant, *Olden Times in Zululand and Natal*, 1929, p. 77 f.

CHAPTER IX
EDUCATIONAL EVALUATIONS

THE conception of African education underlying the present study is frankly one of adaptation of all that is suitable from indigenous culture in order to weave it into the fabric of a new African civilization. This point of view, stated in the Preface and already elaborated with reference to the social structure in Part One, needs no detailed re-statement here.

Umbundu education, as described and analysed in the foregoing chapters, obviously has points of contact with a progressive conception of Christian education. If nothing else, at least the degree of success which it achieves should cause us to search out its secret. It is probable that there is no formal system of education which could show as great a percentage of success as can this primitive system. In terms of artistic or scientific achievement or discovery its results may not bulk very large, but in terms of successful adaptation to environment they are remarkable.[1] In terms of personal and social integration achieved the results are yet greater.[2] The success achieved by Umbundu education requires the attention of the educationist seeking to serve this people.

Among those elements of Umbundu education which may be built upon by missionary education, I wish to consider three: (1) The Umbundu conception of character, (2) Educational method as actual participation in real life situations, and (3) Educational 'content' as life itself—all of life.

Character

The significance of what the Ovimbundu estimate to be desirable character is evident, and no one would dispute the importance of perpetuating and generalizing the more desirable types of behaviour analysed. Only by grafting into these behaviour patterns, which the Ovimbundu recognize and understand, can

---

[1] This subject cannot be given adequate treatment in a chapter on education. Cf. J. H. Driberg, *The Savage as He Really Is* (London: Routledge, 1929), chaps. ii, iii.

[2] As with many primitive peoples, delinquents and misfits are relatively rare. In Umbundu society allowance for dissent is usually large.

EDUCATIONAL EVALUATIONS 135

desirable character be produced among them. This is the only root into which higher values can successfully be grafted. However much present needs may differ from those of the past, and whatever new and superior standards and ideals may now be desirable, if they are to flower and bear fruit in Umbundu life and character, the only available stock is that which is already present. As educators and as missionaries we should be profoundly grateful that it contains so large a balance of that which is valuable.

The Umbundu concept of character as successful functioning, achievement of personality by a process of social integration, is congenial to progressive character education.[1] The ways in which the Ovimbundu have made and continue to make their social adjustments are of interest, not only from the descriptive and analytical point of view, but also to those who would now be their mentors, responsible for helping them to make new adjustments in new situations. The problem is how to conserve the values of traditional integration while at the same time including the values demanded for successful functioning in the present situation.

Educational Method

Whether in the field of social usages and adjustments, or in that of skills and techniques, the method of education most generally used by the Ovimbundu is the method of actual participation in real-life situations. The children learn usages and make adjustments by *doing* that which they are being taught. Babies learn language by talking and being talked to.[2] Children and adolescents learn their various skills by actually participating in community services. What method could be more real and vital than this? What children ever took part in a joint-activity programme more real than an actual trading expedition? Could nature-lore be learned more naturally than in field and veld? Can belief and ceremony be learned more thoroughly than through real participation in dance and ritual? Attitudes and morals are absorbed all unconsciously from fable, proverb, and song and from observa-

---

[1] Cf. H. Hartshorne, op. cit., pp. 184 ff., 214 ff.

[2] This is true everywhere except where the counterfeit article of 'baby-talk' is used (cf. *supra*, p. 96). Babies among the Ovimbundu advance more rapidly than most Europeans because, in addition, they are rarely left alone with no older person to talk to. Cf. the observation of Father Van Wing, quoted *supra*, p. 96.

136   UMBUNDU KINSHIP AND CHARACTER

tion of those older than oneself. Speaking of Africa in general, Dougall writes:

. . . the training was mostly practical and it was concerned with working in company with other members of the unit for common purposes. This . . . is not unlike the modern discovery of the project as an educational technique. . . . The African method was . . . sound in its emphasis on the social nature of all learning. African boys and girls learnt their lessons through participation in the real tasks and ceremonies of the family and the clan. Here Africans were employing the most effective means of moral training for it makes morality . . . an assumption which is so unconscious that it is unlikely to be questioned and can scarcely be forgotten.[1]

Educational Content

The fact that the content of Umbundu education is coextensive with all of the life and culture is of significance in describing and analysing their development. It is no less significant in programme and curriculum planning. The fact that in Umbundu society the child shares the whole sphere of adult life, has undoubtedly been of great importance in producing the particular individual and social development which has taken place. The simpler the type of life and society the easier it may be to maintain the identity of education with all of life. With a culture as complex as is ours, some degree of dichotomy seems inevitable. It is remarkable that the Ovimbundu with their far-flung and complicated trading operations should have avoided a split between the life of the child and the adult. The life of the adult Ocimbundu of the present time is projected upon a somewhat simpler scale than it was at the time of the great trading operations. The factor of European culture has come in to produce a different sort of split between the school and the life of the adult community, but that should not be allowed to prevent the formation of a programme and a policy as close to realities, answering as nearly to the need of the people, and educationally as sound as was the traditional programme. The traditional system of Umbundu education unites with modern educational philosophy in demanding the 'experience-centred' or 'life-situation' programme.[2]

[1] James W. C. Dougall, 'The Development of the Education of the African in Relation to Western Contact', *Africa*, 1938, p. 322.
[2] Cf. G. A. Coe, *What is Christian Education?* (New York: Scribner's, 1929,

EDUCATIONAL EVALUATIONS 137

Instrumentalities

For an experience-centred programme, a great many instrumentalities may be employed. Once education decides that no experience of the people is alien to its sphere, it cannot confine itself within four walls and a time schedule. Umbundu life is relatively simple, decidedly poor, almost infinitely less complex than ours. Nevertheless, many instrumentalities can be made to contribute to education. For the most part, however, they can be made to present their contribution through three institutions: Family, Church, and School. The family was considered in Chapter IV and also the relation of the Church to the Family and to Umbundu life. It remains to consider Family, Church, and School as educational institutions. No one of these, nor yet any other programme such as medical or agricultural, should be allowed to develop in separation from the others lest the unity of life be violated and compartmentalization after our Western fashion set in. The school, then, is to be definitely a church school, and the church itself grows *within* the family and the kinship pattern of the Umbundu social structure. This principle should be taken as fundamental for an experience-centred Umbundu educational programme. Close co-operation between family, church, and school is a recognized necessity everywhere.[1] Once this principle is made basic in the Umbundu programme, the resources of each made available for all, the values of each recognized and utilized by all, then the sound and healthy reorganization of Umbundu life will take on great impetus.

Educational Policy

The first essential is to determine upon an educational policy. I have assumed the necessity for an experience-centred approach not merely because that is 'new' or 'progressive' but because I believe with John Dewey that 'the fundamental issue is not of new versus old education nor of progressive against traditional education, but a question of what anything whatever must be to be worthy of the name *education* . . . what we want and need is

---

1935), pp. 190–8; Kilpatrick, *Education for a Changing Civilization* (New York: Macmillan, 1926), pp. 123–8; John Dewey, *Experience and Education* (New York: Macmillan, 1938), chaps. vii, viii.

[1] Cf. T. J. Jones, *Essentials of Civilization*, pp. 8 f., 21 ff., 184 ff., &c.

138   UMBUNDU KINSHIP AND CHARACTER

education pure and simple'.[1] If the Ovimbundu are to be educated in any sense worthy of the term a clear-cut and well-defined policy must be formulated without any further delay. Almost eight years ago this was urged by Dr. Oldham and Miss Gibson:

'. . . If Christian missions are to achieve their distinctive purpose, and at the same time to co-operate, as they must do, with government in education, they must know clearly what they want. If they have not a clear policy of their own, they will either have to accept one dictated by government or withdraw from the educational field altogether. . . . In each territory in Africa there must be formulated a missionary educational policy adapted to the circumstances in that area. This next step can only be taken by those on the spot. . . .'[2]

Christian missionaries would agree that the missions can best 'achieve their distinctive purpose' through a truly Christian educational system. Necessity compels them in all areas 'to co-operate . . . with government'. This study assumes the necessity for education centred about present Umbundu experience. How can the claims of each of these three criteria be satisfied? The problem may be difficult but is, I believe, possible of solution. Christian education at its best *is* centred in the social experience of the pupils.[3] In meeting the educational requirements of government, Christian education must shape its own policy and purpose with great care lest it fail to retain its creative Christian character, without which it cannot achieve its 'distinctive purpose'.

The opportunity is great, for it is still possible to build a creative Christian educational system among the Ovimbundu. The government has shown little inclination to enter directly the field of mass education of the natives.[4] The missions are the only agency in the

---

[1] John Dewey, *Experience and Education* (New York: Macmillan, 1938), p. 115 f.

[2] J. H. Oldham and B. D. Gibson, *The Remaking of Man in Africa* (London, O.U.P., 1931), p. 16.

[3] Cf. George A. Coe, *What is Christian Education?* Prof. Coe has answered this question better than any writer of whom I know. See chap. viii: '. . . The personality-principle calls for self-organization, for the integration of selves in society, and for a kind of interrelation between persons that can hold through time. . . . Two maxims will sum up the matter: Approach all persons in the spirit of respect or ethical love; approach all facts in the spirit of science. These are two aspects of one principle. . . . For, since the scientific method, as we have seen, is a necessary expression of personality, ethical love, which seeks the self-realization of persons, will directly evoke scientific attitudes and practices in both the lover and the loved' (p. 178).

[4] The government participates through the work of the Roman Catholic missions which it subsidizes heavily.

EDUCATIONAL EVALUATIONS 139

field. It is their evident duty to work out a clear policy, before they 'have to accept one dictated by government'.

It may be objected, and with reason, that the Protestant missions possess insufficient financial resources adequately to undergird an entire educational system. The missions cannot expect appropriations sufficient to underwrite schools for all the children and youth among the 140,000 who are adherents at the present time, not to mention the very considerable accessions of each successive year. Provision for some but not for all would naturally appear to the Africans as unfair discrimination.

For a long time the missions have endeavoured to educate the necessary leaders. All authorities on African education agree in differentiating between the functions of mass education and education of leaders. As long ago as 1930 a definite division of responsibility was urged upon the missions: that the missions concentrate upon education of leaders while the Umbundu Church takes over complete responsibility for educating the masses.[1] Long before that, mission leaders had felt that the village work, education as well as evangelism, should belong to the sphere of the Umbundu Church in order that this work might be carried on without division of authority and approach or compartmentalization. In some regions this method has been adopted, but it cannot become a success unless it is made a matter of policy and applied in the entire field. If the Umbundu Church is given opportunity to take part in shaping policy, I feel sure that it will respond in a manner worthy of all confidence. Its membership is very poor, perhaps few churches anywhere subsist on the average of such a low income-level of membership. However, where the village work is organized on a kinship basis the necessary leaders will be maintained by their own people. The missions, then, should concentrate on the problem of providing the specific types of education needed by the leaders. In addition the missions must supply leadership and vision in its broader phases. For where there is no vision the people perish.

Problems of organization and of the relationship of school and community need not detain us at length at this point. In Chapter IV the advantages of organizing church and school within the kinship system and the natural social structure were shown. The close

[1] See Frank K. Sanders, *Report to the Prudential Committee of the A.B.C.F.M. concerning the W. Cent. Af. Mission* (A.B.C.F.M.: Boston, 1930. mimeog.), p. 8.

140 UMBUNDU KINSHIP AND CHARACTER

connexion between the kinship groups and character has been demonstrated in the description and analysis of Chapters V–VIII. The desirability of conserving the fundamental social attitudes will not be questioned. The tragic results of discarding those outgoing social attitudes are already all too visible both in social relations and in individual character—especially among the detribalized or partially de-tribalized. Given the Umbundu conception of character as achieved in social functioning, no other result could be expected when social ties break down.

Values have been discovered in the social attitudes and in certain types of social behaviour, but it is vain to expect the Church or school to 'use' these or build upon them unless the kinship structure is conserved to become the basis for organization of Church and school. Only on such a basis can these fundamental attitudes be conserved, given standing and prestige, and eventually widened in scope and application. Along with and as a part of the above, encouragement can be given to retain such items as the traditional kinship system of nomenclature, and forms of courtesy and etiquette which would help in the retention of respect, true courtesy, and other worth-while types of behaviour.

In a territory where native political life has been abolished, education and the Church have a much heavier responsibility than where native political life still functions through indirect rule. In the former, only education and the Church remain to 'strengthen the feeling of responsibility to the tribal community'.[1] Fundamental to the formation of sound policy and more basic than the adaptation of Umbundu method or content in education is organization within the kinship system and the natural social structure.

[1] Advisory Committee on Native Education in the British Tropical African Dependencies, *Education Policy in British Tropical Africa* (London: H.M.S.O., 1925), p. 4.

CHAPTER X

PARTICULAR FIELDS OF EDUCATION

Method and Content

'THE belief that all genuine education comes about through experience does not mean that all experiences are genuinely or equally educative. Experience and education cannot be directly equated to each other. For some experiences are mis-educative.'[1] In the book quoted, Dewey develops the thesis that educative experience is that which promotes further significant experiences, i.e. growth toward maturity. The alternatives now confronting the school 'if it is not to drift aimlessly', are either a 'return to the intellectual methods and ideals that arose centuries before scientific method was developed', or 'systematic utilization of the scientific method as the pattern and ideal of . . . the potentialities inherent in experience'.[2]

The scientific organization of an experiential curriculum for Umbundu education is an inescapable necessity. In this study it is only possible to touch upon a few of the most urgent problems and point out the basis for organization.

Social behaviour has the central place in Umbundu education, a fact which is said to be true of African education in general, with 'the particular occasion . . . the medium of the lesson'.[3] The undoubtedly greater effectiveness of that traditional training over the accomplishments of formal western schooling in manners, morals, or 'civics' should lead us to investigate the possibility of making use of the traditional method. Social behaviour can only be effectively taught in real-life situations. For the Ocimbundu child the only real world is the world of his own family and village. His manners and morals must first be those of his own family and village. Without that sure foundation, he can never build a larger structure. Sound technique for training in social behaviour can only be attained when the school has a vital connexion with the family, the village, and the living social structure of the people. When the Church and its schools have established their work within that structure, when these schools are entrusted to African

[1] John Dewey, *Experience and Education*, p. 13.　　　　[2] Ibid., p. 108.
[3] J. W. C. Dougall, op. cit., *Africa*, 1938, p. 321.

142 UMBUNDU KINSHIP AND CHARACTER

teachers who have themselves had traditional training and have maintained their own kinship ties, then we can work out with them sound social methods.

Language teaching is of great importance in the field under consideration. The mission schools have produced remarkable results in their teaching of the Portuguese language, results probably unequalled by schools similarly situated and conditioned elsewhere. Regulations prohibiting the vernacular except in religious instruction, and requiring the use of Portuguese in all schools from the start,[1] have created great difficulties. No responsible person in touch with the situation questions the utility of teaching the language of the European colonial power, but the educational soundness of attempting to use, as a medium from the start, a language which is not used in the home is open to serious question. It is obvious that such a policy must seriously curtail the effectiveness of the school. The vernacular is still allowed for 'religious instruction' but beyond this, almost nothing but instruction in the Portuguese language can be accomplished. This policy compartmentalizes the school work to an unfortunate degree and places such emphasis on the mere acquiring of a language that the whole programme is warped. It is even inefficient as regards the teaching of the language itself, for pupils who have first had systematic instruction in their mother tongue are by that fact better equipped to acquire a European language.[2]

The French colonial authorities, who first applied language regulations of this sort in Africa, have come to realize the necessity for some modifications in practice. Gouverneur-Général Brévié, of Afrique Occidentale Française, in December 1931 stated:

. . . In order that this system of education may produce the best results immediately, we must not hesitate to have recourse to the local

[1] Enforced since 1922 under the provisions of Decree 77 of 9 Dec., 1921 (*Boletim Oficial* No. 50, 1921). The text with an English translation may be found in *Treaties, Acts, and Regulations relating to Missionary Freedom* (London: International Missionary Council, 1923). A law of April 1938 lays down still more difficult regulations regarding the teaching of Portuguese and includes certain provisions which frankly discriminate between Protestant and Roman Catholic mission schools.

[2] 'in Achimota (Gold Coast) . . . by means of convincing tests it has been established that a child educated in his mother tongue in one year obtains a knowledge of English which otherwise would take him six years to acquire' (Gouverneur-Général Olivier, *Six Ans de Politique Sociale à Madagascar*, chap. v, quoted by Paul Crouzet in the *Educational Yearbook 1931*, p. 472).

PARTICULAR FIELDS OF EDUCATION 143

idiom to express ideas which the natives could not otherwise understand. Shall we wait until they know French sufficiently to divulge the secret to them that the anopheles carries malaria and the louse carries epidemics of typhus? Shall we demand of the African a diploma or a certificate of studies of fertilizers . . .? The need of practical education is beyond all question. Let the local idiom be used where French fails to apply.

M. Crouzet goes on to comment:

The latest information from West Africa indicates that in future the native language will not be wholly disregarded as a means of carrying on instruction in the elementary school.[1]

In adult education the vernacular is to be used even more widely in French West Africa where, according to Prof. Labouret, the authorities have come to recognize the necessity of this step if mass education is not to be indefinitely delayed.[2]

As long as the official educational regulations in force in Angola seem not to envisage any real system of mass education, may it not be uneconomic for the Church to continue a widespread system of schools teaching the Portuguese language? In the Cameroun, where similar although less stringent language regulations are in force, the missions carry on only *écoles de catéchisme* in the vernacular in the villages, and concentrate their teaching of French where officially recognized teachers are available.[3] A similar policy might be worked out to advantage for the schools of the Umbundu Church.

I feel that this is desirable not only for reasons of economy, but also in order to improve the quality of language teaching. If the teaching of Portuguese were restricted to those schools taught by properly qualified teachers, that fact alone would improve the quality of the output. In that case, it would also be easier to follow the method of direct and exclusively oral instruction at the beginning, a method which those in touch with the local situation

---

[1] Ibid., p. 473 f.

[2] H. Labouret, 'L'Éducation des Masses en A. O. F.' (*Africa*, 1935), pp. 98 ff.: 'L'orientation est avant tout rurale. . . . Elle (l'école) est destinée à créer une mentalité paysanne, à rattacher la classe à la vie du groupement humain . . . . Dans une autre circulaire, le Gouverneur Général précise ses intentions: "Ce rôle . . . sera soutenu et continué quand il se pourra, par l'institution de cours pratiques d'adultes, *où l'on emploiera au besoin les langues indigènes*. . . . Le cours pratique d'adultes en langue indigène me paraît un excellent moyen en vue de cette action éducatrice de la masse" ' (p. 100).

[3] W. R. Wheeler, *The Words of God in an African Forest* (New York: Revell, 1931), chap. ix; J. H. Oldham and B. D. Gibson, op. cit., p. 130.

144 UMBUNDU KINSHIP AND CHARACTER

have for several years agreed to be the most effective. This is the method whereby babies learn their own language, a method which competent African teachers can easily understand and have adapted with good results.

Physical education and recreation would seem to be a simple matter among a people which spends so large a proportion of its time in out-of-doors occupations and one which, again, has almost universally good posture, and a large proportion of which is of good physique. Comparing the Ovimbundu with their neighbours to the north, the Ovimbundu are greatly superior both in physique and in posture. Umbundu forms of physical education are responsible at least in part. Carrying loads on the head, which is done by all ages and both sexes, has also had undoubted influence. Most important of all is the dance. The dance is very good physical exercise but it is much more than that. It is more than mere recreation. 'The dance is in most primitive societies an important factor in maintaining group solidarity.'[1] This is certainly true of the Ovimbundu. There is nothing which can take its place. It is doubtful whether the solidarity of any group of Ovimbundu can be firmly established or long maintained without the dance. They do adopt various foreign forms of recreation, but the dance meets a deeper need. Whatever new exercises and games may be introduced the physical educator cannot afford to neglect indigenous forms.

Music is of great importance to the Ovimbundu. The Church and mission schools have made much use of this musical ability and bent. The great choirs which give such pleasing renditions of European classical and sacred music would do credit to schools or colleges in any part of the world.[2] Less use has been made of native music but it is still sung, and some teachers have taken real interest in it. Not having described the Umbundu musical forms it is not possible to extend this evaluation. However, it must be noted that European music has been supplied with Umbundu words, and very successfully in some instances. Contrary to the predictions of several authorities, the result, most emphatically, is not 'a kind of musical pidgin'.[3]

[1] Krige, 1936, op. cit., p. 336.
[2] See article by Elizabeth Scattergood Chalmers, 'The Music at the Jubilee', *Missionary Herald*, 1930, pp. 335–8.
[3] See E. M. von Hornbostel, 'African Negro Music', *Africa*, 1928, pp. 30–62. He offers some interesting suggestions on the use of drums. His conclusions on

PLATE XI

Photo. 'Minerva'

a. Musicians of Luanda with xylophone

Photo. M. P. Childs

b. Musicians with flutes

PLATE XII

Photo. D. G. Ridout

a. A baby clinic (Dondi)

Photo. R. S. Webb

b. Bringing a patient in a hammock (*owanda*) (Bailundu)

PARTICULAR FIELDS OF EDUCATION 145

Other fields of education, e.g. agriculture, industries, hygiene, and science, are of much importance. It is not for lack of appreciation that treatment of them is omitted here but rather because the necessary basis for their relation to Umbundu education has not yet been laid by description of economic life, magic, Umbundu outlook on life, &c. At any rate, this study does not pretend to deal with the entire educational field.[1] One other field, the very important one of religious education, remains to be treated.

Christian Education

Christian education, if truly creative,[2] should find a great opportunity in a system built within the Umbundu social structure, the prime concern of which is the personal and social integration of its individual members, i.e. their personal and social relationships. This must be so, because the essential meaning of Christianity and the fundamental task of Christian education are to be found, according to the view assumed by this study, in relations between persons.[3] Evidently Umbundu methods of educating the young and teaching social behaviour through real-life situations offer a splendid opportunity to the Christian educator. Since method is of much importance in religious education, it is indeed fortunate that sound educational method and the social experience of the people to be educated agree at this point.

The content as well as the method of religious education should be rooted in Umbundu behaviour and attitudes. The desirability of utilizing 'the attitudes of the household and the principle of their extension' has already been pointed out.[4] Further description of these attitudes and types of behaviour, together with their synthesis in character, as shown in the description and analysis of Chapters V–VIII, reveal a wealth of sound stock into which Christian character may be grafted. These outgoing and other-

the adaptation of European music seem to be drawn on theoretical grounds and insufficient evidence.

[1] Some interesting attempts toward the construction of African curricula and curricular material will be found listed in the bibliography.

[2] See *supra*, p. 138, note 3.

[3] This view is held in common by authorities such as G. A. Coe and J. H. Oldham who in some matters differ widely. For Dr. Oldham's summary see Oldham and Gibson, op. cit., chap. iv. Prof. Coe's statement of the problem has already been referred to (p. 138). See also his summary, op. cit., p. 296.

[4] *Supra*, pp. 69, 72.

L

146 UMBUNDU KINSHIP AND CHARACTER

regarding attitudes and types of behaviour offer the soil in which Christian life for individuals and for the whole people can take root. Unless the Kingdom of God is so rooted I fail to see how it can ever come.

In view of the tendency of the African Church toward a somewhat excessively legalistic type of life it is especially necessary to take over as much of *positive* value as may be found in indigenous behaviour. There are, however, elements of value in some of the Umbundu prohibitions. Aversion to expression of anger has been dealt with at length.[1] Whatever its psychological basis, the result of this attitude in personal relations is definitely good. When the incidence of angry behaviour within intimate circles is definitely less frequent than among many Americans and Europeans, may not the Ovimbundu be nearer in this respect both to the teaching of Jesus[2] and to sound educational practice?[3] This is only one of many moral restraints of which good use may be made, and upon which sound morality may be built.[4]

The Bible has been and will continue to be the greatest of source books for African religious education. An experience-centred curriculum for a primitive people will find much in the Book which records the experience of another people in an only slightly less primitive stage of development.

Ethnological and intellectual points of contact between the ancient Hebrews and the Bantu have been noted by many writers. It is indisputable that culturally these peoples have more in common than, for example, have the ancient Hebrews and modern peoples. Educated Africans often reveal a superior understanding of biblical narratives. When sound historical and cultural methods are used, biblical narratives often take on a wealth of meaning. Africans sometimes discover meanings which Westerners had not found. It should not be forgotten that it was from questions of his Zulu assistants that Bishop Colenso was led to investigate the historical sources of the Pentateuch.[5]

---

[1] *Supra*, pp. 21; 101 ff.

[2] See Matt. v. 21–4.

[3] See Allport, op. cit., p. 343: 'The proper control . . . of anger is an important pedagogical problem.'

[4] Among South African writers on Bantu moral ideas, see Junod, op. cit., vol. ii, pp. 579–84; also his article in *I.R.M.*, 1927, pp. 85–90.

[5] See J. W. Colenso, *The Pentateuch and the Book of Joshua Critically Examined*, pp. 8, 15 f., 26 ff. Bishop Colenso plainly stated that the questions of his assistants in translation *drove him* to undertake his critical and historical

PARTICULAR FIELDS OF EDUCATION 147

Although the above illustrations refer more especially to the Old Testament, what has been written is largely true of the whole Bible. It goes without saying that a frankly Christian programme will go to Jesus for its chief inspiration. A programme which seeks the social integration of persons and is based on respect for persons, of necessity seeks guidance from 'Jesus' assumption that persons are of infinite worth'[1] and from his showing forth of 'God, the Great Valuer of Persons'.[2]

Use of the New Testament narratives is presupposed. For their proper understanding, as also for understanding the Old Testament, historical treatment and approach are a *sine qua non*. No other method will bring out the 'ethnological and intellectual points of contact'. By no other method can the Ovimbundu truly 'see Jesus'.

Does it not go without saying that the type of religious education presupposed by the foregoing could never be satisfied merely with 'the inclusion of a religious lesson in the curriculum'?[3] Rather it demands a central place in a system dominated throughout by its own valuation of persons. 'Religion would not be an appendage of academic interests, or even a guest or companion, . . . for the whole enterprise, suffused with a sense of the worthfulness of the personal, would be inherently and aggressively religious.'[4]

Treatment of other Umbundu Material

Much of the Umbundu traditional literature—proverbs, riddles, songs, and folk-tales—is well worth using at some place in the educational programme. References have been made to a few items in this chapter and in the previous one, and it is hoped that

---

studies. While his was not the first such study, it was probably the first undertaken by a churchman engaged in active pastoral work and who was led to the study by the questions of those under his pastoral care.

[1] G. A. Coe, op. cit., p. 296.   [2] G. A. Coe, op. cit., p. 296.

[3] 'The inclusion of a religious lesson in the curriculum may not only contribute nothing to the advancement of true Christianity; it may exert a bad influence. If the lesson is badly taught, it may produce in the mind of the pupil a feeling of boredom which begets a distaste for religion. . . . Above all, if there is a contradiction between what is taught in the classroom and what is practised in the life of the school, it is inevitable that the pupils should come to think that religion has nothing to do with life; that it consists in doctrines which one is supposed to believe, but which have little relation to daily existence' (Oldham and Gibson, op. cit., p. 31).

[4] G. A. Coe, op. cit., p. 295.

148 UMBUNDU KINSHIP AND CHARACTER

a fuller treatment may be given at a later time. All of this traditional literature is of great value to students of the culture and merits serious study. One seeking to work with a people, seeking to educate them and attempting to help them to lay 'the basis for a new culture, needs to study every side of their culture. He must seek to understand them as fully as possible. It is necessary to understand the *whole culture*: those elements which a modern programme can use and those which may eventually be discarded. This holds for teacher and learner alike; African education must needs be a co-operative enterprise. As nearly as possible, the whole process should be brought out in the open: all cards laid on the table. If the missionary deems a given custom or institution objectionable, let him first seek to understand it in an objective spirit. If, after getting as complete an understanding as possible, the cultural element still seems objectionable then let native opinion and advice be sought. It often happens that a direct attack upon a given practice only results in driving it underground and in its being practised secretly or in a disguised form. This happens with religious beliefs, with magico-medical practices, with forms of witchcraft or sorcery, and with other elements which have been attacked. When it becomes necessary completely to uproot a given element or practice, a substitute which is at least equally useful and attractive must be provided. Elimination by substitution will probably have a better chance of success if the emphasis is placed not on attacking the undesirable practice but rather upon the desirable substitute. A fairly simple example of substitution which might well be sought is in the objects which parents and elder siblings teach babies to fear. In place of being conditioned to fear spirits, the bugaboo, imaginary animals, and strangers, children could be taught to fear those things which are really dangerous to them.

Initiation camps offer a more complicated example of a substitution which in my opinion it seems desirable to attempt. I have shown that initiation camps probably did not belong to the traditional Umbundu culture but began to be taken over from neighbouring cultures at about the time when the stopping of the rubber trade left men and boys less actively occupied. I have also remarked that in the matter of educational method, initiation rites are contrary to the spirit prevailing in Umbundu education, which uses almost exclusively the real situations of the normal life of the

PARTICULAR FIELDS OF EDUCATION 149

community.[1] Initiation camps appeal to Umbundu youth largely for lack of something better. They have as yet been taken up only by a very small minority.

Can the missions offer a substitute which will meet the very evident need of youth and so forestall the wholesale adoption of initiation camps? Quite recently the missions have initiated a movement which, if properly developed, may be able in large measure to do just that. The movement is that of vacation camps for children and adolescents. It has had a good beginning in several regions and if carefully and persistently directed and developed it may fill a real need in the life of youth. Since initiation rites are not now a recognized part of Umbundu life I do not feel that it would be either wise or necessary to attempt to 'take them over' as has been attempted in other areas. In those few regions where initiation rites have already established a hold, it may be desirable, in connexion with boys' camps, to arrange for the proper surgical circumcision of those who desire it. This has already been done by some of the mission medical officers, but not in connexion with camps.

Fagging is a subject which needs careful consideration. It is my feeling that the method of dealing with it which offers the best chance of success, whether in school or in camp, is to get the boys or girls, through their recognized leaders, to agree upon its institutionalization on a carefully considered and closely restricted basis. Otherwise it is likely to continue or to recur sporadically, secretly or underground, and to perpetrate most unfortunate excesses. This has been the experience in the past.

It would be well to work out camp programmes which may utilize as many indigenous cultural elements as possible, rather than to attempt to translate a purely Western programme. In Umbundu social, educational, and economic life, and in the traditional literature, are many elements of worth which such a Youth Movement could easily utilize, inasmuch as it is not bound by the requirements of the formal school.

[1] Dougall holds this to be true of African education generally. 'Initiation rites serve as the exception which prove the rule' (*Africa*, 1938, p. 322).

CHAPTER XI

EDUCATION AND LIFE

Can Umbundu Knowledge and Practice yet be adapted?

IN the article of the *Year Book of Education 1938*, already quoted,[1] Mr. H. S. Scott poses the question as to whether it may not now be too late to rescue African educational knowledge and practice from oblivion and disrepute. The educated African to-day, he says, only recognizes education in Western garb.[2] This is hardly less true for the Ovimbundu than for other Africans. Nevertheless I am convinced that if action along the lines herein suggested is taken without delay, it has a good chance of success. I have good proof of this from experience, especially with pupils and teachers of the Normal and Religious Education Departments of Currie Institute. In 1936–7 much of the material used in the descriptive part of Chapters V–VII was gathered by pupils and teachers, largely as a class project. The enthusiasm with which they undertook and carried on the project, the interest with which they turned to other phases of their culture, and the reports received afterwards from those who had finished school and returned to their villages, were eloquent proofs of the prestige which their own culture still has for educated Ovimbundu. Adaptation is yet possible, if it is undertaken without too much delay.

What should be Central for the Umbundu Curriculum?

Assuming that 'the organic connexion between education and personal experience'[3] demands 'systematic utilization of the scientific method as the pattern and ideal of the potentialities inherent in experience',[4] we have found that such utilization will only be possible for the Ovimbundu if interpreted to them through that which is central to their own experience. Umbundu education should be organized around those experiences which are central to Umbundu life.

The Latin colonial Powers, proponents of the ideal of assimilation, in order to promote that ideal, have tried to make the national culture central. Because the African pupils knew nothing of the

[1] See *supra*, p. 119.   [2] *Year Book of Education 1938*, p. 697 f.
[2] Dewey, *Experience and Education*, p. 12.   [4] Ibid., p. 108.

EDUCATION AND LIFE

national language, greater efforts were made to teach it to them, and in effect the teaching of the national language has become the central core of the curriculum round which all else revolves and to which all else is made to contribute. This has often meant that really nothing but the language is taught, and at times even that is not taught very well.[1] Clearly, this is a *reductio ad absurdum*, and cannot, must not, continue to be normative. French colonial authorities have come to recognize their mistake and have been moving to modify their policy.

It is in British territory chiefly that African educational progress has been made. Modern British authorities have for the most part advocated one of two 'central cores' around which to organize the curriculum of the African school. One group envisages closer control of education by the state and with Julian Huxley claims that 'biology and geography make the best central core for the academic side of native education'.[2] The other group, acting on the assumption that the bulk of the schools will continue to be in the hands of the missions, and following the lead given in 1925 by the Advisory Committee on Native Education,[3] holds that 'the curriculum must be related to the Christian purpose of a school' while at the same time teaching 'the best science, as scientists understand it, the best history, the best art'.[4] There is a third group, some members of which may agree with the advocates of biology and some with the advocates of religion, but whose distinction is to put forward the need for first finding out the nature of the African's own education.[5]

The present study, assuming this last-named approach, has found social behaviour central to traditional Umbundu education. It would therefore be logical to advocate a curriculum centred around the social studies, or, in other words, around the present

[1] In many outschools manned by African teachers the prestige of the European language bulks so large that, although they may go through the motions of teaching other, especially Bible, lessons, in effect, however, they accomplish little beyond a smattering of language teaching. I know a large mission school (outside the Umbundu area) which follows the government programme for European pupils without any religious or other lessons suitable for African pupils.

[2] Julian Huxley, *Africa View* (New York: Harpers, 1931), p. 322 f.

[3] See p. 140, n. 1.

[4] Oldham and Gibson, op. cit., p. 47. See also J. W. C. Dougall, *Religious Education in Africa* (London and New York: International Missionary Council, n.d.).

[5] e.g. H. S. Scott, op. cit.; E. W. Smith, op. cit.

152 UMBUNDU KINSHIP AND CHARACTER

social experience of the pupils. A social science course somewhat on the pattern of the course of Rugg and Kruger[1] but constructed from the standpoint of the Umbundu village, the kinship system, and creative Christian education would be a very good curricular basis. On such a basis the claims of all three groups mentioned above could be harmonized.

'Systematic utilization of the scientific method'[2] requires that the education of the Ovimbundu be organized around their own social experience. Only on that basis can a generalization of the scientific method be expected. Only through their own experience can the masses of the Ovimbundu come to understand truly the sciences, i.e. utilize in their lives the results of science and of the scientific method. 'Since the scientific method . . . is a necessary expression of personality'[3] creative Christian education also requires both 'systematic utilization of the scientific method' and the centrality of the social experience of the learners.

In a curriculum so based and so centred the teaching of the European language and culture would take its rightful place. It would necessarily abandon the dog-in-the-manger position which it has been allowed to take in many schools. In compensation the European language, instead of being poorly taught in many schools, would be well taught in fewer schools with ultimately far better results.

The social, religious, and scientific course advocated should be a single course, simple at first and gradually increasing in complexity as the learners advance in experience. Since everything must have a name, let it be called religious or Christian education. Its first cycle would naturally form the curriculum of the so-called 'catechetical' or village schools.[4]

This is a practical solution for a difficult problem. It harmonizes the claims of practical anthropology, of sound education, and of real religion.

Community Education

No consideration of a truly experience-centred system of education should close with the school curriculum. Any education which is truly experience-centred and, therefore, according to

---

[1] For this and other social science courses see bibliography.
[2] Dewey, loc. cit.   [3] Coe, loc. cit.
[4] See *supra*, p. 142 f.

EDUCATION AND LIFE 153

Professor Dewey, 'anything . . . worthy of the name education',[1] must include in its purview the whole community. If education is a process which may not be confined within four walls of a school, neither may it be confined to the school curriculum, nor to the children who are enrolled as pupils. The aim of such education must be a better life for the whole community.

For an African educational system rooted in, and in living contact with, the kinship system and the natural social structure of the people, these facts are self-evident and of fundamental importance. No real progress can be achieved or expected if education holds in its purview less than the whole community. The relative failure, in terms of social integration or social progress, of those boarding-schools which have removed children from their communities, is too well known to require review. Especially flagrant examples could be cited from among primitive peoples.[2] Parents must be influenced along with their children. If a community is to go forward, that whole community must be educated.

African adults want education. When they think that it will mean advancement or advantage for themselves, they are eager to secure it. Reading, writing, and a European language have acquired such prestige that nearly everyone is anxious to acquire these tools believed to be badges of civilization and a superior culture. As recently as thirty years ago many Ovimbundu, perhaps a majority, believed that reading and writing could only be acquired by means of magic or even sorcery.[3] Now, however, such beliefs are held by few, if any, and learning is immensely popular. For a long time adults in infants' classes have been a common sight in village schools. It would be commoner yet were it not for lack of leisure time. Other types of education will be no less popular with adult Ovimbundu, once their effectiveness and practical value have been demonstrated in terms which they can understand.

Examples of successful community movements which might be of value for the Umbundu village may be had from several parts of the world to-day. The work of the United States Federal and State Departments of Agriculture in rural regions by means of

[1] See *supra*, p. 137.

[2] Cf. experience of boarding-schools among Indians in the United States.

[3] Rev. Paulino Ngonga Liahuka, as a youth, was accused of causing the death (by sorcery) of an elder sister in order to 'use her eyes' to master the arts of reading and writing (*Missionary Herald*, 1930, p. 63).

154 UMBUNDU KINSHIP AND CHARACTER

farm and home demonstrators and public-health nurses is well known, as is also the work of 'visiting teachers' of the Jeanes Fund in negro communities of the Southern States of America.[1] These agencies have encouraged and accomplished the organization of parents and teachers, of associations for Village or Farm Improvement, and of Mutual Aid and Co-operative Societies. They have brought healthful recreation and a sense of community life to places which seemed to be without help and without hope.[2] The work of rural schools and cultural missions in Mexico deserves all the attention which educational authorities have given it during the past fifteen years.[3]

Community improvement has long been a practical objective of some African missions. Formerly much depended upon the background of the missionaries. Those coming from rural areas have often been more apt to see community needs and to attempt something practical. It is reported that almost one hundred years ago missionaries of the American Board imported ploughs into South Africa. The Phelps-Stokes Fund, which in 1921 and again in 1924 sent educational commissions to Africa, found some missions and many individual mission stations undertaking very practical projects of community improvement.[4] Then and now many mission stations might with justice be given Dr. Butterfield's term of 'Rural Reconstruction Units'.[5] The influence of the educational commissions of the Phelps-Stokes Fund on the work of the missions in Africa has been very great. It has been especially direct in British Africa where the Carnegie Corporation has given funds for the extension of the work of the 'Jeanes Visiting

[1] See C. G. Woodson, *The Rural Negro* (Washington, 1930); also L. G. E. Jones, *Negro Schools in the Southern States* (Oxford, 1928), chaps. vii and x.

[2] See A. D. Wright, *The Negro Rural School Fund, Inc.* (Washington, 1933); and for a convenient summary, J. Davis, *The Jeanes Visiting Teachers* (New York: Carnegie Corporation, 1936).

[3] See *Las Misiones Culturales en 1927* (México, D.F., Secretaría de Educación Pública, 1928); K. M. Cook, *The House of the People* (Washington: Government Printing Office, 1932), pp. 3–32; C. D. Ebaugh, *The National System of Education in Mexico* (Baltimore: Johns Hopkins Press, 1931), chap. iii.

[4] T. J. Jones, *Education in Africa* (Phelps-Stokes Fund, 1922); id., *Education in East Africa* (Phelps-Stokes Fund, 1925). The Commission of 1921 visited the Mission under consideration in this study and rated it favourably from the standpoint of orderly community development.

[5] K. L. Butterfield, *The Christian Mission in Rural India* (New York: International Missionary Council, 1930); *Rural Conditions and Sociological Problems in South Africa* (New York, 1929).

PLATE XIII

Photo. D. G. Ridout
a. Baptismal service by the Rev. J. H. Cilũlũ

b. Umbundu wedding, new style: Elende church in the background

PLATE XIV

b. Old age

a. Woman (educated) carrying baby (*oku veleka*)

EDUCATION AND LIFE 155

Teachers'. In many African villages this work, which has been so successful in the Southern States of America, is being tried out. Such adaptations to African village conditions of this valuable and practical idea should provide convenient and useful lessons for the rural work of all African missions.[1]

The key to this community function of education is the training of teachers. The 'visiting teachers' are considered most necessary while untrained or ill-trained teachers are used in village schools. It is felt that such specialists as farm and home demonstrators and public-health nurses may always be needed for these more technical aspects of communal education, but that ideally the local teacher should himself have 'Jeanes training'.[2] The village teacher himself will best be able to lead in the transformation of his community and should be chosen and prepared with that end in view.

These broader functions of community leadership demand, no less than do those of teacher of the young, that the person who exercises them should be a natural leader of his people. He should belong to the group which he seeks to lead. The principles already discovered regarding the desirability of the teacher's maintaining his kinship ties apply no less surely to the teacher in his broader communal functions. The importance of the kinship principle and of working within the natural social structure of the people again becomes evident.[3]

The Umbundu conception of education as integration of the individual in the ongoing processes of society and the congeniality of such a conception to progressive character education have been noted.[4] The broader communal aspects of education now considered remind us that education also has a function in transforming society. These two functions of education are not antagonistic but complementary. Neither can be neglected if Umbundu life is to have a part in the Kingdom of God. The question as to whether education *can* transform or attempt to transform society is often raised. An education which calls itself Christian cannot escape this responsibility. Christian education cannot attempt to accept only one of these functions; it must take them both. Neither can

[1] The best account of this work is found in Carnegie Corporation of New York: *Village Education in Africa* (Lovedale, South Africa, 1936). See also articles in *Oversea Education*, ii. 32; iii. 34, 191; iv. 183; v. 130; vi. 126, 161.

[2] Cf. *Oversea Education*, vii. 183.

[3] Cf. *supra*, pp. 65 f., 70 f.   [4] See *supra*, pp. 119, 134 f.

156 UMBUNDU KINSHIP AND CHARACTER

be neglected at the expense of the other. May not the union of these two functions of education in a single system, and the leadership of both in the person of the village teacher, help to preserve the unity of Umbundu life?

BIBLIOGRAPHY

FOR CHAPTERS V, VI, VII, AND VIII

Titles previously listed are not repeated, although these chapters may contain references to them.

ALLPORT, FLOYD HENRY. *Social Psychology* (Boston and New York: Houghton Mifflin, 1924).

BARTLETT, F. C. *Psychology and Primitive Culture* (Cambridge: University Press, 1923).
BOAS, F. *The Mind of Primitive Man* (New York: Macmillan, 1929).

DEWEY, JOHN. *Democracy and Education.* An Introduction to the Philosophy of Education (New York: Macmillan, 1916).
—— *How We Think.* A Restatement of the Relation of Reflective Thinking to the Educative Process (Boston: Heath, 1933).
—— *Human Nature and Conduct* (New York: Holt, 1922).
DOUGALL, JAMES W. C. *Characteristics of African Thought* (London: International Institute of African Languages and Cultures, Memorandum X, 1932).
DRIBERG, J. H. *At Home with the Savage* (London: Routledge, 1932).

ENNIS, ELIZABETH LOGAN. 'Women's Names among the Ovimbundu', *African Studies*, March 1945.
EVANS-PRITCHARD, E. E. *Some Aspects of Marriage and the Family among the Nuer* (Rhodes-Livingstone Institute, N. Rhodesia, 1945).

FORTES, M. *Social and Psychological Aspects of Education in Taleland.* Supplement to *Africa*, Oct. 1938.

HAMBLY, W. D. *Origins of Education among Primitive Peoples* (London: Macmillan, 1926).
HARTSHORNE, HUGH. *Character in Human Relations* (New York: Scribner's, 1932).
—— and MAY, MARK. *Studies in the Nature of Character* (New York: Macmillan, 1928–30). 3 vols.
HOERNLÉ, A. W. 'An Outline of the Native Conception of Education in Africa', *Africa*, 1931, pp. 145–63.

JONES, A. M. *African Music* (Rhodes-Livingstone Institute, N. Rhodesia, 1943).

BIBLIOGRAPHY TO DEVELOPMENT AND EDUCATION 157

KRIGE, EILEEN. 'Individual Development', Chap. V of *The Bantu-Speaking Tribes of South Africa*, edited by I. Schapera (London: Routledge, 1937).

MALINOWSKI, BRONISŁAW. *Crime and Custom in Savage Society* (New York: Harcourt, Brace, 1926).
—— *Myth and Primitive Psychology* (New York: Norton, 1926).
—— 'Native Education and Culture Contact' (*I.R.M.*, 1936).
MARETT, ROBERT R. *Psychology and Folk-Lore* (London: Methuen, 1920).
MEAD, MARGARET. *Coming of Age in Samoa* (New York: Morrow, 1928).
—— *Growing Up in New Guinea* (New York: Morrow, 1930).
The Missionary Herald (Boston: The American Board, Monthly).
MURPHY, GARDNER. *Historical Introduction to Modern Psychology* (New York: Harcourt, Brace, 1929).
—— and MURPHY, LOIS B. *Experimental Social Psychology* (New York: Harpers, 1931).

NTARA, YOSIA S. *Man of Africa* (London: R.T.S., 1934).

Olosapo vi Ovimbundu. A Collection of Umbundu Proverbs, Adages and Conundrums (West Central African Mission, A.B.C.F.M., 1914).

RATTRAY, R. S. 'The African Child in Proverb, Folklore and Fact', *Africa*, 1933, pp. 456 ff.
READ, F. W. 'Iron-smelting and Native Black-smithing in the Ondulu Country', *Journal of the African Society*, 1902, pp. 44–9.
RICHARDS, AUDREY A. *Bemba Marriage and Present Economic Conditions* (Rhodes-Livingstone Institute, N. Rhodesia, 1940).
RITCHIE, J. E. *The African as Suckling and as Adult* (ibid., 1943).
RUTLEDGE, A. 'Insight: the Negro's Power of Perception', *Atlantic Monthly*, Sept. 1938, pp. 366–73.

SCHAPERA, I. *Married Life in an African Tribe* (London: Faber & Faber, 1940).
SCOTT, H. S. 'Education and Nutrition in the Colonies', *Africa*, 1937, pp. 458–71.
SMITH, EDWIN W. 'Indigenous Education in Africa', in *Essays Presented to C. G. Seligman* (London: Kegan Paul, 1934).
—— *The Shrine of a People's Soul* (London: Church Missionary Society, 1929).

'Umbundu Folk Tales', translated by W. C. Bell, *Journal of the American Folk-Lore Society*, vol. 35, 1922, pp. 116–50.

VAN WING, R. P. (S.J.). *Études Bakongo: Histoire et Sociologie* (Bruxelles: Goemaere, 1921).
Vocabulary of the Umbundu Language (West Central Africa Mission, A.B.C.F.M., 1911).

The Year Book of Education 1938 (London: Evans). Part X, 'The Development of the Education of the African in Relation to Western Contact', by H. S. Scott.

158   UMBUNDU KINSHIP AND CHARACTER

FOR CHAPTERS IX, X, XI

* Titles with this designation contain curricular material especially suitable for adaptation in the educational system under consideration in this study.

Advisory Committee on Native Education in the British Tropical African Dependencies: *Education Policy in British Tropical Africa* (London: H.M.S.O., 1925).

*The African Life Readers: *Primer*, three *Readers*, and *Teacher's Manual* (London: Ginn & Co.). (The *Primer* was translated and adapted in Portuguese in 1932 by the author of this study in collaboration with Senhor Jayme de La Rosa Raposo, and has been used since then in chart and typescript.)

*BATTEN, T. R. *Tropical Africa in World History.* 4 vols. (London: O.U.P. 1938–9).

BENNIE, W. G. 'The Education of the Native', *South African Journal of Science* (Johannesburg, 1924), xxi. 108–19.

Books for Africa (London: International Committee on Christian Literature for Africa, Quarterly).

BOOTH, NEWELL SNOW. *Teaching a Bantu Community.* (A Ph.D. dissertation at Hartford Seminary Foundation: typescript copy from the Library.)

BOYD, WILLIAM (Editor for the N.E.F.). *Towards a New Education* (London and New York: Knopf, 1929).

BRAUNSHAUSEN, N. *Le Bilingualisme et les méthodes d'enseignement des langues étrangères* (Amay: Centrale du P. É. S. de Belgique, 1933). Cahiers de la Centrale, vol. 7.

BROOKES, EDGAR H. *Native Education in South Africa* (Pretoria: van Schaik, 1930).

BRUNER, H. B., and SMITH, C. M. *Social Studies*: Intermediate Grades (New York: Merrill, 1936–8). 4 vols.

BUELL, RAYMOND LESLIE. *The Native Problem in Africa* (New York: Macmillan, 1928). 2 vols.

BUTTERFIELD, KENYON L. *The Christian Mission in Rural India* (New York: International Missionary Council, 1930).

—— *Rural Conditions and Sociological Problems in South Africa.* (Report to the Carnegie Corporation of New York, 1929.)

CHILDS, JOHN L. *Education and the Philosophy of Experimentalism* (New York: Century, 1931).

*CLARKE, J. D. *Omu, An African Experiment in Education* (London: Longmans, 1937).

COE, GEORGE A. *A Social Theory of Religious Education* (New York: Scribner's, 1916).

—— *The Motives of Men* (New York: Scribner's, 1928).

—— *What is Christian Education?* (New York: Scribner's, 1929).

COLENSO, J. W. *The Pentateuch and the Book of Joshua Critically Examined* (London, 1862, 1888).

BIBLIOGRAPHY TO DEVELOPMENT AND EDUCATION 159

The Colonial Review (London: Colonial Department, University of London, Institute of Education, Quarterly).

Conférence internationale sur le bilingualisme, Luxembourg, 1928 (Genève: Bureau International d'Éducation; Luxembourg: Maison du Livre, 1928).

COOK, K. M. *The House of the People* (Washington: Government Printing Office, 1932).

DAVIS, JACKSON. *The Jeanes Visiting Teachers* (New York: Carnegie Corporation 1936).

DEWEY, JOHN. *Experience and Education* (New York: Macmillan, 1938).

—— *My Pedagogic Creed* (Washington: Progressive Education Association, 1929).

DOUGALL, JAMES W. C. *Christianity and the Sex-Education of the African* (London: S.P.C.K., 1937).

—— 'The Development of the Education of the African in Relation to Western Contact', *Africa*, 1938, pp. 312–23.

—— *Religious Education in Africa* (London and New York: International Missionary Council, n.d.).

*——— *The Village Teacher's Guide*. A Book of Guidance for African Teachers (London: Sheldon Press, 1931).

—— 'School Education and Native Life', *Africa*, 1930, pp. 49–57.

DUBOIS, H. M. (S.J.). 'Assimilation ou Adaptation?', *Africa*, 1929, pp. 1–21.

—— 'La Pédagogie appliquée à nos Noirs d'Afrique', *Africa*, 1929, pp. 381 ff.

Educational Method (Washington: National Education Association, Monthly).

A Escola Primária (Lisboa: A. Sá da Costa e Cia., Fortnightly). (A useful little paper; organ of the Portuguese section of the New Education Fellowship.)

EVANS, J. M. *Social and Psychological Aspects of Primitive Education* (London: Golden Vista Press, n.d.).

*FAHS, SOPHIA L. *Beginnings of Earth and Sky* (Boston: Beacon Press, 1937).

*——— *Beginnings of Life and Death* (Boston: Beacon Press, 1938).

*FISHER, ANTHONY, AMBLER, M. B., and GEORGE, C. L. *Follett Social Science Readers* (Chicago: Follett Publishing Co., 1934–5).

FLEMING, DANIEL JOHNSON. *Helping People Grow* (New York: Association Press, 1931).

—— *Ventures in Simpler Living* (New York: M.C., 1933).

—— *Contacts with Non-Christian Cultures* (New York: Doran, 1923).

GARLICK, PHYLLIS L. *School Paths in Africa* (London: Highway Press, 1933).

GOLLOCK, G. A. *Lives of Eminent Africans* (London: Longmans, 1928).

—— *Daughters of Africa* (London: Longmans, 1932).

160 UMBUNDU KINSHIP AND CHARACTER

GUGGISBERG, G., and FRASER, A. G. *The Future of the Negro* (London: S.C.M., 1929).

*HANNA, ANDERSON, and GRAY. *Everyday Life Stories* (Curriculum Foundation Series, Chicago and New York: Scott, Foresman & Co., 1935–7).
*HELSER, A. D. *Education of Primitive People* (New York: Revell, 1934).
VON HORNBOSTEL, E. M. 'African Negro Music,' reprinted from *Africa*, 1928.
HUXLEY, JULIAN. *Africa View* (New York: Harper; London: Chatto & Windus, 1931).

International Journal of Religious Education (Chicago: International Council of Religious Education, Monthly).
International Review of Missions (London: International Missionary Council, Quarterly).

The Jerusalem Meeting of the International Missionary Council. Vol. II, 'Religious Education'; Vol. VI, 'The Christian Mission in Relation to Rural Problems' (New York and London: I.M.C., 1928).
JONES, L. G. E. *Negro Schools in the Southern States* (Oxford: Clarendon Press, 1928).
Journal of the Royal African Society (London: Macmillan, Quarterly).
Journal of Negro Education (Washington: College of Education, Howard University, Quarterly).
JOWITT, HAROLD. *Principles of Education for African Teachers* (London: Longmans, 1932).
*—— *Suggested Methods for the African School* (London: Longmans, 1934).

KANDEL, I. L. *Conflicting Theories of Education* (New York: Macmillan, 1938).
—— (Ed.). *Educational Yearbook 1931*. Following articles: I. Kandel, 'Introduction'; Ed. De Jonghe, 'Education in the Belgian Congo'; S. Rivers-Smith, 'Education in the Tanganyika Territory'; Paul Crouzet, 'Education in the French Colonies' (New York: Int. Inst. of Teachers Col., Columbia Univ., 1932).
—— (Ed.). *Educational Yearbook 1933*. Following articles: Hocking, 'The Place and Scope of Missionary Education'; Paul Monroe, 'Problems of Education'; W. A. Brown, 'The Problem of Education and Religious Purpose' (New York: Int. Inst. of Teachers Col., Columbia Univ., 1934).
KILPATRICK, WILLIAM HEARD. *Education for a Changing Civilization* (New York: Macmillan, 1926).
—— *Education and the Social Crisis* (New York: Liveright, 1932).
—— *Foundations of Method* (New York: Macmillan, 1929).
—— (Ed.). *The Educational Frontier* (New York: Century, 1933).
KINGON, J. R. L. *L'Éducation des peuples primitives* (Gand: A. Buyens, 1922).

BIBLIOGRAPHY TO DEVELOPMENT AND EDUCATION 161

KRISHNAYYA, G. S. *The Rural Community and the School. The Message of Negro and Other American Schools for India* (Calcutta: Association Press, 1932).

LABOURET, HENRI. 'L'Éducation des Masses en Afrique Occidentale Française', *Africa*, 1935, pp. 98 ff.

The Liberian Geography (London: Ginn & Co.). (The first book of this series was translated and adapted in Umbundu and Portuguese by the author of this study in 1928, and has been in use in typescript and mimeograph form.)

*_Listen_ 'for the village people, teachers and school children of Africa' (London: Int. Comm. on Christian Litt. for Africa, Monthly).

*MACKENZIE, JEAN KENYON. *Talking Woman*. (A translation in Umbundu and Portuguese has been published in Ndondi by the Mission Press.) (London: Int. Comm. on Christian Litt. for Africa.)

McKEE, W. J. *New Schools for Young India* (Chapel Hill: University of N. Car. Press, 1930).

MAYHEW, ARTHUR, *Education in the Colonial Empire* (London: Longmans, 1938).

MEINHOF, CARL. 'The Soul of an African Language', *I.R.M.*, 1927, pp. 76 ff.

Las Misiones Culturales en 1927 (México, D. F., Secretaría de Educación Pública, 1928).

Moga Journal for Teachers. 'Rural Reconstruction through Progressive Education' (Lahore; India: P.R.B.S. Press, Monthly).

MONROE, PAUL. *Essays in Comparative Education* (New York: Bureau of Publications, Teachers Col., Columbia Univ., 1927).

MUMFORD, W. B., *et al. Africans Learn to be French* (London: Evans, 1937).

—— and JACKSON, R. 'The Problem of Mass Education in Africa', *Africa*, 1938, pp. 187–207.

MURRAY, A. V. *The School in the Bush* (London: Longmans, 1929).

Nigerian Teacher (Education Department, Lagos, Nigeria, Semi-annual).

*_Oversea Education_ (London: H.M.S.O. for the Secretary of State for the Colonies).

PALMER, H. E. *Principles of Language Study* (New York, 1926).

PERHAM, MARGERY (Ed.). *Ten Africans* (London: Faber, 1936).

Portuguese works on educational problems:

Educational problems have had the careful attention of a number of capable Portuguese writers, as for example, Dr. Faria de Vasconcelos, professor in the Escola Normal Superior of the University of Lisbon. None of these writings, however, has been directed toward African problems, and for that reason no attempt has been made to include them in this bibliography.

Among leading publishers of educational works are the following: A. Sá da Costa e Cia., and Livraria Bertrand, both of Lisbon; also,

M

162   UMBUNDU KINSHIP AND CHARACTER

in Brazil: Cia. de Melhoramentos de São Paulo (Biblioteca de Educação); and Cia. Editora Nacional (Biblioteca Pedagógica Brasileira), both of São Paulo, Brazil. Among their publications are translations of leading American, French, and Swiss educators.

Progressive Education (New York: Progressive Education Association, Monthly).

Religious Education (Chicago: Religious Education Association, Quarterly).

Re-Thinking Missions: A Laymen's Inquiry after One Hundred Years (New York: Harper & Bros., 1932).

RICHARDS, S. A. 'The Direct Method in Modern Language Teaching', in Adams, John (Ed.), *Educational Movement and Methods* (New York, 1924).

*RIVERS-SMITH, S., SPENCER, W. K., McKAY, H., and PARNWELL, E. C., *Simple Science in Simple English.* Seven small books under various titles (London: O.U.P., 1936–8).

*RUGG, HAROLD, and KRUEGER, LOUISE. *Man and His Changing Society.* The Rugg Social Science Series. Elementary Course. Eight volumes with work-books and teachers' guides (Boston and New York: Ginn, 1936–7).

*—— *Man and His Changing Society.* The Rugg Social Science Series. Junior High School Course. Six volumes with work-books and teachers' guides (Boston and New York: Ginn, 1931, 1937).

RYBURN, W. M. *The Progressive School.* Methods of Education and Teaching (Calcutta: Humphrey Milford, 1938).

SADLER, SIR MICHAEL (Ed.). *Christian Education in Africa and the East* (London: S.C.M., 1924).

SCHMIDT, C. H. *The Language Medium Question.* The relation of language and thought as illustrated by the experience of teaching in a foreign medium (Pretoria, 1926).

SCHMIDT, W. 'The Use of the Vernacular in Education in Africa,' *Africa*, 1930, pp. 137–49.

SCHWEITZER, ALBERT. *Out of My Life and Thought.* An Autobiography. Tr. by Campion, C. T. (New York: Holt, 1933).

Seara Nova (Lisboa: Seara Nova, Editora, Weekly). (A literary review with occasional educational articles of value.)

Série Escola Primária. (Arithmetics, readers, and other text-books by the editors of *A Escola Primária*, constructed according to modern methods; the best text-books available in Portuguese, but they are intended for European pupils in Portugal.)

SHARP, EVELYN. *The African Child* (London: Longmans, 1931).

SHAW, MABEL. *Dawn in Africa.* Stories of Girl Life (New York: Friendship Press, 1929).

SMITH, EDWIN W. *The Christian Mission in Africa.* Based on the work of the Conference at Le Zoute (London: International Missionary Council, 1926).

—— *Aggrey of Africa* (New York: Doubleday, Doran, 1929).

BIBLIOGRAPHY TO DEVELOPMENT AND EDUCATION 163

Southern Rhodesia: *Report of the Commission appointed to enquire into the Matter of Native Education in all its Bearings in the Colony of Southern Rhodesia* (Salisbury, Southern Rhodesia: Government Printer, C.S.R. 20, 1925).
—— *Reports of the Director of Native Development* (Salisbury, Southern Rhodesia: Government Printer: Annual Publ.).

Teachers College Record (New York: Bur. of Pub., Teachers Coll., Columbia Univ., Monthly).
Teachers' Journal (Director of Education, Accra, Gold Coast, Monthly).
THORNDIKE and GATES. *Elementary Principles of Education* (New York: Macmillan, 1929).
Treaties, Acts and Regulations Relating to Missionary Freedom (London: I.M.C., 1923).

WEST, MICHAEL. *Language in Education* (London, 1929).
WESTERMANN, D. 'The Place and Function of the Vernacular in African Education', *I.R.M.*, 1925, pp. 25–36.
WILSON, R. L. *Iniciação de Lectura*. Tip. do Dondi, 1943. (This primer, together with more elementary wall charts and flash cards and two more advanced readers, are constructed on the principle of a restricted vocabulary and have a few helps in Umbundu.)
WINTER, ALBAN J. E. *African Education, Suggested Principles and Methods for African Students* (London: Longmans, 1939).
WOODSON, C. G. *The Rural Negro* (Washington: Associated Publishers, 1930).
The World Mission of the Church: *Findings and Recommendations of the International Missionary Council, Madras, December 1938* (New York: I.M.C., 1939).
WRIGHT, A. D. *The Negro Rural School Fund, Inc.* (Washington, 1933).

The Year Book of Education 1932 (London: Evans), pp. 748–66: 'Education in the British Dependencies in Tropical Africa', by W. Ormsby Gore.
The Year Book of Education 1933 (London: Evans). Section XI, 'Education of the African Native', by E. G. Malherbe, S. Rivers-Smith, and A. I. Mayhew.
YOUNG, R. R. *Suggestions for Training of Teachers in Africa* (London: Longmans, 1931).

ZIEGLER, E. K. *A Book of Worship for Village Churches* (New York: Agricultural Missions Foundation, 1939).

PART THREE

CHAPTER XII

HISTORICAL

'Heureux les peuples qui n'ont pas d'histoire', quotes Father Van Wing in introducing his *Études Bakongo*, and having noted that the Kongo people 'had entered into history' in 1482 with the discovery of the River Congo.[1] It is very doubtful whether there are any people, however primitive, or however remote or inaccessible their dwelling, who could qualify for that blessed state. If this characterization means entering upon the stage of continuous contact with Europe and Europeans, it may mark a definite stage in the life of this people.

The Ovimbundu have not in this sense as old a 'history' as have the Kongo people. Their first contacts with Europeans probably took place in the sixteenth and seventeenth centuries before their formation as a people—before they were Ovimbundu; but it was from the second or third quarter of the eighteenth century that they began to have regular and constant contacts which have continued with increasing frequency down to the present day.

Pre-History

The pre-history of the Umbundu country awaits competent investigation and should prove a fruitful field. Dr. Merlin W. Ennis has collected stone artifacts from several sites, but chiefly from Elende (twelve miles north of the railway station of Cuma), some of which have been placed in the Peabody Museum of Harvard University, some in the Logan Museum of Beloit College (Wisconsin), and some in the National Museum of Bulawayo, Southern Rhodesia. These artifacts have been classified as similar to those of the Chellean culture.[2] The strata from which they

---

[1] R.P. Van Wing, S.J., *Études Bakongo* (Bruxelles: Goemaere, 1921), p. 1.

[2] For a description, see J. J. Williams, S.J., *Africa's God* (Boston College, 1937), V. Congo and Angola, p. 96; also W. D. Hambly, *The Ovimbundu of Angola* (Field Museum, 1934), p. 207. Several Portuguese and Belgian writers have described stone artifacts found near the northern borders of Angola, comparing them with examples discovered at various sites in the Congo. See *Trabalhos do I⁰ Congresso Nacional de Antropologia Colonial*, Pôrto, 1934: J. R. Santos, Jr., 'Rui de Serpa Pinto e a arqueologia de Angola', pp. 433–51;

HISTORICAL 165

were taken yielded no pottery. Polished stone implements have not been found. Rock paintings or reliefs have not been observed.[1] This region has as yet yielded up no pre-historic skeletal remains. Whether any are present only competent and intensive study may reveal. The geological structure must be borne in mind: that this is one of the oldest parts of the earth's surface, having been exposed since primeval times, and without having had the great earth movements which took place in the eastern part of the continent.

The presence of stone ruins has been mentioned by several writers.[2] I have evidence for the existence of ruins at fifteen sites so widely scattered over Umbundu territory that practically every region of major importance is represented. I feel sure that if a careful survey were made, at least twice this number would be found. All those which have been reported thus far are of similar construction—of natural unworked stone, loosely placed, without any attempt to use mud or mortar; all were evidently built for defence, and all the sites were obviously chosen because of the natural advantages of the terrain, as, for example, on an eminence or at the confluence of streams. Some seem to have had earthworks in addition to the walls of stone.[3] Considering the materials used most of them were evidently well built and well adapted to the specific purpose for which they were intended. Some are now in a better state of preservation than others. Major Artur de Paiva reported that in October 1890 the *Ombala* (capital village) of Sambu, then occupied, had formerly been strongly fortified, as evidenced by the remains of 'walls of loose stone and others of earthworks in front of the present palisades'.[4] In one of the Elende forts may be seen evidence of important iron workings.

In May 1936, while on a field trip in the region of Kasongi (Cassongue), I visited a site called Usengo which had been

and J. da Silveira and J. R. dos Santos, Jr., 'Instrumento pre-historico de quartzo, etc.', pp. 532–5; also J. Janmart, *Subsídios para a História, Arqueologia, e Etnografia dos povos da Lunda* (Lisboa, 1946).

[1] Marquardsen–Stahl (*Angola*) mention a 'rock painting', but on investigation it was found to be quite recent.

[2] Hambly, loc. cit.; E. W. Smith, *Africa, What Do We Know of It?* (1935), p. 64 f.; Serpa Pinto, *How I Crossed Africa*, i. 86; Major Artur de Paiva in *Boletim Soc. Geog. Lisboa*, Serie 14, p. 14; Nevinson, *A Modern Slavery*, p. 81; Cameron, *Across Africa*, p. 405.

[3] Paiva, p. 18; also *Annaes do Cons. Ultr.*, Serie I, p. 520.

[4] Paiva, loc. cit. He also reported the stone ruins at a site in Cingolo (*Quingolo*), which I am inclined to believe was the same site previously reported by Major Serpa Pinto in 1877 (loc. cit.).

166 UMBUNDU KINSHIP AND CHARACTER

fortified with loose stone walls built upon a great rock out-crop, projecting portions of which greatly reinforced the wall and made it unnecessary to build a complete circuit. The wall reached a height of nearly six feet in places. Inside the fortress, under an overhanging ledge of rock, I picked up fragments of pottery evidently of Umbundu make, and also pieces of wine jug of the type used by the Portuguese for *vinho verde*. The dry season had just begun and the growth of grass in the ruin was very rank so that it was not possible to make a systematic search for other vestiges of former occupation. Across the valley, at the village of Ndumba, I found an old man seeming to be about sixty-five or seventy years of age, who declared that he had himself helped to build the walls of Usengo in his youth 'before he had married'. He said that they had fortified the place against the exactions of Soma[1] Saviti of Kasongi; that three chiefs had ruled in it,[2] and that the reason for moving was lack of nearby supplies of water and of earth to daub the walls of the huts, the village site being solid rock. This, he said, was all during the reign of Saviti and before the end of the rubber trade, which fixes it approximately between the dates 1890 and 1910. The largest of the three ruins on the slopes of Elende, mentioned by Hambly and by E. W. Smith,[3] is the subject of a legend recounted by Elende villagers which ascribes its building to Ovimbundu or their immediate prede-cessors. The most detailed and circumstantial report of the build-ing and occupancy of one of these ruins is found in an account of the campaign of 1774–6, in which Portuguese troops and native allies fought the kings of Bailundu (*Baylundo*) and Cingolo (*Quingolo*), and their allies.[4] The map of this campaign,[5] drawn in 1776, contains an inset representing a plan of the fortification alluded to, which, according to the report,[6] was too strong to be taken and was besieged until the defenders fled by night, when it was entered, sacked, and thrown down, which last operation occupied nearly two months. Further evidence that the Ovi-mbundu were using stone-walled fortresses during the seventeenth, eighteenth, and nineteenth centuries is found in the fact that the Portuguese reports of these periods generally allude to the forti-

---

[1] King or Chief.
[2] (1) Ekulika, the builder; (2) Ukelengenje; and (3) Satutu, who moved out.
[3] See *supra*, p. 165, n. 2.   [4] *Annaes do Cons. Ultr.*, loc. cit.
[5] Op. cit., facing p. 518.
[6] Op. cit., p. 520 f.; and especially *Catalogo dos Governadores*, pp. 423 ff.

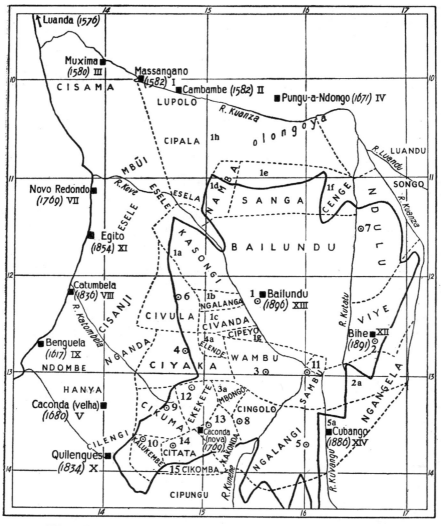

TRIBAL DIVISIONS AND HISTORY OF THE OVIMBUNDU
Heavy continuous line indicates elevation of 1,500 metres (4,920 ft.).
Broken lines indicate Umbundu political boundaries.
⊙ Principal capital towns (*olombala*) numbered 1 to 14.
1a, 1b, 1c, 1d, 1e, 1f, 1g, 1h, tributaries of Bailundu; 2a, tributaries (Ngangela) of Viye;
5a, tributaries of Ngalangi; 3a, tributary of Civaka; 4a, tributary of Wambu.
Portuguese presídios with dates of founding (numbered I—XIV).

HISTORICAL 167

fied towns of the natives as *quipacas*, a word adapted from the Umbundu word *ocimbaka*, meaning a wall. The word for the palisade with which their villages are now enclosed is *olumbo*. Until evidence is adduced to the contrary, it seems that we must conclude that the stone-walled ruins found throughout the Umbundu country were built by Ovimbundu or by their immediate (Bantu) predecessors. As the ruins of Rhodesia and Mozambique seem to have been built by Bantu under Arab or Malay influences, so the Ovimbundu may have modelled their fortifications on the Portuguese forts which they had seen at Caconda, at the coast, along the Kuanza River, or even the walls with which individual traders fortified their establishments. These various forts were first built between 1575 and 1603, and it is probable that individual Ovimbundu themselves took part in some of the building operations.

Tribal Divisions of the Ovimbundu

Before going on with Umbundu history let us fix in mind the principal kingdoms, tribes, or divisions of the Ovimbundu and their present location with reference to one another and to their other neighbours. This may most easily be seen with the aid of the accompanying map.[1] Their mutual relations prior to effective Portuguese occupation, whether of dependence or independence, are also shown. These are the divisions the Ovimbundu were found to have at the beginning of the present century, and these are the divisions still recognized by them, although they no longer retain their former political significance. It is of interest to find that according to Ladislau Magyar, who lived in and travelled through the Umbundu country from 1849 until 1857,[2] essentially these same divisions were then in existence. Under date of 1 August 1799 the Governor of Benguela reported on the 'provinces' and people in the hinterland.[3] It is significant to find that the divisions of the Ovimbundu were then essentially the same as they are

---

[1] Facing p. 164.

[2] Ladislau Magyar, *Reisen in Süd-Afrika* (tr. Hunfalvy), Pesth, 1859. Magyar made 'Quipeyo' (Cipeyo) a part of Bailundu and Sambu a sort of tributary. 'Quibula' (Civula), he said, paid tribute to 'Quiyaka' (Ciyaka).

[3] See *Annaes Maritimos e Coloniaes*, 4a Ser., pp. 147–61 (*parte não official*). This report made 'Quipeyo' tributary to Huambo, 'Ondura' (Ndulu) to Bailundu. Several kingdoms, later tributaries of Ciyaka, were listed as independent.

168 UMBUNDU KINSHIP AND CHARACTER

to-day.[1] The principal Umbundu-speaking groups may be listed as follows:

I. *Independent kingdoms* (in approximate order of their present population):

Mbailundu (*Bailundo*).
Viye (*Bie* or *Bihe*).
Wambu (*Huambo, Huamba,* or even *Hambo*).
Ciyaka (*Quiyaca* or *Quiaca*).
Ngalangi (*Galangue*).
Civula[2] (*Quibula*).
Ndulu[2] (*Andulo, Ondulo* or even *Ondura*).
Cingolo (*Quingolo*).
Kalukembe (*Caluquembe, Caluguembe,* or even *Caluqueme*).
Sambu[2] (*Sambo* or *Sambos*).
Ekekete (*Quiquete*).
Kakonda or Cilombo-coñoma (*Caconda* or *Quilombo*).
Citata (*Quitata*).

II. *Kingdoms generally tributary but not integral parts of the kingdoms to which they owed allegiance*:

Kasongi (*Cassongue*)—generally a tributary of Bailundu.
Ngalanga (*Galanga*)—generally a tributary of Bailundu.
Civanda (*Quibanda*)—generally a tributary of Bailundu.
Namba—generally a tributary of Bailundu.
Sanga—generally a tributary of Bailundu.
Cenge (*Chiengue*)—generally a tributary of Bailundu.
Cipeyo (*Quipeyo*)—a tributary of Bailundu or Wambu.
Mbongo (*Bongo*)—generally a tributary of Wambu.
Elende (*Lende*)—generally a tributary of Ciyaka.

Nearly all of these groups are listed in the report of 1799 to which we have referred, and many of them may be identified on the map of 1776. How long before that had they lived in these their present homes? Since it is already well established that none of the Southern Bantu are autochthonous, we shall not stop to ask

[1] Neither of these accounts mentioned Kasongi, which, according to genealogical evidence, is probably one of the most recently formed of the Umbundu-speaking groups. Both accounts made the non-Umbundu-speaking regions of 'Quibala' (Cipala), Mussende, and Cella tributaries of Bailundu. This was the state of affairs as late as 1893.

[2] See *supra*, p. 167, n. 2.

HISTORICAL

that question concerning the Ovimbundu. Rather, whence did they come and when? Can the lines of their migrations now be ascertained? Can their racial origins be determined with even approximate certainty?

The available evidence regarding origins and migrations of the Ovimbundu is mainly of five sorts: (1) linguistic; (2) legendary, whether of the several groups of the Ovimbundu or of the tribes from which they seem to have sprung; (3) historical; (4) evidence from place-names; and (5) evidence of comparative attitudes and culture-traits as between the Ovimbundu and their neighbours. In addition, we might list evidence of physical measurements and blood-group tests, but such evidence is not yet available for the Ovimbundu.

Tribal Origins

Language Affinities. As I pointed out in the introductory chapter, by linguistic classification the Ovimbundu belong to the western 'province' or group of the Southern Bantu. Linguistically, the Ovimbundu belong with their southern neighbours, the so-called 'Bangala'[1] and with the Ambo and Herero. The northern and eastern neighbours all belong to other language groups. This is a fact that must not be lost sight of, especially since Umbundu has been so often confused with the so-called 'Kimbundu' of the Ndongo or Angola kingdom. We are not surprised to find an author of 1846 declare that 'From the Congo to Cabo Negro (Alexander Bay) these black natives all speak the same language (*bunda*) with small changes of dialect';[2] but when this confusion is compounded in works laying claim to considerable value as linguistic and ethnological studies, as, for example, one which was published by a well-known museum in 1930,[3] a protest is in order.

---

[1] The Ndombe, Nganda, Cilengi, Cipungo, Muila, Mulondo, Humbi, Gambue, &c. I do not know that the term 'Bangala' may be applied with correctness to these people. I only use it for convenience. See 'Notas Etnográficas sôbre os povos indígenas do Distrito da Huila', *Boletim Geral das Colónias*, fev. 1935, p. 41.

[2] Lopes de Lima, *Ensaios sôbre a Statística d'Angola e Benguella*, part i, p. 196.

[3] See F. u. W. Jaspert, *Die Völkerstämme Mittel-Angolas* (Frankfort, 1930). It is reported that the spurious nature of the works of these writers has been exposed by Baumann and others, but although I have searched, apart from a rather ambiguous footnote in Baumann's *Lunda*, I have found no such references, and am unable to say whether this has been done. The origin of the erroneous concept of a Bunda language (also called Bundu, or Mbundu), has been traced, and correctly I think on the whole, by Max Buchner, 'Die Ambakisten' (in

170 UMBUNDU KINSHIP AND CHARACTER

Sir Harry Johnston made this classification abundantly clear in his monumental work published in 1919,[1] and the recent translation and revision of Carl Meinhof's important work on Bantu phonology[2] has used Umbundu extensively for illustrative material. It should now be abundantly clear to all that Umbundu is the northernmost of the Southern Bantu languages, and that in their language the Ovimbundu have elements in common with their southern neighbours.

Traditional Histories. Each of the principal groups among the Ovimbundu has legends with regard to the migrations of their forefathers and the country from which they came. For the most part these legends refer to ancestors of the respective royal families, but some references are also made to the people whom these new-comers found in the country which they came to occupy. All of these legends point to countries of origin in the north or north-east. Several writers have noted this as a fact,[3] but it is necessary to take more explicit notice of each of several legends.

Ndulu has not received as much notice as have some of the other Umbundu kingdoms, but I have come to the conclusion that it is perhaps one of the oldest. The tradition runs that the progenitor of the dynasty, Katekula-Mengo, was an elephant-hunter and that he came with his wife, Ukungu (also called Mbala) from the region of the confluence of the Luandu and the Kuanza rivers. Following elephant-herds down the course of the Kuanza they passed the famous rocks of Pungu-a-Ndongo and in them left the imprints of Katekula-Mengo's bow and of Ukungu's basket, which, it is said, may be seen to this day; for in that early day the rocks had not yet hardened but were like fresh concrete. This couple

---

Zeitschr. f. Ethnol., 1915, pp. 398 ff.). This writer also interestingly and properly shows how the name Kimbundu came to be mistakenly applied to the Ngola or Ndongo language. The error, however, still continues to be propagated (e.g. *vide* A. Miranda Magalhães, 'Os Ambundus de Angola', &c., in *Trabalhos do I⁰ Congresso Nacional de Antropologia Colonial*, Pôrto, 1934, vol. ii, pp. 536–55). This article contains so little of value that a systematic refutation would not be worth while. The writer's notions on the Bantu migrations seem especially fantastic.

[1] *A Comparative Vocabulary of Bantu and Semi-Bantu Languages*, vol. i.

[2] Meinhof, *An Introduction to the Phonology of the Bantu Languages*, translated, revised, and enlarged (Berlin and London, 1932).

[3] J. T. Tucker, *Drums in the Darkness*, p. 34 f. W. D. Hambly (*The Ovimbundu of Angola*) notes this fact at the beginning of his otherwise rather confused chapter on 'Historical Sources'.

HISTORICAL 171

came to the region of Ndulu and wished to settle but could not (i.e. without permission), since they were strangers and new-comers. Thereupon a certain elder of the country, Kakoko by name, caused them to build, first at Ngumba and later at Ndulu-yolosima. Their two sons fought for the succession: Cikolongonjo won and set about to consolidate his position by conquering the va Luimbi, who then left the country. He also won over the region of Kapeyo (*Capeio*), although not by force of arms but through trickery,[1] or superior knowledge. The sixth in the succession and a great-grandson of Katekula-Mengo was Kakulukusu, who, it is said, was a nephew[2] of Cingi I of Bailundu, and was also taken to Luanda when the latter was imprisoned. Historical records show that this was at the end of the campaign of 1774–6.[3] It is chiefly this historical connexion which leads me to place the beginning of Cikolongonjo's rule at about 1680. With regard to the migration of Katekula-Mengo and Ukungu, it seems reasonable to advance the hypothesis that its immediate cause may have been the pro-longed wars between the Portuguese and the kingdom of Angola, which ended in 1671 with the taking of the royal residence in the rocks of Pungu-a-Ndongo and its conversion into a presidio. The highland country of Ndulu offered a remote and peaceful refuge.

The Bailundu tradition states that when Katiavala came from Cipala (*Quibala*), he settled in Mbonga and came to visit Mbulu whose village on the capital hill had at first been built only as a hunter's camp, but, largely by reason of its strategical location, had become, or was becoming, the capital of Bailundu. Mbulu gave Katiavala his daughter to wife, which indicates that Mbulu had also come from the same northern stock. There was a good opportunity when Mbulu and his people were away on a hunt, and Katiavala with his followers occupied the capital, while Mbulu

[1] Kapeyo was ruling over the region now called after him. When Cikolo-ngonjo demanded that he submit, Kapeyo agreed only if he should lose in the *elembe* test, which is used in the dry season by putting out cloths by night to find which will be wet in the morning. In this case they left the *alembe* (pl.) out while they went on a hunt, but on returning Cikolongonjo's *elembe*, which was a kerchief, was wet with the spiritual blessing, whereas Kapeyo's, which was paper (since he evidently had not known the difference) was quite destroyed. Kapeyo, having lost, left the country and settled in Viye. It is significant to find articles of European manufacture mentioned in this tradition, which is one of the oldest of Umbundu records; also to note that the invaders from the north were already familiar with such things while the local inhabitants were not.

[2] Cingi was *inanu* (mother's brother) to Kakulukusu.

[3] See historical chart *infra*, p. 224 f.

172 UMBUNDU KINSHIP AND CHARACTER

took refuge near the Keve River and called his village Eyula,[1] but it was afterwards called Cimbulu after the founder. The dynasty of Katiavala has ruled Bailundu ever since and has also maintained its connexion with Cipala, which was subject to Bailundu until the end of the last century, at the time of effective European occupation. From Cipala has come the queen, the king's principal wife. Katiavala's son Cingi was the third in succession. As has already been noted,[2] he was captured by the Portuguese in 1776 and died in the fortress of São Miguel in Luanda.[3] This date enables us to place the beginning of Katiavala's dynasty at not earlier than about 1700.

The Viye legend has been told by Dr. J. T. Tucker,[4] and before that was given by Major Serpa Pinto.[5] A recent publication of excerpts from the diaries and notes of A. F. Silva Porto gives a slightly different version of the same legend, together with a few notes on the traditional history of Viye (Bie) until the year 1867.[6] Some of these latter are very valuable and enable us to fix more surely the actual or approximate dates of a number of the kings of Viye. Where Silva Porto's data on the earliest days of Viye conflict with those traditionally current, which latter have also been accepted by Serpa Pinto (1878) and by Tucker (1927), I feel that the former must be taken with considerable reserve. Viye, an elephant-hunter of the Humbi people, was tracking his game down the valley of the Kuanza River when he visited the village of Etalala for a beer-drink. There he saw and loved Kahanda, a princess of the Songo people, and they were married. When Viye died he was buried at Kahoko and his spirit is still expected to furnish the country with rain. The younger son, Kahoko, built up the kingdom of that name, which remained subject to Ekovongo, the new capital, built by the older son Ulundu.[7] It is interesting to note the union of the two tribal groups in this legend: the Songo of the north-east and the Humbi who now live in the south.[8] This legend also

[1] From *Yula*, the root of the verb 'to be overcome'.
[2] See *supra*, p. 171.
[3] See historical chart *infra*, p. 224.
[4] Op. cit., p. 34 f.
[5] Major A. A. da Rocha de Serpa Pinto, *How I crossed Africa*, vol. i, p. 156 f.
[6] A. A. F. da Silva Porto, *Viagens e apontamentos de um portuense em África* (Excerptos do seu Diário) (Lisboa: Agência Geral das Colónias, 1942), pp. 165–71.
[7] This name came from Viye's people—cf. the Mulondo, a tribe related to the Humbi.
[8] They had previously lived farther north, however, in the region of Ndondi

HISTORICAL

has it that the people then in the country, apart from the Songo, were 'Ngangela'[1] tribes. Magyar[2] has given different tradition with regard to the origin of the kingdom of Viye. He says that the forefathers came from the land of 'Moropu'[3] about three hundred years previously under the two chiefs 'Kinguri and Schakambundi', and, having conquered 'Masongo', settled on the Luandu River, engaging in agriculture between raids. They had the custom of eating their prisoners, and when there were not enough prisoners they lapsed into internecine warfare and ate each other. Certain leaders began to fear tribal suicide and formed a secret society of buffalo-hunters (*'empakasserros'*), pledged to give up cannibalism by substituting the flesh of the buffalo. When the tribal elder (the 'Jaga') suspected the innovation and objected strenuously, rather than fight the buffalo-hunters moved away and settled on the Kuanza River. After a further subdivision of the tribe, one party, 'under a certain Bihe', went south to the Kukema River, where 'Ganguella' were living, and founded the kingdom of 'Bihe'. Later on, continues Magyar, the people of the 'Jaga' mixed with neighbouring tribes, took on milder manners, and finally found themselves in the land of Kassanji 'near the Kingdom of the well-known Jaga of Kassanji'. This tradition related by Magyar cannot be completely harmonized with the familiar legend of Viye and Kahanda. I have given that tradition as Viye elders told it to me, and have noted that it had already been recorded before. Since these two traditions are at variance, since the version gotten by Serpa Pinto in 1878 is the same one and the only one which is current to-day, and since it is unlikely that in only twenty-one years, between 1857 (when Magyar was in Viye) and 1878, a tradition as interesting as that of the buffalo-hunters should have been forgotten, I am inclined to hypothecate that the source (whether immediate or remote) of the tradition given by Magyar was *not* Viye, but perhaps Songo or even Lunda, both of which regions were visited by Magyar. This report probably contains

where, near Chinguar, is the place called Saviye (Father of Viye); and later, in Ngalangi, whence, according to Ngalangi tradition, came Viye (cf. *infra*).

[1] 'Ngangela' is a deprecatory term by which the Ovimbundu designate the Luimbi, Cimbandi, Lucazi, Nyemba, Ngonzelo, Cokue, and other tribes who live to the east.

[2] Op. cit., p. 266 f.

[3] Dias de Carvalho (*Ethnographia e História Tradicional dos povos da Lunda*, p. 66) explains that this was a term which *os nossos antigos viajantes* applied to Lunda.

174 UMBUNDU KINSHIP AND CHARACTER

traditional elements of truth and value, especially since it agrees with the other traditions in tracing descent to Songo, and since its connecting of Songo with the people of Lunda is substantiated by the traditional histories given by Dias de Carvalho,[1] and by Ferreira Diniz.[2] The tradition of Viye, the elephant-hunter of Humbi, is of further interest through the definite connexion which it gives with the people of the south.

Serpa Pinto's version of the Viye traditional history[3] is interesting for its substantial agreement with the tradition current to-day. He gives a genealogical table containing the same number of kings as the table which I got in 1938,[4] and with only two or three differences which might, even so, be resolved. Serpa Pinto was interested in determining dates, which he might easily have done had he bothered to look up the records. Kangombe, the fourth king who 'mounted the stool' in Ekovongo and grandson of Ulundu, the founder, had been sold to Luanda as a slave by his brother Njilahulu for adultery with one of Njilahulu's wives. In Luanda he became a favourite of the governor, was sponsored by him for baptism, and then took the name of his sponsor, Dom Antonio de Lancastre.[5] Returning to Viye, he took with him some very material help in arms and a few warriors. Dom Antonio de Lancastre held the office of governor from 1772 to 1779. Since there was war in Bailundu, &c., between 1773 and 1776, Kangombe's return was probably toward the end of Dom Antonio's term of office—say, 1778. This being the case, the founding of Viye was probably about 1750.

The Ngalangi tradition also tells of this connexion in another way, but it is of especial interest because it is the only one which attempts to relate the beginning of things. Feti it was, say the Ngalangi elders, who began, that is to say, he came down from above, and whence he came is not known. Inasmuch as he had no wives, he went to a certain lagoon of the Kunene River and there he caught his wives as they came up out of the reeds. To this day, it is said, there may be seen in the rocks by that lagoon the imprints of Feti's foot and of the foot of his dog. Feti's wives were Tembo

[1] Op. cit., p. 94 f.
[2] Ferreira Diniz, *Populações indigenas de Angola* (Coimbra, 1918).
[3] Op. cit., p. 156 f.
[4] Op. cit., p. 160.
[5] The story was related by Silva Porto more than once. *Vide* op. cit., p. 167; also *Boletim Soc. Geog. Lisboa*, 5a Ser., p. 27.

HISTORICAL 175

and Coya and Cĩvi.[1] Now Coya's child was ill and she begged Cĩvi to help by blowing the breath of life back into him. Cĩvi refused because of jealousy: the child died, and ever since then death has clung to us. That, then, is the beginning of Feti. Very soon Feti parted with his son Ngola who went to Luanda to rule; while another child of his, Viye, went to found the kingdom of Viye.[2] When Feti died he left his place to his son Ndumba-Visoso with his wife Katia. Ndumba-Visoso underwent circumcision, since when all Ngalangi kings have submitted to the rite. They founded first one village and then another, and they were hunters, shooting roan antelopes and elephants, for at that time there were many animals in the land. At the instigation of Ngalangi, the younger brother of Ndumba-Visoso, they attacked and drove out the 'va Ngangela', who then occupied what is now the *ombala* (capital or king's residence) of Ngalangi. Taking it for their own, they brought their loads of food: beans, emmer wheat, kaffir-corn, mandioc, and maize;[3] and where they rested their loads the load sticks took root and became the sycamore figs which to this day encircle the capital village. After that the wives of Feti departed: Tembo married in Humbi (or according to another account, in Cilengi or Kalukembe); Coya in Ndulu; and Cĩvi in Ngalangi.[4] There follows an account of an attack on the village by the 'va Ngangela' while the men were away in another country. With only the women at home Katia saved the day with a powerful

---

[1] The name Feti, it is said, comes from the word *fetika* (the verb *oku fetika*, to begin); while Coya is traced to *oya* (the verb *oku oya*, to finish). Thus it is said, *Feti wa fetika, Coya woyapo* (Feti began, Coya finished).

[2] This tradition connecting Ngalangi, Viye, and Ngola (Ndongo) is interesting and perhaps contains elements of truth, whether from tribal recollections or other sources, but it cannot be reconciled with the strictly historical facts since the kingdom of Ngola (Ndongo) was founded before 1550, and when Paulo Diaz de Novaes first came in 1560 he found that Ngola-Mbandi had inherited the kingdom from his father Ngola-Njinga the previous year. The country then came to be called A-Ngola. (See summary in the Introduction to Lopes de Lima, *Ensaios*.) As I have shown, Viye was founded about two hundred years later.

[3] The order is that of the Ngalangi narrator and is probably a recognition of the more recent importation of the last two named. On another occasion he said that his grandmother had told him that in the olden days when people always carried some seed about in pouches on their persons for fear of sudden raids, maize was not known and emmer wheat was the staple food.

[4] This further attempt to establish connexion with neighbouring tribes is significant. The Humbi and the Cilengi belong to the 'Bangala' group of people, while the Kalukembe are Ovimbundu, but seemingly more nearly related to these 'Bangala' than are the other Ovimbundu.

176 UMBUNDU KINSHIP AND CHARACTER

charm which caused the bullets of the enemy to fall to the ground immediately upon leaving the muzzles of their muskets, so that they did no harm, whereupon the women went out and beheaded the enemy with their hoes.[1] When Katia died her husband sent to his brother Ngola to have a figure of her made. Soon after Ndumba-Visoso died and left his place to his sons, first Mulunda and then Kambuenge.

I have given this Ngalangi tradition at length because of its inherent interest and because of the attempts which it makes to show a relationship between the peoples.

The tradition of Wambu is that the first king, Wambu-Kalunga, came from the north from Sela, which is just to the north-west of Bailundu. He came with his cross-cousins Cihamba, Katutu, and Sunguandumbo.[2] The Nganda[3] were then living in Wambu. Wambu-Kalunga was a great warrior and raider. He had a special penchant for human flesh and would catch and eat the children left in the village when their parents went to their fields. He would also dig up and eat recently buried corpses. The elders were greatly disturbed over this custom and sought to kill King Wambu-Kalunga. They managed to get a live man into a rock tomb who speared Wambu-Kalunga when he came at night to get the supposed corpse. His capital was at the rocks of Nganda-la-Kawe (near the present town and railway station at Caála), and to this day his tomb is shown.

Ciyaka tradition names as the founder of its royal family, Cihamba, son or cousin of Wambu-Kalunga. Cihamba was a great hunter and brought back so much game that Wambu-Kalunga gave him one of his concubines and permission to seek a kingdom for himself. His younger brother Katutu accompanied him and each built his village in the mountainous country of Ciyaka, where at that time the Ndombe[4] people were living with their chief Siku. Katutu's village was raided by a party from Wambu. Cihamba

---

[1] The appearance of fire-arms so early in the tradition is interesting, but not surprising, as we shall see when we examine historical accounts.

[2] Another account makes Cihamba and Katutu sons of Wambu-Kalunga, while Sunguandumbo (or Songombanda) is their cross-cousin (*epalume*).

[3] The Nganda belong to the 'Bangala' group and now live just west of the Umbundu country.

[4] The Ndombe are also one of the 'Bangala' people. They are now confined to the Benguela coast-lands, where some of them were already living when the Portuguese first came about 1580. (See *Benguella e seu sertão*, p. 18 f.; *Andrew Battell*, pp. 16 ff.)

PLATE XV

Bailundu: town of Teixeira da Silva

PLATE XVI

a. Ruins at Usengo: section of wall between stone outcrops

b. Rock tomb of the va Sela (Kasongi)

HISTORICAL

came with his five famous hunting dogs and with their aid caught up with the raiders and finished them off. After the battle he collected five baskets of heads and set off for Wambu to present them and find out whether Wambu-Kalunga had sent the raiders. When the bereaved relatives recognized the heads, Wambu-Kalunga had to admit having sent the raid.[1] He also admitted the uncanny ability of Cihamba, to whom he now gave a new name, saying, 'Henceforth, you are Cilũlũ (Ghost), because your anger is altogether too great.' He also gave him the royal insignia[2] for which he should build a spirit-hut (etambo) and sent him away to rule, saying, 'From now on you are the war-leader of Wambu.'

Then Cilũlũ and Katutu returned to Ciyaka and to their hunting. One day when Ċilũlũ returned from a hunt (on which he had gone without his dogs), only four dogs came out to meet him: Ndumbu was missing. When he found that his own sons had eaten the favourite dog which had hunted and fought for him, his sorrow and anger knew no bounds: his heart was black. Straightway he sent for his brother Katutu and insisted that he take the royal insignia and rule in his stead. 'I, Cilũlũ,' he said, 'am Cihamba; from to-day I shall beget no more sons to be kings; to-day I have cursed them and none of them shall rule any more.[3] To-day, oh Katutu, build the spirit-hut, the kitchen, and the chief's hut.'[4]

Later Katutu built the *ombala* of Kawa,[5] and Cihamba came to live with him. One day the queen was gathering firewood on a mountain and found a much better mountain-top site, then

---

[1] Wambu-Kalunga's alleged reason for having sent the raid was that Cihamba had impregnated the concubine given to him, whereas the intention was that relations should have been those of the trial-marriage in which partners occupy the same bed but explicitly avoid conception.

[2] i.e. the small mat, the double-headed ceremonial axe, the bell, and the chalk (to mark the face in ceremony and ritual).

[3] One reason for this particular phase of the tradition was perhaps to explain why the king's brother often inherits rather than a son. There is an Elende tradition designed to explain why the royal succession is in the paternal line rather than in the maternal, as is the case with inheritance among commoners, and also with the royal families of the related people to the south.

[4] *Etambo, ociwo, eyemba,* the three royal buildings. A commoner may have a spirit-hut (etambo), he may have a kitchen (ociwo) for each of his wives, but a house of his own he may not have, only a house for each wife.

[5] This appears in the old Portuguese records as *Quiaca a velha* (see Report of Governor of Benguela for 1799 in *Annaes Mar. e Col.*, 1844, p. 154).

178   UMBUNDU KINSHIP AND CHARACTER

occupied by Siku of the Ndombe people, which site Katutu soon appropriated. This is the present site[1] of the Ciyaka capital.

While reworking some of the material in this paper I had the good fortune to receive help from a member of the royal family of Ciyaka[2] who has more precise data on the succession of that kingdom than I had supposed it possible now to obtain. He not only completed and corrected my list of the kings of Ciyaka, but he also supplied the actual dates for all of them since 1842.[3] Their number would seem to impute to the Ciyaka kingdom a longer history than I have been able to verify for any of the other Umbundu kingdoms, but the absence of historical data from European sources makes confirmation impossible. It would seem, however, that the beginning of the Ciyaka dynasty must date from not later than the first half of the seventeenth century.

Some of the other Umbundu-speaking groups are of considerable importance and interest, but unfortunately there is neither time nor space to give to their origins attention equal to that given to those treated above. The Sambu kingdom has long specialized in the training of medical practitioners and witch-doctors. The tradition is that it was founded by a woman who seems to have come either from Bailundu or from the stock whence came the Bailundu royal family at an even earlier date. From the family of Wambu-Kalunga, in addition to Ciyaka, came those who set up the kingdoms of Elende, which had a woman ruler early in its history; of Cingolo; of Ekekete; and of Cikuma (also called Citata), in whose lands the fort of Caconda a Nova was built in 1769. It was probably after this that the capital of Citata moved across the Katumbela (*Catombela*) River to its present site. Kakonda, the founder of the kingdom generally known by that name, was of Luanda stock but born in Ngalangi,[4] whence he was sold as a slave to Benguela. He ran away with his wife Cilombo[5] and settled in the region near the (present) site of Caconda (a Nova). Kakonda and Cilombo probably settled there only a very short time before the building of the fort, for most of Kakonda's fifteen successors

[1] Called *Quiaca a nova* in the old Portuguese records (see loc. cit.).

[2] Lauriano M. Bahu Ciyaka, a graduate of Currie Institute, teacher of the village of Canja.

[3] *Vide* chronological chart, p. 224 f. *infra*.

[4] It is likely that his ascendants were *pombeiros* (traders) from Luanda and had settled in Ngalangi.

[5] After her, the kingdom was called Cilombo-coñoma (Camp of the Drum).

HISTORICAL 179

had Portuguese names, and tradition speaks of a great accession of mulatto stock, which also is confirmed by observation.

The Umbundu-speaking border groups are interesting. Ngamba was formerly occupied by the Songo and has been peopled by Ovimbundu coming from near the capital of Viye only within the past forty years. Cengi, Sanga, Namba, and Kasongi on the northern flank of Bailundu have probably all only recently become Umbundu-speaking groups. Kasongi is one of the largest groups which paid tribute to Bailundu, and has had a line of Umbundu-speaking kings for more than a hundred years; but judging from genealogical evidence the bulk of the people have not been Ovimbundu that long. Civula is another large group and its uncertain feudal status has been noted. Perhaps the most interesting of the border groups, at least from a linguistic standpoint, is Kalukembe. The royal house seems to have come from Ciyaka and it has been claimed that in Kalukembe the kingship is inherited by the mother's brother's son. This is not supported by the only local traditional history which I have been able to secure and requires further investigation. At any rate it is through the maternal line that the commoners of all the Umbundu-speaking groups inherit, and it is noteworthy that this is also true of the kingship among the 'Bangala' and the Ambo tribes.[1] The 'Bangala' people have clan organizations and are exogamous, so that they may marry in any of the related 'Bangala' groups, and for this purpose they include the Kalukembe but not others of the Ovimbundu.[2] Finally, the variations with which Umbundu is spoken in Kalukembe[3] point to closer connexions with the language-group of the 'Bangala'. There are certain areas which at the present day seem to be undergoing a linguistic 'Umbundu-ization'. This is most evident in the coast towns such as Novo Redondo, Lobito, Catumbela, Benguela,

[1] See Estermann, 'Notas Etnográficas sôbre os povos do Distrito da Huila' in *Boletim Geral das Colónias*, fev. 1935, p. 63; Hahn, *et al.*, *The Native Tribes of South West Africa*, p. 8.

[2] This last item was learned from Mulondo people. The above-cited article deals only with the people of the District of Huila, while 'Bangala' people live also in other adjoining districts.

[3] Compare Umbundu language work of H. Chatelain and others of the 'Mission Philafricaine' in Kalukembe, as versus illustrations of Umbundu used by Johnston, Meinhof, *et al.* Evidently the native 'Mohongo' taken to Paris by Homburger of the Mission Rohan-Chabot, was a native of Kalukembe, for the 'Bailoundou' vocabulary taken from him is of the Kalukembe variation. (See *Mission Rohan-Chabot*, t. III, f. I.)

180 UMBUNDU KINSHIP AND CHARACTER

and Mossamedes. The region of Catumbela, and perhaps of Benguela, seems to have been subjected to migrations of Ovimbundu, or of proto-Ovimbundu, between the sixteenth and the nineteenth centuries, and it is probable that some of these groups early established themselves there permanently.[1] At the present time peoples of many tribes make up the population of these towns and of the surrounding regions, but Umbundu is already the dominant speech, and in Lobito and Catumbela almost no other Bantu language is heard. Certain other areas on the fringe of the Umbundu lands now seem to be in process of 'Umbundu-ization', at least as regards language. This does not seem to have taken place in Musende, in Cipala (Quibala), or in Sela, in spite of the long time during which they owned the king of Bailundu as their overlord. Just now, however, such a process seems to be taking place in Mbuiva (Amboiva), in Cisanji (area of Bocoio), in Nganda, and in Cikomba (Chicomba, south of Caconda).

Some of the neighbouring peoples have traditions of migrations which corroborate the traditions of the Ovimbundu. The Nganda say that they formerly lived in the region of Wambu, around the rocks of Nganda-la-Kawe, and that they moved down-country for two reasons: (1) to escape Wambu-Kalunga and his penchant for eating their children; (2) to be by themselves to practise the rite of circumcision. When they migrated to their present home, the kingdom of Ciyaka, they say, was not yet established.

Traditions of the Herero and Ambo peoples may have bearing on the problem of the migrations of the Ovimbundu. Dr. Vedder concludes from tradition and genealogical evidence that the Herero must have crossed the Kunene 'about the year 1700'.[2] Some of the tribes of Angola with which the Njimba-Herero claim relationship[3] may easily be identified as belonging to the 'Bangala' group, as, for example, the Ovangambue, the Ovangumbi, and the Ovatjerenge, which are plainly the va Ngambue, the va Khumbi (or Nkhumbi), and the va Cilengi, respectively. Other names in the list are very much like some place-names in the Umbundu country.

Traditions of the Songo and Lunda people have already been

[1] According to a Ciyaka tradition. Also see A. Bastos, *Monographia de Catumbella*, pp. 6, 7; L. Cordeiro (ed.), *Benguella e seu sertão, 1617–22*; Ravenstein (ed.), op. cit., p. 19 f.

[2] Hahn *et al.*, op. cit., p. 157.

[3] Loc. cit.

HISTORICAL

mentioned. H. A. Dias de Carvalho collected the traditional history of the people of Lunda, which attempted to show that the Imbangala, the Songo, and the Cokue, or rather their reigning families, were descended from the royal house of the Bongo people of Lunda.[1] Through Ilunga, father of the first Muata Yanvo, this author connects these people, or at least all of them except the Imbangala, with the Luba.[2] Torday offers the hypothesis that Ilunga (or Ihunga) may have been a Bushongo prince.[3] I have heard the hypothesis offered that the Songo were in effect an off-shoot of the Bushongo people, but it seems that such knowledge as we have of the Songo cannot be said to substantiate this theory. Should these theories prove to accord with the facts, we could claim a long traditional descent for the people. of our study in consideration of the careful work done by Torday in tracing the genesis of the Bushongo.[4]

Historical Evidence. Turning from tribal traditions to the solid ground of historical evidence, regarding the migrations in question, it is immediately evident that there is no lack of witnesses. The regions with which we are dealing have been known to Europe since 1482, when the expedition under Diogo Cão first sailed up the Congo River and sent ambassadors representing King John II of Portugal to the king of Kongo. Diogo Cão returned in 1485–6, and then in 1491 there came a great expedition with a specially appointed embassy and a mission of ten Franciscan friars.[5] From this time on the Kongo was not without European observers. The earliest record which we have of native migrations in what is now Angola was the invasion of the kingdom of Kongo in 1568,[6] when it was overrun by hordes of terrible 'Jagas',[7] from the east. The reigning king, Dom Alvaro I (Nenemi-a-lukeni-luambemba), and his forces were so utterly routed that his only resource was to

[1] Dias de Carvalho, op. cit., p. 76 f.

[2] Op. cit., p. 65.

[3] E. Torday, *On the Trail of the Bushongo*, pp. 170, 281.

[4] Ibid., chap. xiii.

[5] See João de Barros, *Decadas* I, liv. 3; Ruy de Pina, *Chronica*, p. 174 f.; Garcia de Resende, *Chronica*, pp. 155 ff.; Fr. Luiz de Sousa, *História de S. Domingos*, pt. ii, liv. vi, c. 8.

[6] There has been considerable disagreement over this date, which has been variously reported as 1558, 1568, and 1570; 1568 seems the most likely date, see Ravenstein (ed.), *The Strange Adventures of Andrew Battell*, p. 119 f.

[7] There are many spellings of this name, according to the language, or even the caprice, of the observer. The commoner forms are: Jagas, Jakas, Iagges, Giaghi, Giaki, and Ayaka. This last is probably the more nearly correct.

182 UMBUNDU KINSHIP AND CHARACTER

take refuge on an island in the lower Congo and send to Lisbon begging aid. In 1570 Dom Sebastião sent out Francisco de Gouveia with six hundred men who, after a year and a half of fighting, expelled the barbarian hordes and reinstated Dom Alvaro in possession of his kingdom, but as a vassal of the king of Portugal.[1] Warriors called 'Jagas' are next mentioned in 1590 as allies of the armies of Ndongo (Ngola) and Matamba, helping to defeat the Portuguese and their native allies under Luiz Serrão at 'Anguolome-aquitambo'.[2] Migrating hordes called 'Jagas' are next mentioned as having been met (about 1600–1)[3] by Andrew Battell, when on a trading expedition on behalf of the Governor of Angola, at Benguela Velha.[4] I quote Battell's own description of this encounter:

In our second voyage, turning up along the coast, we came to the Morro, or cliff of Benguele, which standeth in twelve degrees of southerly latitude. Here we saw a mighty camp on the south side of the river Cova.[5] And being desirous to know what they were, we went on shore with our boat; and presently there came a troop of five hundred men to the waterside. We asked them who they were. Then they told us they were the Gagas, or Gindes, that came from Sierra de lion,[6] and passed through the city of Congo, and so travelled to the eastward of the great city of Angola, which is called Dongo.[7] The great Gaga, which is their general, came down to the waterside to see us, for he had never seen white men before. He asked wherefore we came. We told him that we came to trade upon the coast. Then he bade us welcome, and called us on shore with our commodities. We laded our ship with slaves in seven days, and bought them so cheap that many did not cost one real, which were worth in the city (of Loanda) twelve milreis.

[In a marginal note Purchas adds: 'He, in discourse with me, called them Iagges, and their chief the great Iagge. I think he writ them Gagas for Giagas, by false spelling.']

[1] Domingos d'Abreu de Brito (1592), quoted by Paiva Manso, História do Kongo, p. 138; J. J. Lopes de Lima, in Annaes Mar. e Col., 1845, pp. 93 ff.; Cavazzi, Descrizione de' Tre Regni, pp. 183 ff.; Ravenstein, op. cit., p. 119 f.; A. de Lemos, História de Angola, p. 98; Duarte Lopes, A Report of the Kingdom of Kongo, pp. 96 ff.

[2] Ravenstein, op. cit., p. 148.

[3] Ravenstein, op. cit., p. xiv. Andrew Battell was one of Purchas's Pilgrims.

[4] Now called 'Porto Amboim'.

[5] i.e. the Keve, which generally appears on maps as the 'Cuvo'.

[6] This does not necessarily mean the region of Sierra Leone. There are many places called Lion Mountain in Africa.

[7] Ndongo is the name of the kingdom of Ngola (Angola). Its capital was at Pungu-a-Ndongo, a remarkable group of rocks.

HISTORICAL

Being ready to depart, the great Giaga staid us, and desired our boat to pass his men over the river Cova, for he determined to overrun the realm of Benguele, which was on the north side of the river Cova. So we went with him to his camp, which was very orderly, intrenched with piles of wood; we had houses provided for us that night, and many burthens (loads) of palm-wine, cows, goats, and flour.

In the morning before day, the general did strike his *gongo*, which is an instrument of war that soundeth like a bell, and presently made an oration with a loud voice, that all the camp might hear, that he would destroy the Benguelas, with such courageous and vehement speeches as were not to be looked for among the heathen people. And presently they were all in arms, and marched to the river side, where he had provided Gingados.[1] And being ready with our boat and Gingados, the general was fain to beat them back because of the credit who should be first. We carried over eighty men at once, and with our muskets we beat the enemy off, and landed, but many of them were slain. By twelve of the clock all the Gagas were over.

Then the general commanded all his drums, *tavales, petes, pongos*, and all his instruments of warlike music to strike up, and gave the onset, which was a bloody day for the Benguelas. These Benguelas presently broke, and turned their backs, and a very great number of them were slain, and were taken captives, man, woman and child. The prince, Hombiangymbe, was slain, which was ruler of this country, and more than one hundred of his chief lords, and their heads presented and thrown at the feet of the great Gaga. The men, women and children that were brought in captive alive, and the dead corpses that were brought to be eaten, were strange to behold. For these Gagas are the greatest cannibals and man-eaters that be in the world, for they feed chiefly upon man's flesh (notwithstanding of their) having all the cattle of that country.

They settled themselves in this country and took the spoil of it. We had great trade with these Gagas, five months, and gained greatly by them. . . .

In these five months' space we made three voyages to the city of San Paul, and coming the fourth time we found them not.[2]

On a subsequent voyage Battell was left by 'the Portugals and Mulattos' as a hostage among the 'Benguelas', whence he escaped to 'the Great Gaga', living in his camp and helping to fight his battles during twenty-one months. His description of the life and customs of which he was a daily witness are of great interest, and

---

[1] 'Gingado', elsewhere spelt 'Iergado', is evidently a misprint for *Jangada*, Portuguese for 'raft'.

[2] Ravenstein, op. cit., pp. 19 ff.

184 UMBUNDU KINSHIP AND CHARACTER

seem to bear the stamp of truth in contrast to the evident fabrications of some and the well-meaning confusion of others.

'Jagas' are next reported during the conquest of Benguela[1] in 1617–22 by Manuel Cerveira Pereira. The second and fifth of the five battles described in a contemporary document[2] were with 'Jagas', the latter of which had been an ally of the Portuguese for a time. About this time 'Jagas' were also commonly reported as allies of the Portuguese forces in the conquest of Ndongo and Matamba. References to this state of affairs could be given from many sources, but more significant is the testimony of an eyewitness, one of the conquistadores, who, in a petition to King Philip, dated 16 January 1620, inserted the following:

that the *Jagas* who aid us and are ferocious, who are with us, who are of great effect to overawe the heathen that they may not rise, that Your Majesty should make them a favour of wine, for they desire nothing else, to send them three hogsheads a year at the three principal feasts, for it is necessary to have them for friends, and the said *jagas*, Your Majesty ordering to give them this, they will always give in slaves[3] the value and much more.[4]

Another of the conquistadores also wrote:

The Iacas are stranger folk and who live by robbery and war.

This people came many years ago to these kingdoms and have over-run all the hinterland even to Mozambique. . . .

From them came some to our protection and service, fleeing from their captains. . . .

These people themselves are cruel and great thieves, and were more so after we made use of them: they go about robbing unjustly [*sic*] and captivating the miserable heathen; but, however, the fault is not of the *iaca*, but rather of the governors and captains who command them, and so they should be kept for friends and used well, during the necessary time.[5]

Other contemporary writers could be cited,[6] but enough evidence

[1] The present city of Benguela and its surroundings.

[2] L. Cordeiro (ed.), 1617–22, *Benguella e seu sertão por um Anonymo*, pp. 10, 13; J. J. Lopes de Lima, *Ensaios*, pt. ii, pp. 30 ff.

[3] Lit. 'pieces', a somewhat deprecatory euphemism used in the old Portuguese works.

[4] L. Cordeiro (ed.), 1574–1620, *Da Mina ao Cabo Negro segundo Garcia Mendes Castello Branco*, p. 16 f.

[5] L. Cordeiro (ed.), 1593–1631, *Terras e minas africanas segundo Balthazar Rebello de Aragão*, p. 16 f.

[6] Compare Cavazzi, op. cit., pp. 630 ff.; Duarte Lopes, op. cit., p. 156 f.; Dapper; *Description de l'Afrique*, p. 357 f.

HISTORICAL 185

has been cited to prove conclusively that the 'Jagas' were not one horde but many, and that they multiplied by splitting into other and smaller groups as they went from pillage to pillage. Battell recounts that they killed their own offspring,[1] and this is further attested by other contemporary writers.[2] They ensured their increase by taking the young of their enemies who, as Purchas noted, were trained up as a sort of Janisaries. Battell said that of 16,000 in the camp 'there were but twelve natural Gagas that were their captains, and fourteen or fifteen women'.[3] Purchas added to the first edition of *Purchas, His Pilgrimage* (1613) a note which is helpful in determining, if not their ultimate, at least their proximate, origin, and also their final place of settling. He wrote:

He (i.e., Battell) saith they are called Iagges by the Portugals, by themselves Imbangolas . . . and come from Sierra Liona. . . .
Elembe, the great Iagge, brought with him twelve thousand of these cruel monsters from Sierra Liona, and after much mischief and spoil settled himself in Benguele, twelve degrees from the Zone southwards, and there breedeth and groweth into a nation. But Kelandula, sometime his page, proceeds in that beastly life before mentioned, and the people of Elembe, by great troops, run to him and follow his camp in hope of spoil.[4]

According to this, we may take it that the designation of Iagges, Jaga, Jaka, or Ayaka came from the Portuguese, which means that it came from one or more of the Bantu languages—that it was originally a description given to these hordes or to their leaders by the African people whom they fought and conquered, or even by the African traders[5] who went to the 'Jaga' camps to buy slaves in exchange for cloth, beads, rum, and muskets. The word evidently comes from the verb to fight, *oku yaka*; they fight, *a yaka*,[6] or *va yaka*. Father Van Wing[7] and Emil Torday[8] both hold that there is some real relationship between the tribe of the Bayaka of the middle Kuango and the 'Jaga' hordes, and make that

---

[1] Ravenstein, op. cit., pp. 32, 84 f. Could this have been an (extreme) instance of the well-known fear of menstrual blood found among many people, including the Ovimbundu?

[2] Ravenstein, op. cit., p. 32, note 4.   [3] Ravenstein, op. cit., p. 33.

[4] Ravenstein, op. cit., pp. 84, 85.

[5] *Pombeiros descalços*, barefoot traders.

[6] The Portuguese transcription of this form is *a iaca*, or *a iacca*, with the hard *c* mistakenly changed to *g*, and *i* taken for *j* as was formerly often done.

[7] Van Wing, op. cit., p. 106.

[8] Torday, op. cit., see map facing p. 282.

186 UMBUNDU KINSHIP AND CHARACTER

the origin of this tribal name. It is no less reasonable to suppose that the name has also been preserved in the name of a section of the Ovimbundu—the va Ciyaka,[1] which is an augmentative noun from the same verbal stem.

'He saith they are called . . . by themselves Imbangolas.' This statement has given rise to a great deal of speculation from the time of Purchas to our own. The *Imbangala*, better known as 'the people of Jaga Cassange' or Bangalas, are generally recognized to have been one of the marauding hordes which troubled Angola in the seventeenth century, and it has already been noted that their own traditional history, as given by Dias de Carvalho and by Ferreira Diniz, fits in with this theory. It seems reasonable, therefore, to make this further identification of the 'Jagas' of Battell with the Imbangala of Cassange. There is one more traditional link to add, and that is that the Ovimbundu of Ciyaka recognize the region of Cassange as the location of the oldest ancestral tombs of which they have any tradition. Once when there was a particularly severe drought, tribal elders were sent from Ciyaka to Cassange to worship at these ancient tombs, to anoint the skulls, and to plead for rain.

When Purchas noted in 1613 that 'Elembe settled himself in Benguele', he meant the hinterland of Benguela Velha,[2] i.e. in the regions of Mbũi (*Amboim*), Cipala (*Quibala*), or Sela (*Cela*). As I have shown, tradition connects the kingdom of Wambu with Sela, and the kingdom of Bailundu with Cipala. Although 'Kelandula, sometime his page, proceeds in that beastly life before mentioned', we may be reasonably sure that eventually he also, or his followers, settled in the same general region. Both Elembe and Kalandula are common Umbundu names and the latter is found twice among the kings of Bailundu.

There is further evidence in the similarity of customs as between the 'Jagas' and the royal families of the Ovimbundu, for both Battell and Cavazzi have given fairly full accounts. To show these similarities fully it would be necessary to re-edit Battell, and therefore I shall speak of only a few outstanding points. The cannibalism of the 'Jagas' was perhaps their most striking custom.

[1] The Portuguese transcription of this form would be 'Giaca', but this has become changed to 'Quiaca', as also with many similar names.

[2] See p. 122, n. 4 *supra*. It was only in 1617 that the settlement on the *Baia das Vaccas* was made, and (wrongly) given the name of Benguela.

HISTORICAL 187

The Ovimbundu are not ordinary cannibals, if indeed that term may be applied to any people in Africa, nor do the commoners of the Ovimbundu ever eat human flesh on their own account, but no king may ever reign or be considered as regularly enthroned until he has 'eaten Ekongo'.[1] The cannibalism traditionally ascribed to Wambu-Kalunga is also a case in point.[2] Other human sacrifices practised by the 'Jagas' and described by Battell also have their counterparts in the practices of the Umbundu kingdoms.[3] The mode of the burial of the dead described by Battell[4] is essentially that which has been used, at least until the last few years, for the kings and the other 'holy'[5] men of the Ovimbundu, except that where rock caves are available the use of them has been adopted and in Kasongi cairns were used. The sitting posture and the sacrifice of wives or slaves and cattle (or of substitutes) are the important points, and these have everywhere been used for the classes mentioned, until quite recently.

The custom of keeping boys captured from the enemy and training them to be fearless warriors amid the terrors of the country has a parallel in the Umbundu custom of the king's slaves,[6] who came from another land[7] and would therefore do the king's bidding without fear, favour, or consideration of family feeling. They often reached high position and certain of the king's ministers always came from among them. There seem to be many recollections of the 'Jagas' in the customs of the kings' sons.[8] Names of certain of the officials seem to have survived, as, for example, Mani (*muēlē*) Lumbo, Mani-Curio (*Muēkalia*), Golambolo (*Ngalamboli*), Tendala (*Candala*), Ukuetambo,[9] &c. Careful linguistic studies would doubtless reveal many remains of the speech

---

[1] *Oku lia Ekongo*—lit. 'to eat the Old One'. This is a ritual feast in which the flesh of a specially fattened slave is eaten mixed with the flesh of various animals. See Ravenstein, op. cit., p. 33, note 3. Magyar described this custom, calling it '*Ouri-Kongo*', op. cit., pp. 275 ff.

[2] See *supra*, p. 176.

[3] Compare Ravenstein, op. cit.   [4] Op. cit., p. 34 f.

[5] 'Holy' in the sense of spirit possessed—the king, the hunter, the medical practitioner, and the smith.

[6] *Ocinduli cosoma*, singular. May there be some recollection of 'Kinguri' (=Cinguli) in this word?

[7] In Bailundu the *ovinduli viosoma* (plural) came mostly from Luandu, i.e. the Songo country across the Kuanza—further evidence of connexion with Lunda emigrants.

[8] *Omālā volosoma*, used collectively of all the royal families of the Ovimbundu.

[9] Cavazzi, op. cit., pp. 206 f., 211.

188 UMBUNDU KINSHIP AND CHARACTER

which the 'Jagas' had, although they soon adopted the language of the people whom they conquered. As recently as fifty years ago the mother of the king of Bailundu spoke Umbundu brokenly, since she came from Cipala, and her sons were sent to complete their education with her people where later they were often called to rule.[1]

Recognition by the Ciyaka people that their forefathers came from the region where the Imbangala now live has been noted. It may have been a similar tradition heard in Viye which started Magyar to find out the tradition of 'Kinguri'. Such a tradition was mentioned in Viye as late as 1898.[2] This relation between the Umbundu ruling families and either the 'Jagas' or the Imbangala has been noted by several of the Portuguese writers. Lopes de Lima, in his History of the Discovery of the Congo, adds a footnote on the 'Jagas' as follows: 'The Jagas are almost nomadic peoples . . . coming from the interior of Africa, . . . there are some on the frontiers of the Congo, Angola, and Benguella, where some have fixed their habitations (as those of Cassange, and Bailundo).'[3] Writing in 1797 a certain Col. Pinheiro de Lacerda said of the inhabitants of Ngalangi, Kakonda, Wambu, Bailundu, &c.: 'These are they of the uplands, who are divided into two groups, those of one are called "Quinbundos",[4] (these do not eat human flesh); the others are called "Quimbangalas", who eat it, and when they make their sacrifice, which all attend, all eat the "Macongo".'[5] At that period the diversity of these two component parts of the Ovimbundu people was so apparent that they were even spoken of as separate and distinct peoples.

Place-names. Before leaving the subject of migratory movements a word should be said on the evidence of place-names. There is nothing to prove, except in a few instances where traditions have been collected, that the recurrence of identical or similar names at different places indicates the actual lines of migration followed by the several tribal groups represented. It may be said, however, that this line of evidence, taken together

---

[1] See *Missionary Herald*, 1888, p. 70.

[2] *Missionary Herald*, 1898, p. 108.

[3] *Annaes Mar. Col.*, 1845, p. 93.

[4] Taken from the singular form *ocimbundu*. As already explained, the change of *chi* to *qui* is a commonly met mutilation of the Bantu forms.

[5] *Annaes Mar. Col.*, 1845, p. 488. There follows a circumstantial account of the ceremony of *Oku lia Ekongo*, to which reference has already been made.

HISTORICAL 189

with that which has already been reviewed, might make it possible to determine the demography of the Benguela Highland prior to the formation of the Umbundu kingdoms. It is also further evidence as to the demographic make-up of the Ovimbundu. Some of these recurring place-names evidently represent elements which now constitute separate entities outside the Umbundu kingdoms, although they probably made contributions to the formation of those kingdoms. Others represent elements which probably moved away from the earlier invasions from the north but stayed in their new sites to amalgamate with later arrivals. Some may represent successive splittings-off from a stock which thus settled at various places. Many recurrent place-names could be shown both in this region and outside the language-grouping.

Attitudes toward Other Tribes. Attitudes of the Ovimbundu towards the various neighbouring tribes are instructive. Mention has already been made of the attitude of the southern 'Bangala' people in their inclusion of the Ovimbundu of Kalukembe within their own system of exogamy. The Ovimbundu recognize a common humanity with the peoples who are their neighbours both on the south and on the north. They are all *omanu*,[1] people, or even *vakuetu*, comrades. Similar recognition is not extended to the eastern and south-eastern neighbours who are lumped together under the derogatory term of 'va Ngangela' or *ovingangela*.[2] This eastern region as far as the Great Lakes was the happy hunting-ground of the slave-traders from Viye and from Bailundu. There is a term *olongoya* which is applied to the northern neighbours, but without the derogatory connotation of 'Ngangela'. *Olongoya* has a linguistic connotation as did *barbaroi* in the Greek, and refers to the fact that these neighbours speak what is to the Ovimbundu an unintelligible language. How much of rationalization there may be in these attitudes and prejudices one cannot say, but it seems that in them there is some recognition of tribal origins and relationships, of the fact that across the Benguela Highland migrations have swept from north to south.

Conclusion. In consideration of the above evidence, it is now possible to draw conclusions concerning the origin of the Ovi-

---

[1] *Omanu* is the Umbundu equivalent for the Nguni *abantu*, which has come to be applied to the whole language family.

[2] This Umbundu attitude is best illustrated by the proverb 'As a grass hut is not a house, so an *ocingangela* (singular) is not a person (*omunu*).'

190 UMBUNDU KINSHIP AND CHARACTER

mbundu. They are the result of a fusion of diverse stocks, chiefly of the Southern Bantu and of the Congo or Central Bantu peoples. The ruling families probably were Lunda emigrants for the most part,[1] at least in their origin. It was probably during the seventeenth century that these people entered the Benguela Highland and began to found their respective dynasties. The people whom they encountered in these lands were mostly of Southern Bantu stock, with some 'Ngangela' people in Ndulu, Viye, and Ngalangi. The upper strata of these local populations seem to have moved on with their cattle to join related stocks in the border regions, while the masses seem to have stayed behind to form the nucleus of the Ovimbundu. Especially does this appear to have been the case with the original Southern Bantu stock, for many who were cattle-owners seem to have fled to the drier and more suitable lands in the south and west, while those who stayed must have lost to the invaders such cattle as they had. Only in the south-west (especially Kalukembe) was the Southern Bantu influence of sufficient strength to preserve any semblance of the cattle-culture complex, together with a recognition of kinship from their southern neighbours. Everywhere, it seems, the Southern Bantu nucleus was of sufficient strength to exert a dominant linguistic influence. It is certainly noteworthy that over the whole region a single language has developed with only small dialectic differences[2]—and that without benefit of political union. Commercial intercourse has probably largely supplied the place of the latter.

Historical Development

Dominant Tendency. The origins of the principal groups of the Ovimbundu have been traced in outline from both native and European sources. It now remains to sketch the main lines of

[1] But Viye and Ngalangi traditions *in re* the origin of their ruling families must be borne in mind—traditions also supported by other evidence.

[2] Retention of peculiarities of the parent stock by Kalukembe has been noted. There are certain noticeable differences as between 'up-country' and 'down-country'—roughly divided by the Keve and Kunene Rivers. Each of the outlying regions has its own peculiarities due to local foreign influences. In Kasongi, in Ngalangi, and in Viye these are quite noticeable but can hardly be called separate dialects. Regions of older European occupation—Kakonda and Viye—have taken more from the Portuguese. In consideration of these facts and the further fact that the Viye racial stock had a larger 'Ngangela' element than had other regions, the recent linguistic influence of Viye has been out of all proportion to reality and may be explained by the relatively larger number of missions and missionaries working in that region.

HISTORICAL

their historical development. The traditional history and separate European contacts of each of the several Umbundu kingdoms would occupy far more time and space than the limits of this study permit. I propose, therefore, to give in outline the broader trends of European contacts from the earliest days, filling in such items of traditional history as may be necessary for complete understanding, and to summarize this with a chronological chart in which the dynastic successions of the principal Umbundu kingdoms are included.

There are many books about Angola and several histories of Angola, so-called, but the History of Angola, in the proper sense of the term, remains to be written. None of the books written thus far has taken sufficient cognizance of the economic factors involved, whereas a history of Angola is no history at all if not an economic history. This is particularly true of this territory where two of the greater traders of the continent have met.

The Portuguese are the most tenacious traders of all the Europeans who have gone to Africa. Proof of this is the fact that the Hausa, Indian, Syrian, Armenian, or Greek traders, who almost monopolize the petty trade of most African colonies, in Angola have no footing whatever. From the first, the Portuguese traders began to utilize in their trade the services of natives of the old kingdom of Angola. Early in the nineteenth century the Ovimbundu began to be noticed as traders and soon came to be known[1] as the greatest traders of Bantu Africa, after the Zanzibar Arabs.[2] These latter they met in the Great Lakes region, and they (the Arabs) subsequently began to come down to Benguela or Luanda themselves.[3] In the middle of the nineteenth century the Yankees in their clipper ships played a large part in the trade of the Angola coast. More recently the British have made considerable investments in trade and in industrial developments. After the war of 1914–18 Germans played an important part in the commercial life of the colony. Any history of Angola, then, that makes sense must be an economic history. This is no less true of the history of the Ovimbundu and their European contacts.

---

[1] Under various names, as, for example, Mambari, Biheans, Bailundos, Kimbundus, Mbundus, &c.

[2] Cf. comparisons drawn by Serpa Pinto, op. cit., p. 163.

[3] The Umbundu name for the Zanzibaris is 'va Lunguana'; compare the medieval (1228) name for Zanzibar, Langujah (C. M. Doke in *Bantu Studies*, 1938, p. 135 f.).

192   UMBUNDU KINSHIP AND CHARACTER

European Influences 1600–1770. The first European contact of the Ovimbundu or of the 'proto-Ovimbundu' was without doubt for purposes of trade. The first record which we have of any such contact is in *Andrew Battell in Guinea.* About 1600 the governor, as the chief trader,[1] sent his prisoner Battell on trading expeditions along the Benguela coast. At the Bahia das Vaccas, the Ndombe, a cattle-keeping people, were met. They supplied the Europeans with produce,[2] including cattle and 'the famous sheep which have five quarters',[3] but *not* with the principal article of commerce, for as another of the conquistadores noted, 'In this kingdom there is no slave trade, for it is not their custom to sell each other.'[4] This lack was soon supplied by 'proto-Ovimbundu' when, on the next voyage, Battell with the 'Portugals and Mulattos' found the encampment of 'Jagas' at the mouth of the Keve River, from Battell's account of which we have already quoted.[5] Although hardly recognized as such at the time, this, it seems, was the beginning of a long commercial partnership. As long as the 'Jagas' continued 'to take the spoil of the land', they supplied many slaves[6] for the trade, and after they settled they became traders both in direct European employ and on their own account.

The early European settlements in Africa were made with the hope of finding gold, but although that metal was not found in the Congo or Angola, black gold—human gold—soon proved to be equally profitable. There was a religious motive in the Portuguese discoveries, for from the time of Prince Henry the Navigator, his captains were bidden to 'plant the Cross on some new headland'. With every ship priests went out to convert the heathen. Some priests doubtless did good work but more of them, both individually and as members of the various orders, early came to the conclusion that the best way to convert the heathen was to sell

[1] The governors continued to engage in trade openly, until forbidden by the law of 17 Sept. 1721, and then, says Lopes de Lima, some complied, while others did not (*Ensaios*, part i, p. 84).

[2] A. Battell, p. 16.

[3] L. Cordeiro (ed.), 1574–1620, *Da Mina ao Cabo Negro segundo Garcia Mendes Castello Branco*, p. 34. The reference is to the fat-tailed sheep of the Hottentots and their neighbours. This is perhaps the first reference to it on the west coast.

[4] Ibid., 1593–1631, *Terras e minas africanas segundo Balthazar Rebello de Aragão*, p. 15.

[5] *Supra*, p. 182 f.

[6] Battell, pp. 20, 28; L. Cordeiro (ed.), 1574–1620, *Da Mina ao Cabo Negro segundo Garcia Mendes Castello Branco*, p. 17.

HISTORICAL

him off where he would have the double benefit of regular work and Christian doctrine. In 1560 the Bishop of São Thomé wrote that 'he doubted that the people of the kingdom of Angola could be made Catholics unless the King would allow Trade'.[1] The slaves were baptized by the bishop by the boatload—rowed along the wharf of Luanda. The Jesuits profited greatly by the slave-trade, employing continuously three of their own ships. The religious motive was thus early swallowed up by the commercial and profit motive. Commerce was almost entirely taken up with the slave-trade. Four-fifths of the value of all exports were slaves.[2]

During the first hundred years of the Colony of Angola a million slaves were exported,[3] and three million would probably be a very conservative estimate of the total. As long as the over-sea slave traffic remained legal, little effort seems to have been made to develop other exports. In spite of protests and until 1832, ivory remained a monopoly of the royal treasury with regulations which discouraged its export. Such products as gum copal and orchilia only began to be exported in 1832–8. The only product of any importance which had also been exported in the time of the slave-trade was bees-wax. The slave-trade was first questioned in 1831, it was formally prohibited in 1836, but for many years enforcement was not accomplished. During the 250 years of the oversea slave-trade, Angola was in reality a dependency of Brazil.[4] When Brazil became independent, there was a movement in Benguela for union with that country.[5] So complete was the commercial domination of Brazil that Lisbon merchants had hardly anything to do with the Angolan trade. Lopes de Lima points out that the colony was also spiritually dominated by Brazil, and attributes the noteworthy religious decadence not only to the preoccupation of the clergy with the slave-trade, but also to the fact that from 1677 until 1845 the diocese of Angola and Congo was a part of the Metropolitan archdiocese of Bahia. The one great fact with regard to Angola of the sixteenth, seventeenth,

[1] It had been a royal monopoly and allowed only through Kongo. This letter is from the National Archives of the Torre do Tombo and quoted by Lopes de Lima, *Ensaios*, p. ix.

[2] Statistics given by Lopes de Lima, *Ensaios*, part i, p. 69 f.

[3] Cadornega, *História Geral das Guerras Angolanas* (1680–1), vol. iii, p. 254 (also quoted by Paiva Manso).

[4] Lopes de Lima, *Ensaios*, part i, p. 74; J. P. Oliveira Martins, *O Brasil e as Colónias Portuguezas*, p. 18.

[5] Lopes de Lima, op. cit., p. 127.

O

194 UMBUNDU KINSHIP AND CHARACTER

eighteenth, and much of the nineteenth century, then, was the slave-trade.

Most of the historical treatises on Angola are little more than chronological lists of battles and expeditions. The relation of these events to the main facts, i.e. to the economic facts, has rarely been made. Two or three presídios were founded with the hope of controlling nearby mineral deposits,[1] whether real or supposed, but all the rest were intended as spearheads for trade or to protect existing trade. Many of the military expeditions were raids with an obvious end in view; others were rearguard actions to protect a more or less successful raid of the same sort; others were retaliations for reprisals or vice versa. Practically all of the soldiers who were free men, from the captain-general down, were also traders, and some who were not free were traders on account of others. There may have been a few expeditions which had less immediate connexion with trade, for there were genuine explorers in those early days, even as more recently.

There would be little interest or profit in cataloguing the military expeditions which had, or seem to have had, contact with the Ovimbundu or with their predecessors in the land during the seventeenth and eighteenth centuries. There were only a very few of real significance. During the seventeenth century many raids were made from Massangano across Libolo to the edge of or into the Benguela Highland, and likewise there were many actions between the garrisons of Benguela and Caconda and the inhabitants of the plateau. In 1607 Balthazar Rebello de Aragão set out to cross Africa and had to turn back after going eighty leagues, but his own report was so scanty that even the direction he took cannot be determined.[2] In 1645, while the Dutch controlled Luanda and the coast, there was a raid which was said to have reached Bailundu.[3] The very scanty references to this raid give no description of the inhabitants, but since there seems to be no Bailundu tradition with regard to it, I conclude that the present dynasty (beyond the establishment of which tradition hardly goes) must have been founded since that date. About 1650 there was a raid across Libolo as far as the Keve River which found a cattle-rearing

---

[1] e.g. Benguela Velha and Cambambe.

[2] L. Cordeiro (ed.), 1593–1620, *Terras e minas africanas segundo Balthazar Rebello de Aragão*, p. 15.

[3] *Catálogo dos Governadores*, p. 374; Lopes de Lima, *Ensaios*, part i, p. 99.

HISTORICAL

people living there,[1] which also leads me to conclude that the Ovimbundu as we now know them were not there at that date.

About 1661 there was an expedition from Benguela in order to restore a native ally, the 'Iaga Caconda', against an 'intruding Iaga' who used fire-arms.[2] This is the first record of fire-arms in native hands in the hinterland of Benguela. Muskets and powder were sold from the time of Luanda's founding (1576),[3] but not all tribes took to them quickly.[4] If fire-arms were already in use by natives in the Benguela hinterland in 1661, it is most probable that the founders of the present Umbundu dynasties had them when they came to the country. The first presídio of Caconda was built in 1680, destroyed soon after, and rebuilt nearby in 1685. This was at four or five days' journey from Benguela but not on the Plateau nor within the present Umbundu area. The third presídio, known as Caconda-Nova, was built at its present site in 1769. Most writers have supposed this fort to have been built at its present site in 1685, overlooking the fact that there were not two sites but three.[5]

European Influences 1770–1840. The governor who effected the final moving of Caconda on to the Plateau, D. Francisco de Souza Coutinho, also undertook many other reforms designed to better the economic state of the colony. He brought something of the intentions of the great Marquez de Pombal to this remote tropical dependency. He seems to have been the first governor of Angola to realize the immense superiority of the Benguela Highland,

[1] Cadornega, op. cit., vol. ii, pp. 42–6.

[2] Cadornega, op. cit., p. 176 f. It is of interest that according to this author (1680) this expedition passed the Bay then known as 'Catumbella of Salt Water' or 'Catumbella of the Oysters'. Jaspert made the error of stating that this Bay (Lobito) was 'discovered by the English' about 1900!

[3] Garcia Mendes Castello Branco (1620) protested against allowing this traffic (*Da Mina ao Cabo Negro*, p. 25).

[4] In 1790 the Ovimbundu used fire-arms very well, but the 'Ganguellas' had not then adopted their use (*Annaes Mar. e Col., 5a Ser.*, p. 489).

[5] Lopes de Lima (*Ensaios*) made this error (or omission), and more recent writers have perhaps erred by following him. The correct accounts are given in the *Catálogo dos Governadores*, pp. 396 ff., 416 ff. (also to be found in *Arquivos de Angola*, vol. iii, pp. 507 f., 528). The facts are most clearly brought out by the governor of the District of Benguela in reporting a visit made to Caconda. He gives a short history of the presídio and tells of having seen the ruins of the earlier forts (*Districto de Benguella 1892*, Lisboa, 1894). The report to the Ministry in Lisbon of the governor, D. Francisco Inocencio de Souza Coutinho, explaining (among other things) the moving of this presídio, and dated 18 Oct. 1769, has been published in *Arquivos de Angola*, vol. i, no. 1 (Oct. 1933).

196 UMBUNDU KINSHIP AND CHARACTER

from the point of view of climate, situation, and resources, over the rest of the West African lands with which the Portuguese had relations. He stated in his report[1] that until that time most of the Europeans who entered the Highland were escaped convicts or deserters. He attempted to provide for a more orderly commercial development in these regions not only by building the forts of Caconda-Nova and Novo Redondo,[2] but also by bringing the traders of the interior together at determined places where they could have judges appointed from among themselves, and even parish priests.[3] If the office of 'captain-major and exterior judge'[4] did not originate at this time, at least it was Souza Coutinho who revived it in his appointments and made it a useful instrument for the commercial penetration of the Benguela Highland and of the regions beyond.

Among the regions for which he created such an office was 'Gallangue grande'[5] (Ngalangi). This captaincy-major and the parish of 'S. João Nepomuceno de Gallangue' are mentioned subsequently but only to note the vacancy of both posts. Souza Coutinho was remembered for his many accomplishments, and for his realistic attitudes. He recognized that the law of 1620 prohibiting the entry of traders into the hinterlands[6] was largely a dead letter, and that in so far as it was observed, it only favoured the

[1] Dated 18 Oct. 1769, loc. cit.

[2] The chief reason for building the latter was to put an end to the contraband trade of the English (see reports of the same governor of 12 Jan. and of 16 May 1769 in op. cit., vol. i, nos. 5 and 6 (Mar. 1936).

[3] Order of 23 Sept. 1768, and report of 12 Jan. 1769 in ibid.; report of 18 Oct. 1769; also *Catálogo dos Governadores*, p. 416 f. (*Arquivos de Angola*, vol. iii, p. 528).

[4] The *capitão mor e juiz de fora* was appointed to represent the government in a region not subject to it nor within the range of military occupation. His chief duty was to keep the peace among the Portuguese subjects of his jurisdiction and to attend to legal and orderly inheritance of their goods when they died. He also was supposed to secure for them as much extra-territorial treatment as the native kings and courts would concede. Compare explanation by Francisco de Salles Fereira in *Annaes Mar. e Col.*, 1846, p. 118. Long lists of these appointments for the various regions of the interior, together with many contemporary documents, are given by Ralph Delgado, *Ao Sul do Cuanza*.

[5] He gave it the name 'Linhares' after a Portuguese town, but neither this name nor that of 'Contins' for Caconda was kept.

[6] The purpose of this law was not, as Livingstone supposed (*Missionary Travels and Researches*, p. 369), directly humanitarian, but more especially to preserve the trade for residents of the towns and to avoid the necessity for punitive expeditions which the traders' presence in the hinterland had so often motivated.

HISTORICAL

foreign buccaneers and other contraband trade in the unoccupied ports of the Congo, Loango, &c. He therefore removed the prohibition[1] and counted on the appointment of captains-major to keep the peace. From this time the hinterlands were legally open to traders—to all Portuguese subjects whether white, black, or brown.

Though the hinterlands were now legally open to all traders, life was not thereby made any easier for them than it had been previously for the 'barefoot traders'[2] who had carried on most of the trade hitherto. Once they went beyond the range of the guns of a presídio, they entered what were practically foreign countries which recognized no European principles of law or of conduct. Those who could afford it built themselves small fortresses and manned them with their slaves. Even so, they had to become vassals and feudatories of some native king and pay tribute according to his good pleasure. Those traders who could not afford such an establishment led a very precarious existence, nor could they long maintain a status above that of the natives of the region. Many of these early traders and their descendants were subsequently incorporated into the Umbundu stock, and in some instances whole communities of them.[3] For one reason or another this increased commercial contact led to further wars with the natives. The war of this period which made the greatest impression upon the Ovimbundu was the campaign of 1774–6, to which allusion has already been made.[4] Memories of this war and of the capture of their respective kings have been preserved in the traditions of Bailundu and of Ndulu,[5] and it also seems that these two peoples learned, for a time at least, that it was safer and more profitable to trade with the Europeans than to raid their establishments. Ciyaka and the neighbouring groups do not seem to have followed suit, for they continued to raid the forts of Caconda, Quilengues, and Huila until fairly recent times; nor do Europeans seem to have penetrated Ciyaka for residence until almost the turn of the present century. But in all the Umbundu kingdoms life

[1] Report of 9 May 1765 in *Arquivos de Angola*, vol. i, nos. 5 and 6.
[2] i.e. native African trading agents.
[3] I have genealogical tables and family histories of some of the present-day descendants. The mixed origin of communities in Kakonda has been noted by several writers. A noteworthy example in Viye is the region called Kamundongo—an old Ndongo (Angola) settlement.
[4] *Supra*, pp. 166, 171, 174.   [5] *Supra*, pp. 170, 171.

198 UMBUNDU KINSHIP AND CHARACTER

continued to be difficult for the traders, subject as they were to the conditions of primitive custom and belief.[1]

About the time of the above-mentioned military campaign, events took a turn which in the end greatly advanced commercial life in Viye. I refer to the restoration of Kangombe to his 'stool' with the help of the governor, Dom Antonio de Lancastre.[2] This alliance with the Portuguese government was maintained by Kangombe's successors until 1890. In 1782, and perhaps even in 1770, there were so many Portuguese residents that a 'Captain-major and exterior judge of Bihe' was appointed,[3] a post which seems to have been maintained until Silva Porto's suicide in 1890.

Reference has already been made to an account by Paulo Martins Pinheiro de Lacerda, who evidently lived in Ngalangi and in Wambu about 1790,[4] but although this man wrote a good deal about native life, he had little to say about trade, although it was perhaps his own livelihood. I have accounts of two trading expeditions from Benguela to the country of 'Lovar' or 'Lovale' at the head-waters of the Zambezi in 1794 and 1795, undertaken by Alexandre de Silva Teixeira and Jozé da Silva Costa at the instigation of a slave originally from that region.[5] They passed through Bailundu and Viye, but mentioned these regions only to say that the road was already well known to all backwoodsmen (traders). All available evidence seems to indicate that before the close of the eighteenth century the Ovimbundu were becoming, if they had not already become, traders. If trade had not yet taken first place over raiding and warfare, at least it was well-established in their habits of life. Bailundu tradition says that the first traders to offer cloth and beads and fire-arms for slaves and ivory were the Ndongo, the 'barefoot traders' (*pombeiros descalços*). This was doubtless during the very early days of the eighteenth century, or

[1] Silva Porto's diaries, although referring to a later time, give a good description of difficulties faced (op. cit.). *Soc. Geog. Lisboa, 5a Ser.*

[2] Governor and captain-general, 1772–9. He was the immediate successor of D. Francisco de Souza Coutinho.

[3] For this appointment, which may not have been the first, and the duties of the office, see *Annaes Mar. e Col., 6a Ser.*, p. 118. I have the names of subsequent appointees, and for four of them the following dates of appointment, respectively—1791, 1819, 1838, 1885; also of one previous appointee in 1770 or 1771.

[4] *Supra*, p. 188.

[5] *Arquivos de Angola*, vol. i, no. 4 (Nov. 1935); *Annaes Mar. e Col., 4a Ser.* (1844), p. 159 f.

HISTORICAL 199

even earlier. Long before that the forerunners of the Ovimbundu kings, the 'Jagas', had sold their prisoners to the *pombeiros*. The other side of the national lineage had probably bought salt from Cisama[1] even before the white men came to the land.

Dominant Tendencies 1840–74. The next period in which there was great commercial development among the Ovimbundu began with the fourth decade of the nineteenth century, following upon the abolition of the monopoly in ivory and the development of new products as substitutes for the slave-trade, formally prohibited in 1836. This period saw a considerable increase in the number of traders resident in the region. The new régime at the coast may have caused some to go inland.[2] In Bailundu, and especially in Viye, they were well received by kings and by people who saw in the coming of more Europeans to live among them increased commercial opportunities.[3] For various reasons most of these traders established themselves in Viye,[4] and from this time Viye took first place in trade with the interior and with the coast. But since the caravan road to Benguela must pass either through

[1] Lopes de Lima, *Ensaios*, part ii, p. 55.

[2] Some statistics on these older periods are available, but since they are themselves in disagreement and none of them seem to be very reliable I do not include them here. The Report of the Governor of Benguela for 1799 gives the rather optimistic figure of 78 *whites* (including 5 women) resident in the several interior districts (*Annaes Mar. e Col.*, 1844, p. 161), with correspondingly larger numbers for persons of mixed race and (civilized) blacks. In 1838, according to Lopes de Lima (*Ensaios*, part i, p. 4 f.), the number of *whites* in the same districts was only 14, with no women, and the number of 'brown inhabitants' correspondingly small except in Caconda, for which he gives the number of 2,992—more than in all the rest of the colony! J. R. Graça gave a list of 101 names of inhabitants of Viye alone, 'Portuguese or descendants of Portuguese . . . *including 6 Europeans*'. This was probably near the truth for 1846. Magyar (1849–57) gave very interesting calculations of the population and area of the several Umbundu kingdoms, but no figures on European residents.

[3] A very interesting glimpse of Bailundu in 1837 was given by a political exile, Carlos de Almeida Sandoval (*Annaes do Cons. Ultr., Ia Ser.*, p. 519 f.). Very full accounts of life in Viye have been given by Silva Porto, who first reached Viye in 1840, coming from Luanda (see some of his diaries in *Annaes do Cons. Ultr.*, Ser. I; *Boletim Soc. Geog. Lisboa*, Ser. 5, 6. A small volume of excerpts from Silva Porto's diaries was published in 1942 by the Agência Geral das Colónias under the title *Viagens e apontamentos de um portuense em África*.)

[4] The early continuous connexion of the dynasty with the Luanda government has been mentioned, as also the continuous appointment of a *capitão mor*. The incumbent at the time (appointed 1838) was Francisco José Coimbra, of mixed race from Caconda (*Annaes Mar. e Col.*, 1846, p. 118; *Annaes do Cons. Ultr., Ia Ser.*, p. 112 f.). Both Cameron and the early missionaries mention dealings with his sons. Some of his grandsons and great-grandsons, now reincorporated with the Ovimbundu, still tell of their descent.

200   UMBUNDU KINSHIP AND CHARACTER

Bailundu (and its dependent states), or through Wambu and Ciyaka, while the road to Luanda lay either through Ndulu or Bailundu, these other kingdoms were not slow in following along the path of commercial success. In Ngalangi the king himself took a very active interest in trade and annually sent a royal caravan to Benguela, taking care to get a pass from the captain of the fort at Caconda. Other kings also adopted the practice of the royal caravan,[1] but the kings of the principal kingdoms were slow to give up raiding, plunder, and warfare as a manner of life[2]—a custom which became distasteful to their subjects in proportion as trade became more profitable and attractive.

In addition to those already named, there were other historical events and policies which contributed toward the development of trade during this period. The abolition in 1834 of the monopoly in ivory,[3] which the royal treasury had held since the beginning, was of great importance, and this, in turn, abetted in perpetuating the slave-trade, now a contraband, for ivory always had been brought from the interior on the backs of slaves, and it must not be supposed that this would suddenly be stopped, especially since ivory had just become much more valuable. According to Bastos,[4] slaves for this contraband trade continued to be cheap and plentiful until the eighties, which was probably due in part to the large supply offered. Another reason was perhaps that the contraband oversea trade was largely in the hands of foreigners—Brazilians, Spaniards, and Americans, who were not always reliable in the matter of paying for their cargoes.[5]

---

[1] *Omaka*, which had special routines and prerogatives. Other types of caravans were named from the products which they carried or conducted.

[2] See Lopes de Lima, *Ensaios*, part ii, p. 54: 'Bailundo . . . a warlike people, of the race of "Jagas", whose chief is always on a campaign'; Magyar, *Reisen*, many references, but especially pp. 290 ff., 383–420; Silva Porto, op. cit., p. 82 f., 160; *Missionary Herald*, 1883, p. 339; 1884, pp. 145 f., 504 f.; 1885, pp. 279, 375 f.; 1886, p. 228 f.; 1887, p. 106; 1889, pp. 67, 535; 1890, p. 292, &c.

[3] From 1618 (B. Rebello de Aragão, p. 14) until 1834 (Saldanha da Gama, p. 86), all critics agreed that this monopoly even defeated its own purpose, i.e. revenue; for, they said, the conditions and regulations were so onerous that the natives could not afford to bring ivory to the coast. Available statistics show that there was very little export of ivory until 1835 (Lopes de Lima, *Ensaios*).

[4] A. Bastos, *Monographia de Catumbella*, pp. 18, 25. He gives prices varying from 5 $000 to 18 $000 or even 20 $000, and remarks that slaves were later designated as servants, redeemed ones, contracted labourers, &c. The milreis (1 $000) was then worth about $1.10. Monteiro (*vide infra*) says that in the sixties 'a little nigger' could be had for 5s.

[5] J. J. Monteiro, *Angola and the River Congo*, pp. 181–4. Monteiro attributes

HISTORICAL   201

The town of Catumbela (founded 1836) played an important part in the trade of the Ovimbundu. The first trade of Bailundu, Ndulu, and Viye had been with Luanda and with the presídios on the north bank of the Kuanza, while the rest of the tribe had traded with Caconda and with Benguela. Some trade went to Egito from Bailundu, Kasongi, &c. Catumbela was first built on the left bank of the river of that name, about four miles from its mouth, at the point where caravans from Viye, Bailundu, and from nearer regions to the north of the river crossed to go to Benguela. Immediately some began to stay in Catumbela rather than go on to Benguela, some fifteen miles farther. The nearness of Catumbela to Lobito Bay, a favourite hide-out for slavers and other contrabandists, was another advantage.[1] In 1856 the commercial houses of Catumbela completed a move to the right bank of the river, and after that the caravans from the interior had no further need for going on to Benguela. Just previously, in 1852, Silva Porto had 'broken a new trail' from Viye to Catumbela by way of Bailundu, Civula, and Cisanji, thus avoiding entirely the regions of Ciyaka and Ganda where the caravans were 'continually assaulted, robbed, and at times cut to pieces by the highwaymen of those regions'.[2]

The old road in its descent from the plateau followed more nearly (although not entirely) a natural watershed, but even though the new one had to cross some large and turbulent streams, it was much superior because of the greater safety which it offered. Silva Porto's road was 'new' in that part where it took its final rise to the Highland and in most of the section that crossed the Umbundu country, but not in the section crossing the Cisanji country, nor in the final descent to the coast. In these latter sections it followed the same old slave caravan road, long rutted by the passage of endless loads of human misery.[3] The descent of

---

unreliability to the receivers in Cuba, &c., and not to the ships' masters. There are interesting incidents of American and other contrabandists in the *Boletim Official da Provincia de Angola*, for the years 1850–69.

[1] A. Bastos, op. cit., p. 85. In this bay ships could anchor very close in-shore, and there was a great overgrown mangrove-swamp which hid them from view to seaward.

[2] A. Bastos, op. cit., p. 9. For the date of opening of the 'new road', see *Boletim Soc. Geog. Lisboa, 5a Ser.*, p. 6; op. cit., p. 19 f. (Silva Porto's diary). I have autobiographical notes from old men in Ciyaka which give a very realistic picture of the activities of the robber-barons and their followers.

[3] Bastos, who is almost everywhere very careful of his facts and who gives

202   UMBUNDU KINSHIP AND CHARACTER

this trail along the face of the cliffs behind Catumbela may still be seen to-day.

I have noted how largely Brazil had absorbed the commerce of the colony. This was due in large part, of course, to the slave-trade, but it was also due to the fact that all foreign, i.e. non-Portuguese, ships were prohibited from having any part in the colony's trade, or even from entering its ports. This was an effort to keep all colonial trade for the motherland, and was quite in line with early colonial theory and practice. In this instance it served to enrich Brazil at the expense not only of Angola but also of Portugal itself, and it is rather strange that this ruinous policy should have persisted even after the separation of Brazil. In 1844 the two ports of Luanda and Benguela were opened to ships of all the world. Lopes de Lima remarks[1] that not only did foreign commerce flow in, but Portuguese commerce with the colony also increased greatly. It must not be supposed that Angola at once became a great example of Free Trade, for customs duties remained high. Only the first bars in the fence of monopoly were let down, but for that day it was a great step and it attracted trade.

In 1869 the first experimental export of raw rubber was made: a very small beginning of a very important movement.[2] The imminent importance of this export was not realized by 'the man on the spot'. In 1870 Silva Porto, tired of accusations of witch-craft by his Ovimbundu neighbours and of the increasing demands

a very truthful and realistic picture of conditions, of events, and of trends, errs in supposing that it was only with the opening of this 'new road' by Silva Porto that caravans from the interior began to come to Catumbela. Magyar, who went inland from Benguela in 1849, took the usual road via Catumbela. Even in 1795, when there was no town at Catumbela, but only a few vegetable farms, Teixeira and Mello started for the interior from there (*Annaes Mar. e Col.*, 1844, p. 159). Their itinerary in detail from Catumbela to Viye is not given, but only distances to Cisanji, to Civula, to Bailundu, and to Viye. Since their route was via Civula and Bailundu, rather than via Ciyaka and Wambu (Huambo), and therefore the route of Silva Porto's 'new' road, I am inclined to believe that the latter was probably a return to a route formerly used. Magyar gives a good description of the route via Ciyaka. The route via Bailundu has been described by scores of writers from Silva Porto through Cameron, the early missionaries (of the A.B.C.F.M.), Nevinson, *et al.*, down to 1910, when the road was abandoned for the Benguela Railway. There are now three motor roads from the Highland to the coast, but none of them follows the old slavers' route except in certain short sections.

[1] *Ensaios*, part i, pp. 78, 135.

[2] Bastos, op. cit., p. 24; *Boletim Official*, 1870 (Exports for 1869); *Benguella, Relatório do Districto de*, 1891, p. 29.

HISTORICAL 203

for tribute and other exactions of King Konya Cilemo, successor to the stool of Viye, decided to leave his place at Belmonte (Viye) for Benguela,[1] where he remained for ten years. A year later Guilherme Gonçalves left to his sons his flourishing settlement near Kamundongo (Viye), and sailed for Lisbon, intending to stay indefinitely.[2] These two men were the leading traders established in the Highland, but little idea had they that the small trickle of rubber exports begun in 1869 would so soon inaugurate a new era in Central African trade. It was only in 1882 that rubber took even second place in the exports (after bees-wax),[3] but already in 1872[4] its importance was becoming evident, and by 1877 individual Ovimbundu of Viye had already turned over considerable fortunes in the trade.[5] Bastos seems to be correct in taking 1874 as the beginning of this new era in the trade of the region.[6] For the Ovimbundu, the preceding decades, indeed the preceding century or even centuries, had been a period of preparation for the trade which was now beginning. For them the rubber trade, from 1874 until its close in 1916, was the classical period of commercial activity.

The time of preparation had necessarily developed in the Ovimbundu the intellectual acumen, venturesomeness, a technique of co-operation both within their own social groupings and with outsiders, a knowledge of people, places, and things of their Central African world, together with the other qualities which enabled them to carry on their far-flung trading activities. These qualities merit a fuller description (q.v. *infra*, p. 206 f.). During this earlier period, since many of their travels were naturally exploratory, the Ovimbundu probably travelled more widely than during the time of the rubber trade. There were hardly any territories within the bounds of the Congo River, the Lakes, and the Kalahari Desert which they had not penetrated.[7] Some Ovimbundu went even farther afield as employees of European traders or on their own account. A ready example is Domingos Cakahanga and his companions who, in the employ of Silva Porto during the years

[1] *Boletim Soc. Geog. Lisboa, 5a Ser.*, p. 20.
[2] See Cameron, op. cit., p. 400.
[3] *Benguella*, op. cit., 1887, pp. 24 ff.   [4] *Benguella*, op. cit., 1892, p. 29.
[5] Serpa Pinto, op. cit., p. 161 f.   [6] Bastos, op. cit., p. 24.
[7] Serpa Pinto, op. cit., p. 164; L. Magyar, op. cit., pp. 298, 299. The best proof, however, is the fact of the geographical and tribal names found in the Umbundu language.

204 UMBUNDU KINSHIP AND CHARACTER

1853–4, crossed Africa from Benguela to the mouth of the Rovuma.[1]

Nor was this the only transcontinental journey effected by Ovimbundu traders.[2] Such long-distance expeditions were not always the most profitable, and certainly the relatively shorter journeys of the time of the rubber trade must have been much more lucrative. Indeed, the judgement of Magyar was that the Ovimbundu generally got more enjoyment and excitement than monetary gain from their expeditions.[3]

Mention has been made that the several Umbundu kingdoms fell in line with the trading activities of Bailundu and Viye. By the beginning of the period of great activity this had eventuated in a loose system of alliances or mutual understandings to the effect that the traders and caravans of each would be tolerated in, and allowed passage through, the territory of the other. At times their 'trade-agreements' seem to have embraced all the Umbundu-speaking peoples, but violations were frequent,[4] and complaints of violations seem to have been almost the regular state of affairs as between Viye and the Ciyaka-Cingolo-Citata group. There also developed regional industrial and commercial specializations. In Magyar's time there was a great metal industry at Ekovongo, the capital of Viye, making hoes for trade with the interior,[5] but by 1875 this work seems to have ceased,[6] for although hoes were still

[1] Cakahanga kept a diary which was edited by Silva Porto and published under the title 'Third Voyage' in the *Boletim Official* of Angola, 1856–7, and later in the *Annaes do Cons. Ultr. Ia Ser.* A summary of this diary appeared in the *Proceedings of the Royal Geographical Society* of London, 1860, pp. 136–49, but the translator and editor mistakenly believed that Silva Porto had himself crossed Africa, and added to the confusion by calling the Ovimbundu 'Arabs from Zanzibar'. Silva Porto himself only went as far as Naliele, and it seems that there were 'Arabs' or Swahili in the party, but how far they accompanied it is not clear. That the diary was kept by Cakahanga is evident, for the 'Arabs' could write no language known to Silva Porto.

[2] See Magyar, op. cit., p. 297.

[3] Ibid., p. 299. This referred only to Magyar's time, 1849–57, but I feel it to be a judgement capable of wider extension. Serpa Pinto says that in 1878 he met many who 'turned over capital of a thousand to twelve hundred pounds sterling and some even more; one indeed . . . arrived during my sojourn . . . from the interior where he had traded on his own account to the extent of . . . about £3,500!' (op. cit., p. 161 f.). However, there were also losses and often, so that Magyar's dictum is worth remembering.

[4] e.g. see account of dispute between Ekuikui (Bailundu) and Njambayamina (Viye) in *Missionary Herald*, 1886, pp. 228 f., 452, 508; 1887, p. 463.

[5] L. Magyar, op. cit., p. 297.

[6] See negative testimony of Cameron, of Serpa Pinto, and of early missionaries.

HISTORICAL

made, there as elsewhere throughout the Umbundu-speaking
territory, their wholesale manufacture was only carried on in
Ndulu. This was a natural specialization, for the best and most
easily accessible deposits of iron ore are in the Ndulu country,[1]
whose smiths have become justly famous. In exchange for hoes
they received palm-oil or cattle from other regions, or salt, rum,
or goods from the coast. Other regional specializations were—
Kasongi and the Sele country for palm-oil, Cikuma for bees-wax
(also obtained from the interior), cattle from Ngalangi, Kalukembe, Cilengi, and farther south. Ciyaka, Civula, and Bailundu
took much corn-meal to the coast in those early days. 'Trade-
agreements' were also made beyond the Umbundu-speaking area.
At first these were strictly one-way affairs, allowing the Ovimbundu traders to operate in many lands, near and far, since this
was to the advantage of the rulers of those lands. At the same
time, the men from Bailundu and Viye did and said everything
possible to discourage the interior peoples from venturing out on
their own account.[2] Later, when the trade, as well as knowledge
of the whites and their trade, spread, arrangements were made
between the king of Viye and various interior chiefs allowing them
to send their own caravans through to the coast, and gifts were
exchanged periodically.[3]

Their very early introduction to articles of European use and
manufacture has undoubtedly had great influence upon the
development of the Ovimbundu. Their early and thorough
familiarity with fire-arms certainly played a decisive role in their
national formation and subsequent history. The introduction
of domestic plants and animals from abroad is an important
subject, but too broad for treatment at this time. The early
introduction of European-manufactured goods has had profound

[1] See article on smelting and smithing in Ndulu by F. W. Read in *Journal of
the African Society*, 1902, pp. 44-9.

[2] Livingstone tells of the displeasure of the Ovimbundu ('Mambari') at
meeting the Makololo near Luanda. The Ovimbundu tried to frighten them
from trading with the whites with tall tales, making the whites out as impossibly
clever magicians and wizards (op. cit., p. 384). Cameron and his east-coast
carriers experienced the displeasure of Viye people owing to jealousy of the
same sort, but no longer so openly expressed (op. cit., p. 406).

[3] The Muata-Yanvo of Lunda was one of those who had such a 'trade-
agreement' with Viye. Silva Porto notes in his diary on 14 Jan. 1880 that an
embassy from the Muata-Yanvo had arrived with a tusk of ivory for Cilemo
(*Boletim Soc. Geog. Lisboa, 5a Ser.*, p. 148).

206 UMBUNDU KINSHIP AND CHARACTER

influences. The stock to which the common people belong were wearers of skins, which is true of many of them to the present time. The people from whom the ruling houses came have a highly developed weaving industry. The 'Ngangela' neighbours, who have also contributed elements to the racial make-up of the Ovimbundu, make and use bark-cloth. The Ovimbundu evidently gave up the use of skins for clothing more than a hundred years ago.[1] This fact, and the additional one that they never developed weaving or bark-cloth industries, was probably due to their early and widespread use of trade-cloth. Rum came with the slave-trade from Brazil. They were almost inseparable. The ships which fetched the slaves came laden with rum distilled in Brazil. The rum was used in buying the slaves, and much more of it was consumed by Ovimbundu—traders, chiefs, and retainers—than by the interior people. Thus, while the slave-trade had such a disruptive influence in the life of the interior tribes, rum did much to corrupt the Ovimbundu. Native tradition[2] and the accounts of early travellers agree on this point. Rum continued to come from Brazil and from other countries or oversea colonies all through this early period, but import was partly supplanted by distillation at the coast, and this process was soon learned by the Ovimbundu themselves.

The part which the Umbundu trade had in spreading the goods and uses of the outside world is a fascinating subject and one which would repay study. Ethnographical and historical knowledge of Central Africa is not yet so extensive or precise that the dates and places of these movements can be plotted with certainty. Professor C. M. Doke records that Nkumine, who ruled the Lamba sometime before 1840, sold many of his people 'as slaves to the Mbundu traders from the West Coast for calico, guns, and powder'.[3] It is important to remember that throughout this period the Ovimbundu were for all this part of Africa the chief intermediaries in the slave-trade. These activities affected the ultimate

---

[1] See Magyar, *passim*.

[2] A Ngalangi tradition says that from the time of King Ndumba II (*c.* 1840) rum was so plentiful that it was poured into troughs, whence it was lapped up by all—men, women, and children. A constant difficulty encountered by the early missionaries was the objection of chiefs and their counsellors to the missionaries' refusal to give liberal presents of rum, as did all the traders.

[3] C. M. Doke, *The Lambas of Northern Rhodesia* (London: Harrap, 1931), pp. 36, 37.

HISTORICAL 207

physical composition of the Ovimbundu themselves, and also their character and accepted attitudes. Livingstone told of the beginning of their trade with the Makololo in 1850, and how they had visited the Barotse 'in ancient times'.[1] These items fit into the picture of that early period of trading activities which is had from studying Umbundu traditional history in the light of documents such as Silva Porto's diaries, Magyar's account,[2] the historical monograph of Augusto Bastos, the comments of travellers,[3] and of the early missionaries.

Period of the Rubber Trade, 1874–1911. Turning now to the rubber trade, that time may conveniently be divided into three periods: from 1874 until 1886, during which only 'first-class' rubber (from the plants themselves)[4] was exported; from 1886, when the discovery of 'second-class' or 'red rubber' (from a root)[5] caused a great boom which lasted until 1900; and, finally, the period of decline until the rubber export stopped in 1916, though for the Ovimbundu it had already practically stopped several years earlier.

Of the older exports only bees-wax and ivory survived along with rubber. The former of these was somewhat neglected, while the importance of the latter continued in Benguela only until about 1893 when the frontier of the Congo was closed. Bastos remarks that after 1900 not a single tusk appeared.[6] Already in 1880 Silva Porto had to go beyond Lunda to the middle Kasai before he found ivory.[7] At that time most of the ivory trade was in the hands of Viye traders. Between 2 November 1879, when Silva Porto left Catumbela, and 26 November when he reached Belmonte (Viye), there passed him about forty caravans on their way to the coast. Of these, ten carried ivory, practically all of which

---

[1] D. Livingstone, op. cit., p. 91 f. The business-like methods of the Ovimbundu were commented upon later, see op. cit., p. 271.

[2] The picture which Magyar (*Reisen in Süd-Afrika*) gives of Umbundu life in that early period is very good, but for an understanding of many terms used a knowledge of Portuguese and Umbundu is quite necessary. His truthfulness with regard to the slave-trade must be questioned when confronted by evidence from Valdez, Monteiro, and especially from Bastos.

[3] Valdez, op. cit.; Monteiro, op. cit.; Graça, op. cit.; Serpa Pinto, op. cit.; Capello and Ivens, *From Benguella to the Territory of Yacca.*

[4] Principally *Landolphia*, which are big woody climbers; also the tall and stately *Funtumia elastica.*   [5] Especially the *Carpodinus chylorrhiza.*

[6] Bastos, op. cit., p. 39. From this time until 1913 Angola continued to export ivory in ever-decreasing quantities, but from the port of Mossamedes and therefore not from the Umbundu country.

[7] *Boletim Soc. Geog. Lisboa*, 6a Ser., pp. 189 f., 256.

208   UMBUNDU KINSHIP AND CHARACTER

were from Viye,[1] since Viye was nearest to what was then the source of supply—Luva, Katanga, Barotze, &c. Caravans from other regions could and did pass through Viye, but they found it more economical and advantageous to go to other regions for other commodities. Bees-wax was to be found in most of the neighbouring regions and was brought to the coast by traders of all the Umbundu kingdoms. The same may be said of the 'first-class' rubber.[2] It was found chiefly in the forest regions of the interior, and the distance and consequent time involved made it a product hardly more profitable than bees-wax. Rubber was then simply one product along with the others, and until 1886 its export had its ups and downs.

Red Rubber, 1886–1900. In 1886 a caravan of Ovimbundu came down to Catumbela with loads of 'red rubber' for the first time. They had gotten it in the sandy country to the east of the Kuanza River, and a great deal nearer than the region of the 'first-class' rubber. At first, the price paid for this 'red rubber' was lower than for the other, but whereas a caravan could not procure loads of the first in less than eight months, the 'red rubber' could be gotten within three months.[3] Subsequently the red rubber was found to have certain superior qualities so that the higher price came to be paid for it. Immediately the export of rubber from Benguela increased enormously and reached undreamed-of totals.[4] Beeswax

[1] *Boletim Soc. Geog. Lisboa*, 5a Ser., pp. 5, 6, 10, 16.

[2] There are very interesting summaries and descriptions of the commercial activities of the period—both native and European—in the *Relatorios do Districto de Benguella*, 1887, 1891 (Ministerio da Marinha e Ultramar, Lisboa, 1888, 1894).

[3] See a note in *Proceedings of the Royal Geographical Society*, 1888, p. 450 f.

[4] The values of the three leading products exported from Benguela from 1886 to 1891 were as follows (from *Relatorios do Districto de Benguella*, 1887, 1891):

Product			1886	1887	1888
Rubber	.	.	65,210$153	286,937$018	664,786$870
Wax	.	.	187,483$964	158,945$996	109,734$140
Ivory	.	.	37,692$536	36,923$042	29,997$968

Product			1889	1890	1891
Rubber	.	.	665,746$552	781,057$860	1,042,112$070
Wax	.	.	133,436$344	93,680$580	123,645$876
Ivory	.	.	31,701$133	11,298$782	45,392$534

For further statistical reports of this period, see also *Portugal, Ministerio da Marinha e Ultramar, Relatório, Propostos de Lei*, &c. (Lisboa, 1899), p. 266 f.

HISTORICAL

dropped off; of ivory there was no more. From 1893 on, says Bastos, rubber was practically the sole export of the District of Benguela and of its hinterland.[1] In 1891 more than one million milreis' worth of rubber was exported from Benguela, sixteen times as much as was exported only five years before, and three and one-half times the value of the *three* leading exports in 1886. Until 1891 this increase was not at the expense of other exports, but rather in addition to them.

All of this rubber, and the other exports as well, came to the coast in caravans of the Ovimbundu or their neighbours. In its inception and its great development it was an enterprise of the Ovimbundu. Everyone who was able to carry a load joined a caravan. It had always been the custom to take boys on trading expeditions, as young as they could go—say, from their tenth year—as a part of their education. Now girls were also taken and hardly any but the women stayed at home to raise the crops and provide rations for the caravans. European residents experienced great difficulty in securing necessary porters,[2] and this was one reason for finally putting through the wagon-road from Benguela to Caconda.[3] It was extended to Viye during the military campaign of 1890. The fever of the rubber trade reached into all the villages of the land and took in everyone able to travel. Mission schools had been established since 1881, but they had but few pupils until 1900. There were also other reasons for this, but a principal one was the attractiveness of the rubber trade.[4] Even the kings found it more difficult to gather armies for their wars: trade had become more attractive than the possibility of plunder.

Of all the kings who ruled the various Umbundu kingdoms during this time, the one who is best remembered is Ekuikui (II) of Bailundu (1876–93). Tradition has begun to ascribe to him and to his reign some things which properly belong to earlier

---

[1] Bastos, op. cit., p. 34. He does not include *serviçaes* in the exports, since they all went to the mainland or island plantations, but he remarks that at this time the price rose to even 90 $000 (p. 33). The rise in price was perhaps due to the smaller supply owing to the preoccupation of the Ovimbundu with the rubber trade. [2] See *Missionary Herald*, 1889, p. 350.

[3] *Benguella*, 1891, op. cit., p. 10.

[4] The reports of the governor of Benguela, to which reference has been made, also mentioned this fact, saying that although the American missions were intelligently directed, their results were small, since parents would not send their children to learn while they could pick up loads of rubber (1887, p. 19; 1891, p. 20).

P

210 UMBUNDU KINSHIP AND CHARACTER

times, which is a sure sign of his greatness in Umbundu estimation. Ekuikui's reign marked the end of an era and the beginning of another, not only for the people of Bailundu, but for all the Ovimbundu. The rubber trade had begun just before he came to the stool and his reign saw its intensive development. Tradition is probably right in placing the beginning of intensive agricultural pursuits during Ekuikui's time, for the great development of trade, need for rations for the long journeys, and a market for foodstuffs at the coast provided the necessary stimulus to cultivate beyond immediate seasonal need. Ekuikui carried on the tradition of warfare[1] which was so large a part of his ancestral heritage, but he had the good sense to attempt no large-scale operations either against his relatively powerful Ovimbundu confrères, or against European establishments. There was plenty of provocation[2] and no lack of warlike counsel, but he probably realized that the tenor of the times was against such operations. Had his contemporaries of Viye and his own successors been possessed of equal good sense, the Ovimbundu might have been saved some very difficult times and not a little bloodshed. The military occupation of Viye came about in 1890, after a disastrous war brought on by foolishly high-handed treatment on the part of King Ndunduma[3] and his counsellors of a little expedition bound for the interior under Captain Paiva Couceiro, and of Silva Porto,[4] resulting in the suicide of the latter. The ruler and people of Viye relied on a largely magical defence against Boer sharpshooters and Portuguese field artillery with Krupp guns. When finally Ndunduma came in and gave himself up[5] he was exiled to São Tiago in the Cape Verde Islands,

[1] For King Ekuikui's wars see *Missionary Herald*, 1882, p. 225; 1883, p. 339; 1884, pp. 145 f., 504; 1885, pp. 279, 355, 375; 1889, p. 67; 1890, p. 292.

[2] See op. cit., 1886, pp. 228 f., 452, 508.

[3] *Ndunduma* (Thunderer) was the name assumed by Cikunyu when he took office after a *coup d'état* in 1888 (see *Missionary Herald*, 1889, p. 242 f.).

[4] Antonio Francisco Ferreira da Silva Porto, appointed 'Captain-major and exterior judge' of Bihe in 1885. He had authority only over the European residents, but he knew the country and people well and had tried to bring about a peaceful occupation of the country; neither the Government in Benguela nor the native authorities, however, would take his advice. His suicide brought the importance of the Umbundu country to the fore, and he became a Portuguese national hero.

[5] It was the Rev. W. H. Sanders, in charge of Kamundongo Mission Station, who sought Ndunduma and got him to surrender in order to avoid further slaughter. For a report of this 'war' see *Relatorio do Districto de Benguella*, 1891, pp. 12–14; also *Missionary Herald*, 1891, pp. 47, 63 f., 88, 108 f.; Dr. J. Johnston, *Romance versus Reality in South Central Africa*, pp. 59–63. F. S. Arnot (*Bihe*

HISTORICAL 211

and the country settled down to the rule of 'the Fort' with Ndunduma's successor named by the captain-major. The occupation of Bailundu was effected at that same time,[1] while Ekuikui yet ruled, but for several years only a nominal force was employed.[2] In 1896 Ekuikui's successor, Numa II, attacked the fort, and the captain-major burned the *ombala*[3] in retaliation. From 1890 European traders settled in both Viye and Bailundu in ever-increasing numbers.[4] Then came the 'Bailundu War' of 1902,[5] after which the occupation of the whole Umbundu country was quickly completed.

The operations of 1890 had only interrupted the ivory trade. The campaign of 1902 completely paralysed trade in and with the interior, and greatly aggravated a depression which the District of Benguela was feeling because of a fall from the high prices which rubber had enjoyed in 1898–9.[6] After the war it seemed that trade would soon regain its former levels, and the export statistics show that for a time it did so, but closer inspection and a consideration of other factors which entered into the situation show that this was the beginning of the end. The price of rubber never regained its former level, so that the high value of exports reported represents an even larger quantity than before. The increased quantity largely represented a greatly debased product, for the native traders and producers understood nothing

---

and Garenganze, pp. 19–23) also wrote of these incidents but with more of the personal element and perhaps less accuracy.

[1] *Relatorio, Benguella*, 1892, p. 13 f.

[2] In 1892 there were 2 soldiers in Bailundu, 135 in Viye, 21 in Caconda (*Benguella*, op. cit., 1891, p. 15). Bailundu tradition says that (native) soldiers were first brought in disguised as porters with loads of goods.

[3] *Ombala*, capital village.   [4] A. Bastos, op. cit., pp. 36, 43.

[5] This war was named in Umbundu after the Bailundu war leader, *Mutu ya Kevela*. He is named among the kings, but it was only during the war that he assumed power. The immediate causes were excesses on the part of European residents against the natives, especially in connexion with 'the recruiting of contract labour'. The best work on the subject is in the nature of a report written by the man who was then governor, Cabral Moncada, *A Campanha do Bailundo* (Luanda, 1903). General ideas may be had from *Missionary Herald*, 1902, pp. 353, 400, 452 f., 520 f.; 1903, pp. 22 f., 69 f., 122, 211 f.; H. W. Nevinson, op. cit., p. 157 f.; and J. T. Tucker, *Drums in the Darkness*, p. 122 f. The account given by Keiling (*Quarenta Anos de África*) is of interest for certain details of this war, but its statements are inaccurate and its judgements unreliable. The missionaries sought to dissuade the natives from taking up arms, and once the fighting had begun they provided medical services for both sides and sent food-supplies to the garrison of the beleaguered Portuguese fort.

[6] A. Bastos, op. cit., p. 39 f.

212 UMBUNDU KINSHIP AND CHARACTER

of price fluctuations and sought by every means to maintain the former level of returns. The European traders aided and abetted this process in order to bolster up their credit, for from 1887, when the boom began, most of them were operating on shoe-strings. The result was almost immediate. Benguela rubber was classified as 'third-class' at a price one-fourth the former rate.[1] This was the end of the rubber trade. With the establishment of plantations in the East Indies, in South America, and on the African west coast, which produced a uniformly high quality, the native-produced wild rubber of Angola ceased to have any quotation whatever.[2]

Export statistics show that the totals in quantity and value of rubber exported were nearly as large in 1916 as in 1888, and that in 1918 and 1919 they fell to almost nothing,[3] but for the Ovimbundu the rubber trade ended in 1911—'the year of the great hunger in the Ngangela country'. They remember that many caravans which went out at the beginning of that year's dry season never did return, or that only a few of their stronger members returned—mere skeletons and shadows. *Ngandi*[4] tried to eat wax and died; *Ngandi* killed and ate his younger brother, saying, 'It is better that one of us should live to return, rather than both die.' The caravans usually carried actual rations for only a few days of the outward journey (to last through the 'Hungry Country'), and relied on buying the food needed for the rest of the time. This experience put an end to a trade which was already passing out of the hands of the Ovimbundu—owing to the multiplication of European trading establishments, not only throughout the Umbundu country but even in the 'Ngangela' regions, and the building of the Benguela Railway, which finally put an end to porterage and the trading caravans of former days.[5]

---

[1] A. Bastos, op. cit., pp. 40 ff.

[2] In 1942, after the capture of Malaya and the Dutch East Indies by the Japanese and the consequent acute shortage of rubber, the gathering of wild rubber in eastern Angola was resumed, most of the product going to Britain. Some, however, has gone to the national factories at Luanda and in Portugal, and consequently there is a stimulus to maintain the production of wild rubber in the colony, but unless more humane methods are used with the native producers the present limited supply is bound to fall off.

[3] Statistics of export and import are given by F. Trancoso, op. cit. The figures for rubber from 1888 to 1919 are on p. 36.

[4] *Ngandi*, the Umbundu equivalent for 'John Doe' or 'So-and-so'.

[5] The Benguela Railway (*Caminho de Ferro de Benguela*) began construction in 1904; in 1910 it reached Cuma (198 miles) in Ciyaka, well up on the Plateau

HISTORICAL

It must not be supposed that trade has been abandoned. Every sale or exchange of field or garden produce is a serious trading operation. Produce will often be carried a very long way for a very small advantage, or even for no apparent gain. The successively lower economic levels to which the colony, and especially the natives, have fallen since the close of the rubber trade is a factor. Individual trading, involving journeys into even such distant regions as Ovamboland, is a latter-day development since European rule has made for greater personal security.

Another factor which operated to end all large-scale trading operations of the Ovimbundu was the disappearance of the traffic in human beings. It has been shown that even before they ruled over the Ovimbundu the 'Jagas' were leading intermediaries in this traffic, and the Ovimbundu have continued in this role right down to the period under review. Whatever name or form it bore at the coast, in the interior the traffic was the same. At the height of the rubber boom this traffic, along with other activities, suffered a decline, being somewhat less profitable than rubber. At that time came the peak of the rum trade and the demoralization which it brought turned the point of the 'contract labour' traffic in upon the Ovimbundu themselves. Such Umbundu customs as getting into debt, the pawning of relatives, and also such factors as times of food scarcity, quickly taken advantage of by the traders, served to exacerbate the hardships, and the result was the native uprising of 1902 known as the 'Bailundu Campaign', but extending beyond the limits of Bailundu. The effects of this uprising upon trade have already been noted. Pending investigation of its causes, the export of 'contract labourers' was stopped,[1] but the practice was soon resumed. The scandalous conditions then obtaining in the neighbouring 'Congo Free State' almost from its founding until 1908 greatly aided and abetted the slave-traffic, however much this new frontier may have interfered with trade in ivory and rubber. Trade with the *revoltés* was particularly lucrative to Ovimbundu and other traders of Angola. Powder and arms were an especially important item in this trade.

and just under the rim of the Highland. In 1916 construction stopped at Chinguar (312 miles and on the edge of Viye) until after World War I. It was completed to the Angola frontier in 1929 and the Belgian section finished in 1931, with transcontinental connexion at Elizabethville.

[1] Cabral Moncada, op. cit.; Massano de Amorim, *Relatorio sôbre os acontecimentos do Bailundo* (Loanda, 1903); *Missionary Herald*, 1903, p. 69.

214   UMBUNDU KINSHIP AND CHARACTER

It was only with the beginning of World War I that trade in powder and fire-arms was stopped. For more than a century Portuguese patriots and thinkers had been insisting upon the necessity for ending the export of man-power, so evidently impoverishing in its effects on the life of the colony.[1] Law succeeded law, and regulation followed regulation, but there was little real change.[2] With the Republic,[3] however, real changes began. Conditions were investigated,[4] and although complete and immediate reform could hardly have been expected, changes did begin. Provisions for manumission upon presentation to authority were made and carried out. Repatriation from island and mainland plantations began to be undertaken. This was the origin of small communities of Cokue and other 'Ngangela' people now living at various points in the Umbundu country. From the plantations they were repatriated to 'their places of origin', which were, however, not their own homes but the places whence they had been sold into servitude. Under various regulatory practices, contract labour has been continued down to the present day. The depression which came to Central Africa in 1930 reduced the demand to a minimum, and for a few years it did not represent a serious problem in the life of the Ovimbundu. There was a time of great activity in road building (approximately 1915–32) when the demands for labour were a serious problem to Umbundu life. Soon after the opening of World War II a strong demand for colonial products revived the industries of Angola and stimulated the creation of new ones. The consequent demand for labour and the means used to supply it have come to constitute the most severe trial which has yet come to the Ovimbundu. Their docility has made this service bear more hardly on them than on some other people of the colony. Their

[1] e.g. Saldanha da Gama, *Memoria*, 1814; Sá da Bandeira, 1839; Lopes de Lima, *Ensaios* (1846), pp. xxxviii, 6 f., 44 f.; Casmiro, *Africa Nostra*, p. 60 f.

[2] The principal laws were promulgated as follows: 1836 (Formal abolition of the traffic); 1839 (Authorizing co-operation with the international naval squadron); 1840, 1841, 1845 (Supplementary ordinances); 1875 (Law of Liberation and regulation of contract labour); 1878, 1889 (Further regulations); 1899 (Dealing with 'corrective labour'); 1902, 1903 (Further regulation of recruitment).

[3] Proclaimed in Portugal, 5 Oct., 1910.

[4] A Commission came from Lisbon that same year and took testimony throughout the colony. For conditions just previous to the Republic, see Nevinson, op. cit.; C. A. Swan, *The Slavery of To-day* (1909); H. R. F. Bourne, *Slave Traffic in Portuguese Africa* (1908); W. A. Cadbury, *Labour in Portuguese West Africa* (2nd ed. 1910); C. Harding, *In Remotest Barotseland* (1905).

HISTORICAL

geographic position in the centre of the colony has also made it harder for them to evade it. Nevertheless, many have emigrated. In 1941 and again in 1944, when the writer visited South Africa, he found thousands of Ovimbundu on the Rand and many more in the Rhodesias and the Congo. Many are also known to have gone to the South-West Territory and to Bechuanaland, and some even to such distant points as Natal's north coast and French Equatorial Africa.[1]

Recent Developments

Currency, in the sense of money, is quite a recent introduction to the Ovimbundu. To the end of their trading activities, cloth ('trade goods') was the standard of exchange. Although dependence upon world markets caused prices to fluctuate with the course of the rubber trade, as we have seen, there was not, however, the great range which follows the fluctuations of the money market through a course of inflation and deflation. The Ovimbundu had had some dealings in money before the time of World War I, when there was a silver coinage, so that the depreciation which set in about 1921 was all the more confusing to them. This is not the place to discuss the finances and banking of Angola, but it must be noted that the conversion of the 'Escudo' into the 'Angolar' in 1928 at the rate of Ag. 0,80 to Esc. 1 $00 greatly increased the sense of confusion among the natives. This was only to be expected when the native tax remained at Ag. 80,00 where it was Esc. 80,00 before, whereas daily wages to contract labourers became Ag. 0,80 where before they were Esc. 1 $00. The confusion was considerable.[2]

Taxes began to be levied soon after military occupation, but for some years they were very small, especially in relation to opportunities for earning. When the head-tax reached Esc. 80,00 it remained at that figure for some years. In 1935 a 'work tax' and

---

[1] This state of affairs is frequently and quite freely commented upon in the Angola papers. For a recent notice see local correspondence entitled 'Notícias do Cuma' in the *Voz do Planalto* (Nova Lisboa) for 17 Aug. 1946. One of the most serious recent indictments is contained in an article in O *Farolim*, Luanda, 5 Nov. 1945, by Padre J. Alves Correia. This distinguished writer asserts that the present labour policy is 'killing the goose which lays the golden egg'.

[2] For finance, currency, banking, and economic conditions in general, see Department of Overseas Trade, *Economic Conditions in Angola*, H.M.S.O., 1929. There are also reports for 1923 and 1925, but the one for 1929 covers the previous decade.

216   UMBUNDU KINSHIP AND CHARACTER

another small amount were added, so that it is now Ag. 91,00.[1] This is not high in comparison with the figures for the Union of South Africa and some other African territories, but opportunities for earning in Angola are small. Wages and prices of produce are low indeed. These problems of labour and of taxation are much the same in many South and Central African territories. Their present-day poverty bears very hardly upon the Ovimbundu who saw much more prosperous times in the days of their large-scale trading.

Land. The ownership and occupation of land by natives does not present the acute problem in Angola which it does in several African territories. Natives have not been herded on to reserves, for rigid segregation is not the Portuguese idea, nor has there yet been occupation of land by European settlers on a scale sufficient to encroach upon the land needed by natives, save in a few localities. A large proportion of the concessions provisionally taken out by Europeans in 1919–25 have reverted to the State for failure to meet requirements, as, for example, to bring a stated proportion under cultivation. Many schemes for European colonization in the Benguela Highland have been projected from time to time. The Portuguese law protects the native in his holdings, but since European settlers often find ways to circumvent the intent of the law, and since an increasing European colonization is apt to be a threat to native holdings, a simplification of the machinery whereby the natives may secure sure title to communal or to individual holdings is highly desirable.[2]

Whatever else may be said, however, it is good to be able to report that at the present time the Ovimbundu have their land. This fact has been a very important factor in their transition from

[1] About $4.00 at present exchange. In 1937 the economic year was changed to the calendar year, and in most districts payment of an extra half-year's tax was required. About 1941 the tax was again raised, to Ag. 108,00, and in 1945 it was again put up, to 120,00. These figures are for most of the districts inhabited by the Ovimbundu. In some areas, especially frontier areas, the amounts levied are considerably lower.

[2] For the present official status of the questions of administration, land, labour, &c., see Comte J. de Penha-Garcia, *Organisation politique et administrative de l'empire colonial portugais*, Inst. Col. Int'n'l (1936); ibid. (ed.), *Les Colonies portugaises* (1931); a useful summary of the same will be found in Lord Hailey, *An African Survey* (London: 1938), pp. 213–16, 796 f. There is a discussion of these problems in J. T. Tucker, *Angola, Land of the Blacksmith Prince* (1933), chap. 8. See also Valdez dos Santos, *Angola, Coração do Império* (Lisboa: Agência Geral das Colónias, 1945).

HISTORICAL 217

the occupations of warfare and of trade to the more settled agricultural life. And it is the possession and cultivation of land which provides a minimum basis for those who are also able to engage in any sort of trade, either commercial or one of the handicrafts.

Health. A sanitary history, or the course of health among the Ovimbundu throughout their national existence, would be of interest if it could be made known. Legend tells of a time in the distant past when sickness was rare and death came hardly ever, if at all. It is said that hasty burials were not permitted because there had been cases of the supposed corpse returning to life. Some have taken this to mean that the tribe came from a more healthful region than the one which it now occupies, but it seems rather to be a traditional recognition of the fact that many of the diseases and bodily ills which at present afflict the Ovimbundu are of comparatively recent date. The time of arrival of some of these unwelcome guests can be estimated. Some are the subject of traditional tales as, for example, the jigger[1] (*pulex penetrans*), which a Ngalangi tradition says came to them from Bailundu, and Bailundu tradition says was first recognized in the time of Ekongo-liohombo (*c.* 1875) or Ekuikui II (*c.* 1876–93). Now the jigger is well known in Africa as an importation from South America, and the time of its first appearance could probably be determined. This parasite is widely present in tropical Africa, but there are some regions which it has not (yet) reached.[2] Its coming to Angola is probably, therefore, of recent date. Silva Porto, writing in 1879, said, 'This evil is of recent date on the coast . . . (*pulex penetrans*).'[3] The first notice of this pest which reached the pages of the *Boletim Official* of Angola was in 1875. If this date really represents the time when the jigger first appeared in Angola, it seems strange that it should have been so late, in view of the slave-ships ferrying back and forth from Brazil for the previous three hundred years.

Small-pox[4] might also be thought of as a recent arrival for, according to a note in the *Boletim Official*, it first appeared in Novo Redondo in June 1864, having been brought from Luanda by ships' crews.[5] Its first appearance on the Plateau, however,

---

[1] *Ewundu* or *ocindiundiu* is the Umbundu name, from *oku wunda*, to hide (the hidden one).

[2] e.g. Amboland, according to Umbundu testimony.

[3] *Boletim Soc. Geog. Lisboa*, 5a Ser., p. 10.

[4] *Ocingongo* is the Umbundu name.

[5] *Boletim Official da Provincia de Angola*, 1865, no. 5.

218   UMBUNDU KINSHIP AND CHARACTER

was prior to this, for it was mentioned by Magyar.[1] Among the imported diseases are grippe, pneumonia, tuberculosis, and other complaints of the lungs and bronchia; the venereal diseases (especially syphilis); several so-called 'children's diseases' such as measles, scarlet fever, mumps, &c.[2] Typhoid fever is only beginning to appear, although it has long been known at the coast, at Malange (to the north), &c.[3] Diseases of other regions, as tropical ulcers, sleeping sickness, &c., are found only in patients coming from regions affected with those ills.

In comparison with the diet of other non-cattle-keeping tribes of West and Central Africa, the diet of the Ovimbundu is fairly satisfactory. Certain it is that the articles imported by the Portuguese from America and elsewhere have done much to enrich the diet of this people. Only the mention of maize,[4] their staple and mainstay, makes this evident. Their early and close contact with the Portuguese gave them the advantage of many plants[5] brought by those rural-minded conquistadores,[6] which found their way inland only much later. (Mrs.) Alice K. Strangway has made an interesting study of Umbundu diet and has come to the conclusion that its principal deficiencies are fats and calcium. The Ovimbundu need to learn to make better use of the resources which are already theirs or at their command, as, for example, peanuts and soy-beans. Other improvements such as a more general use of milk and other animal foods can only come with education and an improved economic situation.

Magyar's account (1849–57) of the Ovimbundu gives the impression of a people in better health, suffering from fewer ills, and

[1] L. Magyar, op. cit., p. 290.

[2] There are Umbundu names for all the foregoing, with several names or euphemisms for some, except for the lung and bronchial complaints which are spoken of simply as *vonulo* (in the chest), and scarlet fever which is called *osalambu* (from the Portuguese *sarampo*).

[3] In 1936 there was an epidemic of typhoid at Bela Vista among Europeans and natives. Infection was traced to Catumbela (at the coast).

[4] Maize has a true Umbundu name, *epungu*, as is the case with most of the early importations which the Ovimbundu adopted, save tomatoes (*amatia*).

[5] There is a good discussion of the American plants introduced into Africa in Ficalho, *Plantas úteis da Africa Portugueza*, pp. 32 ff. In *Benguella e seu sertão*, 1617–22, p. 17, the anonymous writer states that 'all kinds of vegetables of our Portugal do very well . . . such as: large corn (i.e. *mayz*), beans of various kinds, pumpkins . . . and melons'.

[6] Cá da Mosto tells of trying to grow wheat in Senegal (João de Barros, quoted by Ficalho, op. cit., p. 29 f.).

HISTORICAL 219

generally more resistant than those whom we know to-day. Some of the imported diseases have probably been with the Ovimbundu since they first encountered Europeans, others are more recent, but all seem to be more deadly to Africans than to Europeans. This is especially true of the lung complaints, against which the Ovimbundu have little resistance, and the manner of their life makes tuberculosis very difficult to check.

Diseases native to the region also constitute a great problem, notably malaria in its several forms, leprosy, bilharzia, yaws, goitre, nutritional diseases, &c. The medical staffs of the government services and of the missions are well aware of the magnitude of the problem. The resources at their command, however, are terribly inadequate. It is urgently necessary that resources be found and made available.

Religious Development. Before bringing this historical survey to a close it is necessary to take note of certain developments with regard to religion. It was noted in passing that representatives of the ruling families had, on occasion, returned to the lands of their exodus to worship their ancestors at the ancient shrines. From this it is evident that the ancestors of the ruling families became the gods of the kingdoms over which they ruled. The commoners kept their own ancestral deities, family by family. Special cults of various sorts have grown up. From the texts of a hundred to a hundred and fifty years ago it is evident that many of the religious practices of the Ovimbundu were then similar to those which are observed at the present time. Some practices described in those texts, on the other hand, seem to have ceased or to have been altered beyond recognition. The very presence of the Europeans must have affected the rites and their observance, for their attitudes, whether of approval or of disapproval, registered over so long a period, must have produced some effect.[1] Degrees of intensity of this European contact, varying from region to region, must have had their influence in the development of regional differences. Some such differences have been noted.[2]

---

[1] Battell records that the 'Jagas' would not let him witness certain rites. Pinheiro de Lacerda, writing in 1797, says that he burned more than one hundred *oratorios* called *chacapombo* (*Annaes Mar. e. Col.*, 1845, p. 491).

[2] W. H. Sanders put down to their closer contact with Europeans the fact that the king's councillors of Viye were not 'a very dignified set. . . . They seemed to have none of that decorum which prevails among the head men of Bailundu' (*Missionary Herald*, 1886, p. 143).

220   UMBUNDU KINSHIP AND CHARACTER

The field of Umbundu reactions to cultural influences is a wide
and an important one. Whatever contact the Ovimbundu or their
progenitors may have had with the early Roman Catholic missions,
little impress seems to have been made. The cross has been
adopted as an object used in divination. Certain rites *seem* super-
ficially to resemble the procession with the Host, but there is no
indication of the assimilation of any ethical or conceptual element
from Christianity during the early or formative period.[1]

Christianity first came to the Ovimbundu with the arrival of
three missionaries at Bailundu in March 1881.[2] This was during
the reign of Ekuikui and proved to be not the least important
event of that reign. It is not within the scope of this study to give
a history of the work of this Mission.[3] Its inception was planned
as carefully as the times permitted, and although its subsequent
development did not always proceed according to plan, its progress on the whole has been of an orderly nature, and it has
produced noteworthy results which have been evaluated by deputations, by commissions, and by other visitors from time to time.[4]

The amount of interdenominational co-operation achieved in
this field is worthy of note. There are the missions of the

[1] There were missions of the Jesuits, Capuchins, Carmelites, &c., in Angola
from 1575 until about 1800, and there were priests as chaplains of the various
presídios visited by the Ovimbundu during most of their history. Major Artur
de Paiva, writing in 1890 (see *Boletim Soc. Geog. Lisboa*, 1895, p. 15 f.),
describes the ruins of a Roman Catholic mission which he found in Cingolo
(*Quingolo*) and which he judged to have dated from the end of the eighteenth
century. I have found no reference in any historical work to the founding or
operation of such a mission. It may have been built about 1770 when Governor
Souza Coutinho ordained a number of towns in the Benguela hinterland, but
the absence of specific reference to it seems to indicate that its existence was short.
[2] Messrs. Bagster, Sanders, and Miller sent out by the A.B.C.F.M. (Boston)
to inaugurate a mission in Bihe, for that region was well known from the
reputation of its traders, while Bailundu and other Umbundu regions had
scarcely been heard of.
[3] For a brief summary of the early years see Strong, *The Story of the American
Board*, pp. 336 ff.; also two articles in vol. 126 (1930) of the *Missionary Herald*,
pp. 424–9; J. T. Tucker, *Drums in the Darkness*, gives a historical treatment of
the work of this mission.
[4] There have been two 'deputations' sent to the West Central Africa Mission,
in 1911 and in 1930, reports of which were issued by the A.B.C.F.M. Secretaries
have visited the mission in 1924, '28, '30, '34, '38, and '46, and have given their
impressions either in the *Missionary Herald* or in the *United Church Record and
Missionary Review*. The report of the African Education Commission dealt
with the work of this mission (T. J. Jones, *Education in Africa*, pp. 40, 239 f.,
245 ff.). Among visitors who have written of this work see Nevinson, op. cit.,
chap. 7; J. Johnston, op. cit., chaps. 2, 3, and 4.

HISTORICAL

A.B.C.F.M. (Congregational) and of the United Church of Canada, which for practical purposes work as one mission. This mission co-operates with several smaller organizations and with the Angola Evangelical Alliance. This prevailing spirit of co-operation has been noticed by travellers.[1] Another characteristic has been 'regard for plan, order, and "cultivation of the field" ', according to the African Education Commission.[2] Of yet greater significance has been the extent to which this mission has been able to seize upon and develop indigenous initiative. This showed in the early organization of the Church, which was encouraged to develop its own life from the start. The utilization of indigenous forms, especially of social organization, has been a source of real strength.

Further development in this direction is greatly to be desired. For such further development, and indeed for all orderly growth, more knowledge of Umbundu life and attitudes, and an orderly synthesis of knowledge already in hand is a *sine qua non*. It is hoped that the present writer's study may help to supply the lacunae. A recent Roman Catholic handbook for missionaries in Africa has urged that for each ethnic and linguistic region a mission should have specialists in each field of research.[3] Although this advice may be considered 'for the present a counsel of perfection', it is the direction toward which missions are working,[4] an ideal which they must realize in the not too distant future. If Protestant missions in Africa are to maintain the place of leadership which, because of their evangelistic zeal they have had, they cannot neglect this zeal for knowledge which is demanded to-day.

The Roman Catholic Diocese of Huambo (*Pères du Saint-Esprit*), which embraces most of the Umbundu territory, seems to have had no specialists of the type named above who have devoted themselves to a study of the Ovimbundu. Père Ernest Lecomte

---

[1] Compare Nevinson, op. cit., p. 140, 'there are two . . . notable orders at work in Angola—the American mission (Congregationalist) under the "American Board", and the English mission (Plymouth Brethren) under divine direction only. . . . Of all the sects that I have known, these are the only two that I have ever heard pray for each other, and that without condemnation.'

[2] Dr. T. J. Jones, op. cit., p. 40. Recommendations for further developments according to carefully considered plans were made by Dr. F. K. Sanders in his *Report of Deputation*, 1930 (A.B.C.F.M.).

[3] H. Dubois, *Le Répertoire Africain* (Rome, 1932), pp. 157 ff.

[4] See article by J. H. Oldham, 'The Educational Work of Missionary Societies', in *Africa*, Jan. 1934, p. 47 f.

222 UMBUNDU KINSHIP AND CHARACTER

produced an Umbundu grammar,[1] but does not seem to have published material of an ethnological nature. Père Keiling (who died in 1937) and Père Batteix were both listed in *Le Répertoire Africain* as specializing in the 'Ganguella' language.[2] The Umbundu missions of this Diocese date from 1890 (Caconda), 1896 (Bailundo), 1912 (Cuando), and later. From early days this mission has had quite evident political aspects—from 1889 when a military expedition was sent against the 'Ganguella Soba[3] Tchiuaco' to re-establish Père Lecomte and the Cubango mission station which had been attacked and expelled,[4] up to the recent government charters and mission statutes, which heavily subsidize the religious work of the Roman Catholic missions in Angola. The constitution of the Portuguese Republic decrees the separation of Church and State and full religious liberty. The large subsidies and other special privileges given to the Roman Catholic Church in Angola, however, create difficulties beyond the mere allocation of tax-money. In other parts of Africa the Roman Catholic missions co-operate with the Protestant in many spheres of action. It is to be regretted that such co-operation seems not to be desired in Angola. Is it a sort of monopolistic political aim which keeps the Roman Catholic missionaries of Angola aloof? The rare instances in which a more friendly spirit has been manifested only add point to the question. The appreciative and co-operative spirit shown by Padre J. Alves Correia[5] may be cited.

Roman Catholics and Protestants have both been very successful from a numerical standpoint.[6] Success in building a truly indigenous Church, or in providing it with suitable and capable leadership from its own ranks, is another question hardly to be judged from statistics. More elusive still is the question whether,

[1] *Boletim Soc. Geog. Lisboa*, 1897. This grammar has gone through several editions and is still in use. The orthography is evidently intended to facilitate the use of the language by one whose native tongue is French and rather complicates matters for an African, and, indeed, for anyone whose language is other than French.

[2] H. Dubois, op. cit., p. 340.

[3] *Soba*, a native chief (from *Soma*).

[4] *Benguella*, op. cit., 1891, pp. 10 ff.

[5] See his books, *A Larguesa do Reino de Deus* (Lisboa, 1932); *A Vida Mais Alta*, &c.

[6] Roman Catholics have about 280,000 and Protestants about 140,000 adherents among the Ovimbundu, according to the census taken in 1940 (Colónia de Angola, *Censo Geral da População*, vol. ix; Luanda, Imprensa Nacional, 1943).

HISTORICAL 223

or how far, Umbundu life may have been actually penetrated by a Christian spirit in matters of faith and morals. It is not surprising that after less than seventy years, or very much less in most regions, belief in witchcraft should still have a strong hold upon the minds of the Ovimbundu. Somewhat disturbing, however, is the fact that according to the latest observations, belief in and the hold of witchcraft seem at the present time to be increasing. These observations tally with what seems to be taking place in other parts of Africa.[1] According to observers in Africa and in other parts of the world the hold of witchcraft upon a people seems to increase with a decrease of security, whether relating to the economic basis of life, to health and disease, or to life's religious undergirding. In such a case, it is clearly the duty of all agencies concerned to co-operate for the removal of the cause of insecurity. Here the chief agencies are government, commerce, and missions. It is to be hoped that for the good of the Ovimbundu they may be brought together.

[1] See *Africa*, vol. viii, no. 4, which number is devoted to studies of witchcraft. See especially the article, 'A Modern Movement of Witch Finders', by A. I. Richards, pp. 418 ff.

SYNCHRONIZED CHART OF THE PORTUGUESE HISTORY OF

DATES	EVENTS RECORDED
1482	Diogo Cão discovers the Congo.
1485–6	Diogo Cão's second voyage.
1490–1	Embassy to King of Kongo and Franciscan Mission.
1560	First expedition to Kingdom of Angola under Dias de Novaes.
1568	'Jagas' overrun Kingdom of Kongo.
1575	Luanda founded by Dias de Novaes and Jesuits.
1590	'Jagas' allied with Angola and Matamba defeat Portuguese.
From 1600	Some 'Jagas' allies of Portuguese, others met south of Kuanza and on Benguela Coast.
1617	Benguela founded.
1620	Hinterland forbidden to traders save *pombeiros descalços*.
1640–8	Dutch hold Luanda, Benguela, &c.; Portuguese hold Massangano.
From 1645	Raids from Massangano across Libolo to and across Keve River and to Bailundu.
From 1660	Raids inland from Benguela find some natives using fire-arms.
1671	End of Kingdom of Angola; presídio at Pungu-a-Ndongo.
1680	One million slaves exported since 1576 (Cadornega). First Caconda Fort founded in Hanha.
1685	Second Caconda Fort rebuilt nearby; many attacks on this fort and on nearby natives by native kings from interior.
1718	Further attacks on Caconda and its neighbours; king of 'Gallangue' captured and exiled; his successor said to have become vassal of Portugal. (Delgado.)
1760	Expulsion of Jesuits.
1769	Third Caconda fort built, on present site; presídio of Novo Redondo founded; various 'towns' ordered established in Benguela hinterland and Captains-major named. Formal prohibition of hinterland to traders removed.
1770–1	J. J. Rodrigues (first) Captain-major of Bihe.
1774	Great military campaign from Luanda and from Benguela against Bailundu, Cingolo, Ciyaka, &c.
1776	Return of military forces; king of Bailundu and two nephews captured.
1778	Kangombe baptized as 'Antonio de Vasconcellos' in Luanda and restored to stool of Viye with Governor's help.
1782	J. Gregorio de Freitas, Captain-major of Bihe.

OCCUPATION AND OF THE TRADITIONAL
THE OVIMBUNDU

NATIVE TRADITIONAL HISTORY AND THE UMBUNDU
ROYAL SUCCESSIONS

'Kinguri' leaves Lunda to seek new home; his subsequent wanderings (Magyar).

Traditional origins of the Imbangala, of the Songo; in 'Libolo', in 'Quibala', &c. (Dias de Carvalho; Ferreira Diniz, &c.).

Ngalangi tradition of Feti the First, who found his wives in the reeds, and how they became the mothers of many peoples.

Wambu-Kalunga, the cannibal chief, founder of Wambu, progenitor of Ciyaka, Cingolo, Citata, Kalukembe, &c.

Ndulu tradition of Katekula-Mengo, elephant-hunter, who left imprints in the rocks of Pungu-a-Ndongo.

Katiavala from the north, comes to Bailundu.

Viye and Kahanda.

UMBUNDU ROYAL SUCCESSIONS

	Ciyaka	Ndulu	Bailundu	Ngalangi	Viye
1650	Cilūlū I (Cihamba)[8] Kapango				
		Cikolongonjo			
	Atende I				
	Ukolongonjo I	Kavelavela	Mbulu (Ciliva)[8]		
1700	Ndumbu I (Konya-ya-Cipembe)[8]	Etande	Katiavala I Njahulu		
	Luanjangombe I	Cihuaya	Somandalu	(Kasenje)[2]	Viye
	Mukuku	Cingi		(Cihongo)[2]	(Civava)[2]
1750	Cilūlū II				(Ndalu)[2]
	Handa I	(Ndulu)[7]	Cingi I[1] c. 1760–76	Ndumba Visoso	Ulundu
	Ngalangi Katutu I	Kakulukusu[1]			
					Eyambi Njilahulu
1775	Ndumbu II		Cingi II (Ciliva)[8]		
	Kanutumulua				Kangombe[1] 1778–c.1795
	Kamela			Mulunda	
	Ukolongonjo II	Lumanyula			

For notes see page 231.

Q

226   UMBUNDU KINSHIP AND CHARACTER

DATES   EVENTS RECORDED

1795   Mello and Teixeira, third journey to 'Loval' via Bailundu and Viye.
1808–15   First recorded crossing of Africa (via Lunda, not Viye) by two *pombeiros*.
1817   Native wars in Benguela hinterland.
1819   João Nepomuceno Correia, Captain-major of Bihe.
1823–5   'Golden Age of Slave Trade'—average annual export 11,457 (Lopes de Lima).
1832–8   First export of new products: gum copal and orchilia.
1834   Abolition of royal monopoly in ivory.

1836   Formal abolition of slave trade, but enforcement held up for many years, owing to feeling in the colony.
1837   Lt. Sandoval in Bailundu, whence he describes native life.
1838   F. J. Coimbra, Captain-major of Bihe.
1840   Silva Porto reaches Bihe, coming from Luanda.

1844   Ports of Luanda and Benguela opened to foreign shipping; Prize Court in Luanda to implement suppression of slave trade.
1845   Presídio of Huila founded.
1846   Expedition of J. R. Graça to Lunda, passes through Viye.
1849–57   Ladislau Magyar in Viye.

1852   Silva Porto opens 'new road' from Viye to coast via Bailundu and Balombu (Civula).
1853   'Arabs' in Benguela, coming overland from Zanzibar. Livingstone meets Silva Porto and parties of 'Mambari' (Ovimbundu) at Naliele on the Zambezi.
1854   Livingstone meets 'Mambari' near Golungo Alto, visits Luanda, and returns to Zambezi valley and east coast.
1856–7   Attacks on southern presídios. Great attack on Huila by Ciyaka, Cingolo, Kalukembe, &c.

1865   Slaves now called freedmen (*libertos*) and apprenticed to their masters.
1869   First (experimental) export of rubber.

1870   Silva Porto leaves Viye for Benguela because of exactions of King Cilemo. Export of slaves to Americas now stopped; many sent to local plantations (Bastos).

1875   Lt. Cameron passes through Viye, Bailundu, &c., and reaches coast.
1878   Serpa Pinto, Capello, and Ivens in Caconda and in Viye. Great trading activity in Bailundu and in Viye.
1879–81   Trek Boers who left Transvaal in 1876 settle at Humpata.
1879   Silva Porto returns to Viye and goes on to 'Moyo'.
1880   Bagster, Sanders, and Miller land at Benguela (November), reach Bailundu following March to open W.C.A. Mission of A.B.C.F.M.
1882   Rubber takes second place in exports (after wax).

HISTORICAL

UMBUNDU ROYAL SUCCESSIONS

	Ciyaka	*Ndulu*	*Bailundu*	*Ngalangi*	*Viye*
1795					Kawewe
	Atende II				
		Cindele	Ekuikui I	Kambuenge	Moma (*Vasovava*)[8]
	Cikoko I		Numa I		
	Kuvombo-inene		Hundungulu		
			Cisende I		
	Ndumbu III	Mbundi	Njunjulu	Ndumba II (*Cihongo*)[8]	
			Ngungi		
1835			Civukuvuku[3]		Mbandua[3] 1833–9
	Handa II (*Kaciyombo*)[8]				
			Utondosi		Kakembembe[3] (*Hundungulu*)[8] 1839–42
1842	Njimbi[4] 1842–50	Siakalembe	Mbonge[3] 1842–61		Liambula[3] 1842–7
				Ndumba III[3] (*Epope Kateyavilombo*) c. 1844–c. 1860	
					Kayangula[3] 1847–50
1850	Canja I[4] (*Luanjangombe III*)[8] 1850–70				(Mukinda[2]) 1850–7[3]
1857		Lusãse			Nguvenge[3] 1857–9
				Etumbu Lutate	Konya Cilemo[3] 1860–83
1861			Cisende II[3] 1861–9 Vasovava[3] 1869–72		
1870	Njundo[4] 1870–98	Elundu Civava[4] c. 1870–c. 1890			
			Ekongo-liohombo[3] 1872–6		
1875			Ekuikui II[3] 1876–93	Ndumbu[5]	
1880					Ciponge[3] (*Njambayamina*)[8] 1883–6

228 UMBUNDU KINSHIP AND CHARACTER

DATES	EVENTS RECORDED
1884	Sanders opens Kamundongo station in Viye; Mission expelled from Bailundu by King Ekuikui upon a trader's misrepresentation; Mission appeals to Gov.-Gen. at Luanda; Arnot's arrival at Bailundu influences Ekuikui; Mission invited to return.
1885	Silva Porto, Captain-major of Bihe.
1886	Ovimbundu traders discover new source of rubber—more easily available and more abundant: great boom begins.
1887	Rubber takes first place in exports.
1888	Occupation of Congo by 'Free State' stops ivory trade. Currie opens Canadian Congregational station at Chissamba.
1890	King Ndunduma orders Paiva Couceiro's expedition out of Viye; suicide of Silva Porto. Punitive expedition under Artur de Paiva occupies Viye and receives surrender of king. Roman Catholic mission opened at Caconda. Plymouth Brethren begin work at Kuanjulula (Viye).
1891	Teixeira da Silva begins military occupation of Bailundu. Many traders arrive for settlement in Bailundu and in Viye.
1892	R.C. 'Mission of Bihe' opened at Kacingi (outside Umbundu area).
1895	R.C. Mission station of Bailundu opened.
1896	King Numa attacks Bailundu Fort.
1897	Mission Philafricaine (Swiss) opens station in Kalukembe.
1899	Peak of rubber trade.
1900	Slump in rubber trade; no more ivory (A. Bastos).
1902–3	Revolt in Bailundu put down and remaining Umbundu regions soon occupied.
1904	Benguela Railway begins construction at Lobito. Rubber slump aggravated by debasing product. W.C.A. Mission opens Cileso (Ndulu) Station.
1906	W.C.A. Mission opens Elende (Ciyaka) Station.
1908	R.C. Mission station of Huambo (Wambu) opened.
1910	The Republic proclaimed in Portugal; worst abuses of contract labour abolished; civil administration begins to replace military in interior. Benguela Ry. reaches Cuma; porterage to coast gradually ends.
1912	Gen. Norton de Matos, Governor-General.
1914	W.C.A. Mission opens Currie Institute, normal and training school for young men.
1915	German forces take Portuguese forts on southern border; Portugal enters war against Germany. Benguela Ry. reaches Chinguar (edge of Viye) and suspends construction.
1916	W.C.A. Mission opens Means School for training of young women.
1917	Bailundu troops used to quell Sele revolt.
1919	Gen. Norton de Matos, High Commissioner; period of many public works and of much road-building activity (until about 1930).
1921	Decree 77 severely limits teaching and use of vernaculars. Beginning of currency devaluation with great fluctuations.
1922	Benguela Ry. resumes construction. Galangue (Ngalangi) mission station opened by representatives of coloured Congregational churches of the U.S.
1924	Seventh Day Adventists open work in Mbongo.

HISTORICAL

UMBUNDU ROYAL SUCCESSIONS

	Ciyaka	*Ndulu*	*Bailundu*	*Ngalangi*	*Viye*
1885					Ciyoka[3] 1886–8 Cikunyu[3] (*Ndunduma*)[8] 1888–90
1890		Civange		Ekumbi	Kalufele
			Katiavala II[3] 1893–5		
1895			Numa II[3] 1895–6	Cihonga II	Kaninguluka
		Cipati	Hundungulu Kalakata	Ciyo	
	Cilūlū III[4] 1898–1904				
1900		Cisululu Kasuanje	Kalandula		Ciyuka[4] 1901–3
		Siakanjimba	(Mutu-ya Kevela) [3, 7] 1903		Kavova[4] 1903–15
1904	Handa III[4] 1904–11	Ndingilinya	Cisende III[3] 1904–11		
		Sihinga Congolola		Cipala	
1910					
	Atende III[4] 1911–15		Njahūlū[4] 1911–35		
1915	Cikoko[4] 1915–18				Ngungu[4] 1915–28
		Cisokokua		Kangombe	
1920	Cilūlū IV[4] 1920–5			Ngangawe	
				Cuvika	

230 UMBUNDU KINSHIP AND CHARACTER

DATES   EVENTS RECORDED

1926   'Corporative Régime' gains power in Portugal, May 28; Roman Catholics given
        large government subsidies and many advantages; they open many new
        mission stations from this time on.
1927   United Church of Canada takes over part of work of W.C.A.M. Umbundu
        Church of Christ organized to include work of three Protestant Missions.
1928   Currency conversion with 25 per cent. devaluation. Angola Boers return to
        Damaraland. Mission Philafricaine opens Evanga (Ganda) station.
1929   Completion of Benguela Ry. to frontier.
1929–30 First ordinations in Umbundu Church of Christ.

1930   W.C.A. Mission celebrates Jubilee with attendance of 12,000 Africans, many
        Europeans, and deputations from abroad.
1931   Completion of Katanga Ry., making connexion across Africa; opening of
        through traffic. Portuguese Baptists open small work at Nova Lisboa.

1935   Provincial Exposition at Nova Lisboa.
1938   H.E. President Carmona of Portugal visits Colony.
1939   World War II, Portugal neutral.

From⎫
1941 ⎭ Rapid rise of prices, rise in wages less marked.
1945–6 Visit of Minister of Colonies includes Protestant Missions.
1946   West Central Africa Regional Conference, Léopoldville, Congo Belge: African
        and European delegates from French, Belgian, and Portuguese colonies.

HISTORICAL

UMBUNDU ROYAL SUCCESSIONS

	Ciyaka	Ndulu	Bailundu	Ngalangi	Viye
1925				Cikuetekole	
	Handa IV[4] (*Kalumbombo*)[8] 1926–8	Cihopio[4] d. 1935			
				Mbumba-Kambuakatepa	
					Ciyuka[4, 6] 1928–40
	Sakulanda[4] (*Luanjangombe IV*)[8] 1929–39				
1930					
				Cingelesi[4] 1931–3 Ndumbu II[4] 1933–5	
1935		(Sangombe Esita)[7] 1935–	Musita[4] 1935–8	Congolola[4] 1935–	
			Cinendele[4] 1938–		
	Cilūlū V[4] 1939–40				
1940	Tomasi[4] 1940–				

NOTES

[1] Dates fixed by agreement of native tradition with historical reference.

[2] These names mentioned by European writers; native tradition with reference to them not known.

[3] Dates fixed from historical reference.

[4] Dates from native sources.

[5] Tradition mentions a solar eclipse during this reign, which would be 1886 or 1889.

[6] This is the same king as the one listed for 1901–3: he reigned twice.

[7] The names in parentheses are of men not of royal lines and not regularly enthroned, but usurpers, war leaders, or 'guarders of the stool'.

[8] The italicized names in parentheses after the names of certain kings are appelatives which they took on assuming office.

232 UMBUNDU KINSHIP AND CHARACTER

BIBLIOGRAPHY

FOR CHAPTER XII

Alguns documentos do archivo nacional da Torre do Tombo acerca das navegações e conquistas portuguezas (Lisboa, 1892).

ALVES CORREIA, J. *A Larguesa do Reino de Deus* (Lisboa, 1932).

AMORIM, MASSANO DE. *Relatorio sôbre os acontecimentos do Bailundo* (Luanda, 1903).

Angola, Relatórios dos Governadores Gerais (Lisboa or Luanda).

Annaes do Conselho Ultramarino, 1854–61 (Lisboa, Imp. Nac., 1867).
  Vide especially:
  Descripção de viagem feita de Loanda . . . em . . . 1845, por J. R. Graça, Ser. I, pp. 101 ff.
  Angola: Viagem feita . . . a Caconda, por J. J. Liborio, alferes (1856), Ser. I, pp. 446 ff.
  Uma viagem de Angola em direcção a Contra Costa pelo Sr. A. F. F. da Silva Porto, Ser. I, pp. 273 ff. (This is the diary of Domingos Cakahanga.)
  Angola: Noticia do sertão do Balundo, por C. de A. Sandoval (1837), Ser. I, pp. 519 ff. (To this note there is also added an account of the campaign of 1774–6 by the Governor, dated 1 June 1776.)
  Angola: Concelho de Caconda (Report of 1861), Ser. III, pp. 45 ff.

Annaes Maritimos e Coloniaes. Parte não official, 1844–6 (Lisboa, Imp. Nac.). *Vide* especially:
  Descripção da Capitania de Benguella (1799), 4a Ser., pp. 147 ff.
  Noticia da Cidade de Benguella, e dos costumes dos gentios habitantes daquelle Sertão (1797, por M. Pinheiro de Lacerda), 5a Ser., pp. 486 ff.

Arquivos de Angola, 1933–9; 1942– (Luanda, Imp. Nac.).

BAUMANN, H. *Lunda, Bei Bauern und Jägern in Inner-Angola* (Berlin, 1935).

Benguella, Relatorios do Governador do Districto de, 1887–91 (Ministerio da Marinha e Ultramar, Lisboa, 1889, 1893).

Boletim Official da Provincia (Colónia) de Angola (Luanda, 1845–).

BOURNE, H. R. FOX. *Slave Traffic in Portuguese Africa* (London, 1908).

BOWDITCH, T. E. *An Account of the Discoveries of the Portuguese in the Interior of Angola and Mozambique* (London, 1824).

BUCHNER, M. 'Die Ambakisten', *Zeitschr. f. Ethnol.*, 1915, pp. 394–403.

CADBURY, WM. A. *Labour in Portuguese West Africa*, 2nd ed. (London, 1910).

CADORNEGA, A. DE O. *Historia Geral das Guerras Angolanas*, 1680–1, 3 vols. (Lisboa: Agência Geral das Colónias, 1940–2).

CAPELLO, H. A. DE BRITO, and IVENS, ROBERTO. *From Benguella to the Territory of Yacca*, trans. A. Elwes (London, 1882).

CASMIRO, A. *África Nostra* (Lisboa, 1924).

HISTORICAL 233

Catalogo dos Governadores do Reino de Angola. (Collecção de Noticias para a Historia, &c.) (Lisboa: Acad. Real Sciencias, 1826.) (Also reprinted in *Arquivos de Angola*, vol. iii, 1937.)

CAVAZZI DA MONTECUECOLO, GIOVANNI ANTONIO. *Istorica Descrizione de Tre Regni Congo, Matamba, et Angola* (Bologna, 1687).

CHATELAIN, A. *Héli Chatelain, L'Ami de l'Angola* (Lausanne, 1918). (Parts 6 and 7 contain interesting historical and ethnological notes, if one has the patience to search them out.)

CHATELAIN, HÉLI. *Folk Tales of Angola*. Mem. Amer. Folklore Soc., 1894.

CORDEIRO, LUCIANO (Ed.). *Memorias do Ultramar*:

1574–1620. *Da Mina ao Cabo Negro* segundo Garcia Mendes Castello Branco.

1593–1631. *Terras e minas africanas*, segundo Balthazar Rebello de Aragão.

1617–22. *Benguella e seu sertão*, por um anonymo.

1607. *Estabelecimentos e resgates portuguezes na costa occidental da Africa*, por um anonymo.

1620–9. *Producções, comercio e governo do Congo e de Angola*, segundo Manuel Vogado Sotomaior, Antonio Diniz, Bento Banha Cardoso, e Antonio Beserra Fajardo.

1516–1619. *Escravos e minas de Africa*, segundo diversos. (Lisboa: Imprensa Nacional, 1881.)

CORREIA, E. A. DA SILVA. *História de Angola*, 2 vols. (Lisboa, 1940).

CRAWFORD, D. *Thinking Black* (London, 1913).

CUSHMAN, DR. MARY FLOYD. *Missionary Doctor* (New York: Harpers, 1944).

CUVELIER, J. 'Missionaires Capucins des Missions de Congo et d'Angola du XVIIᵉ et du XVIIIᵉ siècles', *Congo*, vol. i, pp. 344–60; vol. ii, pp. 504–22, 684–703; also a note on the same subject in ibid. 1935, vol. i, pp. 392–8. (Consists mainly of lists of names and dates.)

DAPPER, O. *Description de l'Afrique* (Amsterdam, 1686).

DELGADO, RALPH. *A Famosa e Histórica Benguela* (Lisboa, 1940).

—— *Ao Sul do Cuanza*, Occupação do Antigo Reino de Benguela. 2 vols. (Lisboa, 1944).

DIAS DE CARVALHO, H. A. *Ethnographia e Historia Tradicional dos Povos da Lunda* (Lisboa, 1890).

DOKE, C. M. *The Lambas of Northern Rhodesia* (London: Harrap, 1931).

DUBOIS, H. M. *Le Répertoire Africain* (Rome, 1932).

FELNER, A. *Angola, Colonização dos planaltos e litoral do sul de Angola*. 3 vols. (Lisboa, 1940).

FICALHO, CONDE DE. *Plantas uteis da Africa Portugueza* (Lisboa: Imp. Nac., 1884).

GOYAU, G. 'Les débuts de l'apostolat au Congo et dans l'Angola, 1482–1590', *Revue d'histoire des Missions*, Paris, no. 4, 1930, pp. 481–514.

HARDING, C. *In Remotest Barotseland* (London, 1905).

234 UMBUNDU KINSHIP AND CHARACTER

JANMART, J. *Subsídios para a História, Arqueologia, e Etnografia das povos da Lunda* (Lisboa, 1946–Cⁱᵃ de Diamantes).

JASPERT, F. U. W. *Die Völkerstämme Mittel-Angolas* (Frankfort, 1930).

JASPERT, W. *Das Geheimnis des schwarzen Erdteils* (Berlin, 1930).

—— *Through Unknown Africa*, trans. A. Platt (London, 1930).

JOHNSTON, J. J. *Reality versus Romance in South Central Africa* (New York, 1893).

KEILING, P. LUIZ. *Quarenta Anos de África* (Braga, 1934).

LABAT, J. B. *Relation Historique de l'Étiopie occidentale, . . . description des royaumes du Congo, Angola, et Matamba* (Paris, 1732).

LACERDA, DR. J. *Lands of Cazembe*, trans. A. Elwes (London, 1894).

LAUFER, B., HAMBLY, W. D., and LINTON, RALPH. *Tobacco and its Use in Africa* (Chicago: Field Museum, 1930).

LEMOS, ALBERTO DE. *História de Angola* (Lisboa, 1932).

LOPES, DUARTE. *A Report of the Kingdom of Kongo and of Surrounding Countries; drawn out of the . . . Portuguese by Filippo Pigafetta* (Rome, 1591). Newly transl. by M. Hutchinson (London: Murray, 1881).

MENDONÇA, RENATO. *A influência africana no português do Brasil* (S. Paulo: Bib. Ped. Bras., 1935).

MIRANDA MAGALHÃES, P. ANTÓNIO. *Manual de linguas indigenas de Angola* (Luanda, 1922).

Missionary Herald. Monthly, 1880–1947 (Boston). (See index under Africa, West Central Africa, Angola, Bailundo, Kamundongo, &c.)

MONCADA, CABRAL. *A Campanha do Bailundu* (Luanda, Imprensa Nacional, 1903).

MORAES, EVARISTO DE. *A Escravidão Africana no Brasil* (S. Paulo: Ed. Nac., 1933).

MOREIRA, EDUARDO. *General Report of Journey in the Portuguese African Colonies, 1934* (London: World Dominion, 1935). Pamphlet.

—— *Open Letter to the Bishop of Angola and Congo* (ibid., 1935). ibid.

OLIVEIRA MARTINS, J. P. *O Brazil e as Colonias portuguezas* (Lisboa, 1893).

PAIVA, ARTUR DE. *Excerptos dos seus jornais*, 2 vols. (Lisboa: Agên. Geral Colónias, 1940). ˙

PAIVA MANSO, VISCONDE DE. *Historia do Congo (Documentos)* (Lisboa, 1877).

PENHA-GARCIA, COMTE J. DE. *Organisation politique et administrative de l'empire colonial portugais* (Bruxelles: Inst. Col. International, 1936).

—— (Ed.). *Les Colonies portugaises* (ibid., 1931).

PLANCQUAERT, R. P. *Les Yaga et les Bayaka du Kwango* (Bruxelles, 1932).

PROYART. *Histoire de Loango, Kakongo et autres royaumes d'Afrique* (Paris, 1776).

RAMOS, ARTHUR DE. *As culturas negras do novo mundo* (R. Janeiro: Civ. Bras. Ed., 1937).

HISTORICAL 235

Reports of the West Central Africa Mission, 1914–27. American Board of Commissioners for Foreign Missions (Mission Press, Kamundongo and Dondi).

SALDANHA DA GAMA, ANTONIO DE. *Memoria sôbre as colonias de Portugal... em 1814* (Paris, 1839).

SERPA PINTO, A. A. DA ROCHA DE. *How I crossed Africa,* trans. A. Elwes (London, 1881).

SILVA PORTO, A. F. F. DA. *A travessia do continente africano* (Lisboa: Agên. Geral Colónias, 1939).

—— *Viagens e apontamentos de um portuense em África.* Excerptos do seu diário (ibid., 1942).

Sociedade de Geografia de Lisboa. *Boletim,* 1878– . *Vide* titles listed on p. 15 and also:

As viagens dos portugueses na África e Ásia, Relação cronológica, 51ª Ser., pp. 26 ff.; 52ª Ser., pp. 332 ff.

SWAN, C. A. *The Slavery of To-day* (Glasgow: Pickering, 1909).

TAMS, GEORG. *Visit to the Portuguese Possessions in South-western Africa,* trans. from the German, H. E. Lloyd. 2 vols. (London, 1845).

TORDAY, E. *On the Trail of the Bushongo* (London: Seeley, 1925).

—— 'The Influence of the Kingdom of the Congo on Central Africa', *Africa,* 1928, pp. 157–69.

Trabalhos do 1º Congresso Nacional de Antropologia Colonial (Pôrto, 1934).

TRANCOSO, F. *Angola (Memória).* Com. Exec. da Conf. da Paz (Lisboa, 1920).

TUCKER, J. T. *Currie of Chissamba* (Toronto: Un. Church of Canada, 1945).

The United Church Record and Missionary Review (Toronto), 1925–47. (This periodical continues the *Monthly Leaflet* which had represented the Canadian Congregational Missionary Society.)

VALDEZ, F. TRAVASSOS. *Six Years of a Traveller's Life in Western Africa.* 2 vols. (London, 1861). (*Vide* vol. ii, and esp. chap. 9.)

VERHULPEN, E. *Baluba et Balubaises* (Anvers, 1936).

WILLIAMS, J. J., S.J. *Africa's God*: V. Congo and Angola (Boston Coll., 1937).

WILSON, J. L. *Western Africa, Its History, Present Condition, and Prospects* (New York: Harpers, 1856).

INDEX OF AUTHORS AND SOURCES

Africa (Journal of the Int'n'l African Inst.), vii, xi, 11, 19, 46, 54, 57, 64, 65, 67, 68, 70, 71, 119, 141, 144, 149, 221, 223.
African Society, *Journal of the*, 205.
African Studies (Johannesburg), 86.
Allier, R., vi.
Allport, F. H., 119, 124, 125, 126, 127, 128, 131, 146.
Alves Correia, Padre J., 215, 222.
Amorim, M. de, 213.
Angola, Colónia de: *Censo Geral da População*, 7, 9, 30, 222.
Angola et Rhodésie (Mission Rohan-Chabot), 19.
Annaes do Conselho Ultramarinho, 22, 165, 166, 199, 204.
Annaes Maritimos e Coloniaes, 17, 24, 57, 108, 167, 177, 188, 195, 196, 198, 199, 219.
Arnot, F. S., 210–11.
Arquivos de Angola, 195, 196, 197, 198.
Atlantic Monthly, Sept. 1938, 125.

Baker, A. G., 73.
Bantu Studies, xi, 191.
Bartlett, F. C., 123.
Bastos, A., 44, 115, 116, 180, 200, 201–2, 207, 209, 211, 212.
Battell, Andrew, 176, 181, 186, 192, 219.
Baumann, H., 169.
Benedict, Ruth F., v, 123.
Benguella, Relatorios do Districto de, 195, 202, 203, 208, 209, 210, 211, 222.
Bible, quotations from, 81, 146.
Boletim Geral das Colónias, 4, 8, 169, 179.
Boletim Official, 142, 201, 202, 204, 217.
Boletim da Sociedade de Geografia de Lisboa, see under Sociedade.
Booth, N. S., vi.
Bourne, H. R. F., 214.
Brooks, C. E. P., and S. T. A. Mirlees, 4.
Bryant, A. T., 133.
Buchner, M., 169–70.
Burr, M., 3.
Butterfield, K. M., 154.

Cadbury, W. A., 214.
Cadornega, A. de, 193, 195.
Cameron, V. L., 4, 165, 203, 205.
Capello and Ivens, 207.
Casmiro, A., 214.

Catalogo dos Governadores, 166, 194, 195, 196.
Cavazzi de Montecuecolo, G. A., 182, 184, 186, 187.
Census of Angola, *see* Angola, Colónia de: *Censo Geral da População*.
Chalmers, E. S., 144.
Coe, G. A., 136, 138, 145, 147, 152.
Colenso, Bishop J. W., 146–7.
Cook, K. M., 154.
Cook, P. A. W., vii, 30.
Cordeiro, L. (ed.), 180, 184, 192, 194, 195.

Dart, R. A., 8.
Davis, J., 154.
Delgado, Ralph, 196.
Dewey, John, 119, 122, 137, 141, 150, 152.
Dias de Carvalho, Henrique de, 173, 181, 186.
Districto de Benguella, Relatorios do, see under *Benguella*.
Doke, C. M., 8, 191, 206.
Dougall, J. W. C., viii, 65, 136, 141, 149.
Driberg, J. H., vi, 134.
Duarte Lopes, 182.
Dubois, H., vii, 221, 222.

Ebaugh, C. D., 154.
Economic Conditions in Angola (H.M.S.O. 1928), 215.
Education Policy in British Tropical Africa, 140.
Educational Yearbook 1931 (New York), 65, 142.
Educational Yearbook 1933 (New York), 65.
Eiselen, W. M., 54, 67, 70.
Ennis, E. L., 86.
Estermann, C., 8, 19, 179.
Evans-Pritchard, E. E., vi.

Ferreira Diniz, Dr. J. de O., 4, 174, 186.
Ficalho, Conde de, 218.
Fitzgerald, W., 9.
Folk-tales, Umbundu, 23, 32, 84, 90, 127–8, 147.
Fortes, M., 121, 123, 127, 129.

Geographical Society, Royal, *Proceedings* of, 204.
Gluckman, M., vi.
Goodwin, A. J. H., 3.

INDEX OF AUTHORS AND SOURCES 237

Graça, J. R., 199, 207.
Gutmann, Bruno, 64, 67, 70.

Hahn, *et al.*, *The Native Tribes of South West Africa*, 54, 104, 105, 115, 179, 180.
Hailey, Lord, 216.
Hambly, W. D., 22, 29, 34, 38, 46, 48, 53, 55, 82, 83, 90, 105, 121, 164, 165, 170.
Harding, C., 214.
Hartshorne, H., 123, 135.
Hartshorne, H., and M. May, 130.
Herzog, G., 34.
Hoernlé, A. W., 18, 54, 64, 119.
Hornbostel, E. M. von, 144–5.
Huxley, Julian, 151.

International African Institute, x, xi, 19.
International Review of Missions, 64, 146.
Irle, J., 43, 54.

Janmart, J., 164.
Jaspert, W., 169.
Johnston, Sir H. H., 8, 170.
Johnston, J., 210, 220.
Jones, L. G. E., 154.
Jones, T. J., 63, 65, 137, 138, 154, 220, 221.
Journal of the American Folk-Lore Society, 90, 95–6, 125, 128.
Journal of the Royal Anthropological Institute, 22.
Junod, H. A., 35, 54, 63, 117, 146.

Kalei, Daniel, 104.
Kalupeteka, R., 81, 112, 113.
Kandel, I. (ed.), 65.
Kavita Evambi, R., 41, 45, 81, 107, 111, 113.
Kayalo, I., 81.
Keiling, Padre L., 211, 222.
Kilpatrick, W. H., 137.
Krige, E. J., 41, 56, 113, 121, 144.
Kuczynski, R. R., 30.

Labouret, H., 143.
Lang, A., et C. Tastevin: *La Tribu des Va-Nyaneka*, 43.
Lemos, A. de, 182.
Letcher, O., 4.
Levy-Bruhl, L., vi.
Likuluta Samikanjo, 28, 53.
Livingstone, David, 19, 196, 205, 207.
Lopes de Lima, J. J., 169, 175, 184, 188, 192, 193, 194, 195, 199, 200, 202, 214.
Loram, C. T., 65.

Magyar, L., 23, 24, 25, 40, 54, 83, 111, 112, 130, 167, 187, 204, 206, 207, 218.
Mair, L. P., 42.
Malherbe, E. G. (ed.), vii, 65.
Malinowski, B., 57, 68.
Manso, Paiva, 182.
Marquardsen u. Stahl, 4, 165.
Mead, Margaret, 122, 126, 127.
Meinhof, C., 170, 179.
Memorias do Ultramar, 195.
Miranda Magalhães, A., 170.
Mirlees, S. T. A. (Brooks and ———), 4.
Mission Rohan-Chabot, 19, 43, 179.
Missionary Herald, The, 66, 128, 131, 132, 144, 153, 187, 200, 204, 209, 210, 211, 213, 219, 220.
Missiones Culturales, Las, 154.
Moncada, C., 211, 213.
Monteiro, J. J., 33, 200–1, 207.
Mumford, W. B., 71.
Murphy, G., and L. B., 127, 128.

Native Tribes of South West Africa, see Hahn *et al.*
Nevinson, H. W., 3, 35, 131, 165, 214, 220, 221.
New Standard Dictionary, 35.
Ngonga Liahuka, P., 38, 153.
Ngulu, Abrão, 66, 81.

Oldham, J. H., 64, 221.
Oldham, J. H., and B. D. Gibson, 138, 143, 145, 147, 151.
Oversea Education, 155.

Paiva, A. de, 165, 220.
Pedro Paulo, 81.
Penha Garcia, J. de, 216.
Practical Orthography of African Languages (Int'n'l African Inst.), x.
Proceedings, Royal Geog. Soc., London, 204, 208.
Proverbs, Umbundu, 21, 31, 33, 39, 58, 59, 85, 93, 94, 95, 106, 107, 110, 122, 135, 147, 173.

Ravenstein, 180, 182, 183, 185, 187.
Read, F. W., 205.
Report of Deputation to W. C. Africa Mission, 66.
Rhodes–Livingstone Journal, no. 2, 30.
Richards, A. I., 223.

Sá da Bandeira, Marquez da, 214.
Saldanha da Gama, A. de, 214.
Sanders, F. K., 139, 219, 221.
Santos, J. R. dos, 164.
Schapera, I., vii, 18, 51, 54, 67, 113.
Scott, H. S., 119, 150, 151.

238 INDEX OF AUTHORS AND SOURCES

Serpa Pinto, A. A. da R. de, 165, 172, 191, 203, 207.
Shantz, H. F., and C. F. Marbut, 4.
Shaw, Mabel, 69, 71.
Shropshire, D. W. T., 63.
Siku Nunda, A., 81.
Silva Porto, A. F. F. da, 128, 172, 174, 198, 199, 200, 204, 205.
Silveira, J. da, 164.
Smith, E. W., v, xi, 46, 133, 151, 165.
Smith, E. W., and A. M. Dale, 44, 133.
Sociedade de Geografia de Lisboa, *Boletim*, 128, 165, 174, 198, 201, 203, 205, 207, 208, 217, 220, 222.
Songs, Umbundu, 113, 114.
Stahl (Marquardsen u. ——), 4.
Statham, J. C. B., 4.
Stauffer, M. (ed.), 65.
Stayt, H. A., 54.
Strong, 220.
Swan, C. A., 214.

Torday, E., 181, 185.
Trabalhos do 1º Congresso Nacional de Antropologia Colonial, 164, 170.
Trancoso, F., 212.
Treaties, acts and regulations relating to missionary freedom, 142.
Tucker, L. S., 22.

Tucker, J. T., 33, 170, 211, 216, 220.

Umbundu–English Vocabulary (1911), 113.
Umbundu sources, 81 et seq., 99 et seq.
United Church Record and Missionary Review, 220.

Valdez dos Santos, A. C. T., 216.
Valdez, F. Travassos, 207.
Van Wing, R. P., 96, 103, 135, 164, 185.
Va-Nyaneka, La Tribu des, 43.
Vedder, 43, 54, 105, 115.
Village Education in Africa, 155.
Voz do Planalto, 215.

Wagner, G., 64.
Westermann, D. W., xi.
Wheeler, W. R., 143.
Williams, J. J., 164.
Woodson, C. G., 154.
Wright, A. D., 154.

Year Book of Education 1938 (London), v, 119, 150.

Zeitschrift für Ethnologie, 1915, 170.

INDEX

Abortion, 85.

Acknowledgements, ix f.

Adaptation, 150.

Adjustment, 123 seq., 128; social adjustment, 65, 134 f., 141 f., 151 f.

Administration, European, 195 seq.

Adolescence, 111–18; trial marriage, 112–14; age-groups, 114–15; initiation, 115–17; general characteristics, 117; period of stress, 126 f.

Adult life, 117.

African Education Commission (Phelps Stokes Fund), 154 f., 221.

African words used, xi.

Age, factor of, in household, 41; hierarchy of, 58; — mates, 98, 114, 128; — -groups, 114 f.

Agriculture, 8, 106 ff.; province of the Queen, 20; teaching of, 145.

Ambo, 169, 179, 180.

American Board of Commissioners for Foreign Missions (A.B.C.F.M.), ix, 10, 65, 139 n., 154, 202 n., 221.

American trade with Angola, 191, 200.

Analysis of Umbundu development, 119–33.

Ancestor-spirits, see King, Medicine and magic, Priesthood, Reincarnation, Ritual, Sorcery, Tabus.

Andulu, see Ndulu.

Anger, 124, 146; and sorcery, 125, 131; outlets for, 125 ff., 131; not desired in character of King, 21, 125.

Angola Evangelical Alliance, 221.

Angola, kingdom of, 171, 175 n., 181.

Animal Husbandry, see Domestic animals.

Arabs from Zanzibar, 204 n.

Artifacts, stone, 164.

'Assimilation', vii.

Associations, see Age-groups.

Attitudes, between members of household, 41 f.; between relatives by marriage, 51 seq.; extensions and utilization of, 69, 145; towards other tribes, 189. *See also* Character, Education, Kinship, Social life.

Avoidances, 51–3.

Baby, 86–91; naming, 86–7; food and drink, 88 f., 90; medicine, 88 f.; cultivation of field for, 90; carrying of, 90; nursing, 90 f.; recognition of parents, 91; teaching to sit, 91; the sitting baby, see Childhood.

Babyhood, 89 seq.

Bagster, W., 220 n.

Bailundu, kingdom of, 168 f., 197; traditional history, 171; first Portuguese expedition to, 194 f.; campaigns against, 166, 171, 174, 197; penetration by Portuguese traders, 199, 210; military occupation, 211.

Bangala, 169, 176 n., 179, 180, 186, 189.

Bantu, the southern, 169 f., 190.

Basket-making, 109.

Batteix, Père, 222.

Baylundu, see Bailundu.

Bee-hunting, 31, 110.

Beer, 33.

Bees-wax, trade in, 207 f.

Behaviour, patterns of, among kin, 41–2, 49–51; among affinal relatives, 51–2.

Benguela, 183, 186, 192, 198, 199, 201, 208 f.

Benguela Highland: climate, 3 ff.; communications, 9; fauna, 7; geography, 1 ff.; geology of, 1 ff.; pests, 6 f.; rainfall, 4 f.; regions adjoining, 2 f.; rivers, 3; vegetation, 5 f.

Benguela railway, 212.

Benguela Velha, 182, 186, 194 n.

Betrothal payments, see Marriage.

Bible, use of, 146 f., 151 n.

Bie, Bihe, see Viye.

Birth, 81–5; in the house, 83 f.; in the field, 84; announcement of, 84; congratulations to parents, 84; of twins, 85.

Blood-brotherhood, 129.

Blood relatives, see Relatives.

Bongo, see Mbongo.

Brazil, domination of Angola by, 193, 202; slave trade with, 200.

British trade in Angola, 191.

Bush-buck, flesh tabu to royal families, 43.

Bushongo, 181.

Caconda, presidio, 195; 'a Nova', 178, 195; trading-post, 201; wagon road from Benguela, 209. *See also* Kakonda.

Caluquembe or Caluqueme, see Kalukembe.

Camp and club programmes, 148 f.

240 INDEX

Cannibalism, 173, 176, 183, 186 f., 188.
'Captain Major and exterior judge', origin of office, 196. *See also under* Viye.
Caravan roads, 199 ff.
Cassongue, *see* Kasongi.
Catechetical schools, 143 f., 152 f.
Cattle culture, 190, 192.
Cattle-keeping, 109.
Catumbela, 180, 195 n., 200 n., 201, 207.
Cenge, kingdom of, 168.
Ceremonial occasions, 35; *see* Ritual.
Character, of baby revealed by manner of crawling, teething, and first words spoken, 92; formation in family, 99–104; by wider kinship contacts, 105 ff.; built upon attitudes formed in family, 41 ff., 51 ff., 68 f., 145; of kings and other leaders, 21, 124, 131, 132; Umbundu estimate of, 130 ff., 134, 135; Christian character, 145 f. *See also* Development, Education, Kinship, Social life.
Chellean culture, 164.
Chief, *see* King.
Chiengue, *see* Cenge.
Child (*omōlã*), 49 f., 81–118; elder child (*huva*), 126 seq.; eldest child (*nuñulũ*), 40, 127, 128; younger child (*manja*), 41 f., 127; child sacrifice, *see* Human sacrifice; child insurance, 104.
Childhood, 92–105; early childhood (the toddler), 92–7; later childhood, 105–10.
Chokwe, *see* Cokue.
Christian education, 138, 145, 147.
Christianity, 220.
Chronological chart, 224 ff.
Church, village work of, 66, 67, 72; responsibility and sphere of, 139, 140. *See also* Missions.
Cilombo-coñoma, kingdom of. *See* Kakonda.
Cingolo: walled and fortified capital of, 166; campaign against, 166; kingdom of, 168.
Cipala, 168 n., 171, 172, 180, 186, 188.
Cipeyo, kingdom of, 167 n., 168.
Cisama, an early source of salt, 199.
Citata, kingdom of, 168.
Civanda, kingdom of, 168.
Civula, kingdom of, 167 n., 168.
Ciyaka, kingdom of, 168, 204; traditional history, 176, 178; connexion with the 'Jagas', 186, 188; raids by, 197; late penetration by traders, 197.
Cleanliness, 95.

Climate, 3–5.
Club and camp programmes, 149.
Coevals, 42, 115, 128. *See also under* Age.
Cokue, 181.
Communications, 10.
Community, education, 152 f.; improvement, 154; leadership by teacher, 155; school and, 139. *See also* Education, Social life.
Concubines, 40.
Conflict, 128, 129.
Congo Free State, 213.
Congo river, discovery of, 164, 181, 224.
Congregational Church Missions, *see* American Board of Commissioners for Foreign Missions.
Continent of Africa, early expeditions to cross, 204.
Contract labour, 213 f.
Conversation, 35.
Cord of navel, 83, 84.
Court of justice, royal, 21; village, 36.
Crawling, 92.
Crops, *see* Agriculture.
Cross-cousins, marriage of, 53 f.
Cuba, slave trade with, 201 n.
Cultural disintegration, 73.
Currency, 215.
Curriculum, *see* Education.

Dance, the, 33 ff.; function and value of, in education, 114, 144.
Delinquency, 134 n.
Déracinés, 69, 71 n., 74.
Development, historical, *see* Historical development.
Development, individual, 81–118; analysis of, 119–33; *see also* Adolescence, Babyhood, Childhood, &c.
Dialectical differences in Umbundu, 179, 190 n.
Diet, 97, 218.
Disability, 129.
Diseases, 6 f., 129; of cattle, 7; imported, 217, 218.
Divination, *see* Medicine and magic.
Divisions, tribal, 167–9.
Domestic animals, 31, 109.
Drums, for the dance, 34.
Dutch, 194.

'Educability' of the Bantu, vii.
Education, of the baby, 95 ff.; of the child, 98–110; psychological, 99; in social usage, 100–3; by training in skills, 104, 106; of the adolescent, 111–18; of leaders, 70 ff., 139;

INDEX

241

socio-psychological, 106; coterminous with life and culture, 121 f.; native African, 119, 134, 139; agricultural, 145; Christian, 138, 145–7; community, 152 f.; content of, 141 seq.; curriculum, 141, 150 ff.; central core of, 151; function, in transformation of society, 155; physical, and recreation, 144; religious, 73, 145 ff. *See also* Character, Childhood, Development, Social life.

Educational content, 136, 141–9; evaluations, 134–40; instrumentalities, 137; method, 135, 141; organization, 139 f.; policy, 137 ff.

Egito, 201.

Ekekete, kingdom of, 168.

Ekuikui II (King of Bailundu, 1876–1893), 209 f., 217.

Elende, 164, 165; kingdom of, 168.

Emigration, 215.

Ennis, Dr., and Mrs. M. W., x, 164.

Environmental factors, 5 ff.

Epata, 42.

Epilepsy, 129 n.

Esela, 8 f.

Etiquette, *see* Childhood, Manners, Social usage.

European, administration, 9, 150, 151, 214 ff.; influence, 192, 195, 205 f., 219; military occupation, 194, 197; settlements, 192, 197, 199; trade, 198 ff., 203 ff.

Fagging, 149.

Family, attitudes, 41 f., 69, 73, 145; extended, 42 ff.; restricted, 40 ff.; life, adjustments in, 125 seq.; in relation to village, 29 seq. *See* Kinship.

Famine, 212.

Father (*tate*), 41 f., 44 f., 82, 84, 91, 92, 99, 109.

Father's sister (*tatekãi*) and brother's daughter, 48, 50, 112.

Fear, 99 f.

Fertility, function of King, q.v.

Fire, ceremonial f., of King, 20; ceremonial lighting of, 38 f.

Fire-arms, first recorded use by Natives in Benguela, 195; trade in, 206, 213.

Fishing, 110.

Folk-lore, Cinderella motif in, 128; in education, 114; 147 f.

Foreign commerce, ports of Angola opened to, 202.

Fortress, 166, 167.

Friendship, 128.

R

Galanga, *see* Ngalanga.

Galangue, *see* Ngalangi.

'Gallangue Grande', 196.

Games, 34.

Genealogical table, 62.

Geological structure, 1 f., 165.

German trade in Angola, 191.

Government, European, 9, 195 seq.; tribal, 21–3.

Grudges, 125.

Gunpowder, 198, 206, 213 f.

Habitat, 1–16.

Hambo, *see* Wambu.

Headman of village, 36, *see also under* Village.

Health, 217 seq., *see also* Diet, Diseases.

Hebrews, points of contact with Africans, 146.

Herero *oruzo* and *eanda*, 43; 'child-insurance', 104; linguistic connexion with Ovimbundu, 8, 169; traditions of, 180.

Hierarchy of age, *see* Age.

Historical development, 190–215.

History of African peoples, 164.

Household, 40 ff.

Houses, boys build their own, 111.

Huamba or Huambo, *see* Wambu.

Human sacrifice, 21 f., 128, 187 f., *see also* Cannibalism.

Hunger, 212.

'Hungry country', 3, 212.

Hunting, 110; of bees, 110; deities of, 21; inaugural hunt for King, 21.

Hygiene, 145.

Identification, 129.

Imbangala, 181, 185 f., 188.

Incest, 53.

Individual development, *see* Development.

Individualism, 63.

Inferiority conflict, 129 f.

Inheritance, of property, 44 f., 60; of office, 44, 60; of ancestral traits, 102.

Initiation rites, 59, 115 ff., 148.

Insignia, royal, 177.

Intelligence, of Ovimbundu, vi f.; Umbundu concept of, 122.

Iron-working, 110, 204 f.

Ivory trade, royal monopoly of, 207; abolition of monopoly, 198 ff., 211; connexion with slave trade, 200.

'Jaga' (used as title), 173; explanation of term, 185 f.

'Jagas', migrations of, 181–90; sell captives to Portuguese, 182 ff., 184, 199; customs of, 186 ff.

242 INDEX

Jealousy, 128.
Jesuits and slave trade, 193.
Jesus, teachings of, 146 f.

Kakonda, kingdom of, 168, 178 ff.;
people of, 197 n. *See also* Caconda.
Kalukembe, kingdom of, 168, 179,
190.
Kamundongo, origin of, 197 n.
Kangombe, King, *see under* Viye.
Kasongi, 25, 165 f., 168, 179.
Katumbela, *see* Catumbela.
Keve river, 192.
King, functions of, 20–3; of Wambu,
176 f.; use of magic by, 22; status
of, 23; may not eat in public, 102 f.;
type of character desired in kings,
124, 131.
Kingdoms, 17–24, 167 ff.; independent, 17 f., 168; tributary, 23 f.,
168; border, 179. *See also* Tribal
divisions.
Kinship, 40–61; groups, 42–6; classificatory system, 46–51; genealogical
table, 62; ties, significance of, 67 ff.,
70; village as unit, 29, 32. *See also*
Education, Marriage, Social structure.
Kongo, kingdom of, 164, 181. *See also*
under Congo.

Land, 216 f.
Language, learning of, 96; teaching
of, 143 f.; policy, 142 seq. *See also*
Linguistic, Umbundu, &c.
Leaders, training of, 70 ff., 139.
Leadership in Christian Community,
70 ff.
Learning in real situation, 121 ff.
Lecomte, Père Ernest, 221 f.
Lende, *see* Elende.
Libolo, 194.
Life-cycle, summary of, 81–118. *See*
Birth, Babyhood, Childhood,
Adolescence, Adult life.
Lineage, dual lines of descent, 42–5.
See also Kinship.
Linguistic affinities and groups, 8 f.,
169 f. *See also under* Umbundu.
Loango, 197.
Lobito Bay, 195 n., 201.
'Lovar' or 'Lovale', first expedition to,
198 f.
Luba, 181.
Lunda, 180 f., 205 n.
Lying-in period, 85, 87 f. *See also*
Birth.

'*Mambari*' (name applied to Ovimbundu), 19, 191 n., 205 n.

Manners, Umbundu teaching of, 96,
100 seq., 102 ff. *See also* Social
behaviour, Social usage.
Marriage, 51, 53 f., 56, 111, 112–14,
117, 130; relatives by, 51–6; of
cross-cousins, 53 f., 56; terms of
relationship by, 55 f.; trial marriage,
112. *See also* Adolescence, Kinship.
Mat-making, 109.
Mbailundu, *see* Bailundu.
Mbongo, kingdom of, 168.
Media, *see* Medicine and magic.
Medicine and magic; King's resort to,
22; divination, 22, 88; sorcery, 22,
56 ff., 107 f., 110, 129 n.; medical
practice, 88 f., 110; media, process
for becoming, 121.
Men's club-house, 26 f.; education of
boys in, 102 f.
Menstruation, 109 n., 112.
Metal industry, 204 f. *See also* Iron-
working.
Migrations, 181–8. *See also* 'Jagas',
Traditional histories.
Military occupation, of Bailundu,
211; of Caconda, 211 n.; of Viye,
210 f.
Missions, 10, 65 f., 72–4, 138 f., 142
seq., 149; Protestant, 220 seq.;
Roman Catholic, 219 f., 221; outstations, 72.
Morphology, 1.
Mother (*mai*), 41 f., 81 seq., 86, 89–91,
93 f., 98 seq.
Mother's brother (*manu*) and sister's
son, 44 f., 50.
Murder, ritual, *see* Ritual, *also* Canni-
balism.
Music, African v. European forms,
144; function of, in education, 114;
teaching of, 144; traditional songs,
35.
Mussende, 168 n., 180.
Mutu ya Kevela, war of, 211 n.

Namba, kingdom of, 168.
Naming of Umbundu baby, 86 f.
Ndombe, 176, 192.
Ndongo, 198.
Ndulu, kingdom of, 168; traditional
history, 170 f.; iron-working in,
204.
Ndunduma (King of Viye, 1889–90),
210 f.
Neglect, feelings of, 127 f.
Neighbouring peoples, 8 f., 180 f.
Ngalanga, kingdom of, 168.
Ngalangi, kingdom of, 168, 198;
traditional history, 174 ff.; royal
trading caravan, 200.

INDEX

243

Nganda, 180.
'*Ngangela*' people, 173, 175, 189 f., 206, 212, 214.
Novo Redondo, 196.

Ocimbundu, meaning of term, xi.
Old age, 117.
oluina, 42–5.
oluse, 42–5.
Ondura, *see* Ndulu.
Origins, tribal, *see* Tribal origins, &c.
Orthography, xi, 19.
Out-stations, *see* Missions.
Ovimbundu, meaning of term, xi; linguistic affiliations of, 9; tribal divisions of, 9 n., 18 ff., 23 f.

Parenthood, 117.
Parents, respect for, 41 f.; association of children with, 98 f., 106; parent-child adjustments, 126 ff. *See also* Birth, Kinship.
Pentateuch, historical sources of, 146.
Personality, social determination of, 119 ff.; Umbundu theory of, 119 ff.
Place-names, 118.
Placenta, disposal of, 84.
Plants, cultivated, native and imported, 175, 218. *See also* Agriculture, Diet, &c.
Plymouth Brethren, Mission of, 221 n.
Policy, educational, *see* Educational.
Political life of the Ovimbundu, 17 f. *See also* King, Kingdoms, &c.
Polygyny, 30 f., 42.
Pombal, Marquez de, 195.
Pombeiros, African trading agents, 36, 197 ff.
Population (census figures), 7, 9, 23 f., 30 n., 222.
Ports of Angola, 202.
Pottery-making, 109.
Pregnancy, 82; pre-marital, 113.
Pre-history, 164–7.
Priesthood, of the King, 20, 117 f.; of *oluina*, 46; of *oluse*, 46; of village headman, 36, 38 f. *See* Kinship, Professions, Ritual.
Primitive mentality, vi f.
Professional training, 106 seq.
Professions, 31, 110.
Property, *see* Inheritance.
Psychological education. *See* Education.
Puberty, 111.
Pungu-a-Ndongo, 170 f., 182 n.

Queen, the (*inakulu*), 20, 24.
Quiaca, *see* Ciyaka.
Quibala, *see* Cipala.

Quibanda, *see* Civanda.
Quiboque, *see* Cokue.
Quibula, *see* Civula.
Quilombo, *see* Cilombo-coñoma.
Quimbundo (or Quinbundo), explanation of term and its origin, 188.
Quingolo, *see* Cingolo.
Quipeio (or Quipeyo), *see* Cipeyo.
Quiquete, *see* Ekekete.
Quissama, *see* Cisama.
Quitata, *see* Citata.

Rain, rainfall, 3 ff.; rain-making, 20.
Recreation, 144 f. *See also* Dance, Education, Games, Music.
Reincarnation, 120 f.
Rejection, feelings of, 127 f.
Relationship, 28, 42–5, 46, 47 seq.; classificatory, 46; terms of, 47–9, 55.
Relatives, 42–5; by marriage, 51–4, 56; children stay with, 104 f.
Religion, *see* Medicine and magic, Priesthood, Ritual, Sorcery, Tabus.
Religious developments, 219–23.
Religious education, 73, 145 seq.; place in curriculum, 147. *See also* Education.
Religious orders, 192 f.
Republic proclaimed in Portugal (1910), 214.
Respect, for elders, 41; for and by relations by marriage, 51 f.; for children, 104, 120 f.
Riddles, 35.
Ritual, employed by king, 20 ff., 177 n.; by village headman, 36, 38 f.; and the dance, 33; function of kinship organizations, 43 ff.; employed by individuals, 57 ff., 107, 110, 121; sacrifice, human, 21 f., 128; of children, 22, 128; initiation rites, 59, 115 ff., 148 f. *See also* Medicine and magic, Priesthood, Tabus.
Ritual murder, *see* Human sacrifice.
Roman Catholic missions, *see* Missions.
Rope-making, 110.
Rubber trade, 113, 202 ff., 207–15; first export, 202 ff.; 'First-class rubber', 207; 'Red rubber', 208–11; decline, 211–15; gathering of wild rubber, 193, 212 n.; effects of, on social customs, 198.
Ruins, 165 seq.
Rum trade, 206, 213.

Saint Esprit, Pères du, 221.
Sambo or Sambos, *see* Sambu.
Sambu, ruins of capital, 165; kingdom of, 168.

244 INDEX

Sanders, W. H., 210 n., 219 n., 220 n.
Sanga, kingdom of, 168.
Schools, 70 f., 139, 144, 145, 209; out-station, 66; and community, 139.
Seasons, *see* Climate, Rain.
Sela, 8, 180.
Sex, factor of, in household, 41; division of society, 98; teaching, 103.
Sibling (elder), as nurse, 94 f.; domination by eldest, 127 f.
Siblings, adjustment between, 128. *See also* Kinship.
Silva Porto, A. F. F. da, 199 n., 210.
Sister's son, 44 f., 48, 50, 55 f., 109.
Skills, children's acquisition of, 104, 106–10, 135.
Slave trade, 182, 192 f., 194, 200, 201, 206, 209 n.; formal abolition of, 199; end of, 213 ff.
Slavery, 30, 42, 131.
Smithing, 110, 204.
Snuff, *see* Tobacco.
Social science course, 151 f.
Social structure, 17–73; historical allusions, 17; social life, 32–5.
Social usage, training of children in, 96, 100–4. *See also* Character, Education, Kinship, Village.
Songo, 8, 181, 187 n.
Songs, *see* Music.
Sorcery, 22, 56 ff., 107 f., 110, 129 ff., 202, 223.
Sources, viii f.
Southern Bantu, 8 f., 169 f., 190.
Souza Coutinho, Dom. F. I. de, 195 ff.
Spaniards, in slave trade, 200.
Speech, learning of, *see* Childhood.
Spirits, *see* Ancestor-spirits.
Substitution by elimination, 148 f.
Succession, royal, 22; to office in *oluse*, 44.

Tables, of blood relationship, 47 seq.; of relatives by marriage, 55 f.; genealogical, 62.
Tabus, 43, 124.
Taxation, 215 f.
Teacher, as community leader, 155.
Teeth, chipping of, 105.
Teething, *see* Childhood.
Tenderness, 131.
Thatching, 110.
Theory of personality, *see* Personality.
Tobacco, 33.
Toddler, *see* Childhood.
Totemic tabus, *see* Tabus.
Trade, 8, 21, 45, 61, 105, 108 f., 113, 136, 182, 191–215; dominance in

Angola, 191–4; first trade with Ovimbundu, 204 f.; agreements, 204 f.; goods, 206; with Central Africa, 206 f.; effects of wars, 211; end of large-scale trade, 212 f. *See also* Ivory, Rubber, Rum, Slave trade &c.
Traders, 191, 196 f.; 'barefoot traders', 197.
Traditional histories, 170–81. *See also* Tribal origins.
Trial marriage, 112 ff., 177 n.; decadence of, 113 f.; *see also* Adolescence, Marriage.
Tribal divisions, 17–24, 168, 179; Tribal origins, 169–90.
'Tribe of God', 69.
Triplets, 85.
Twins, 85.

Umbundu, xi; conception of education, 119, 134 ff., 155 f.; culture, 148, 156, 221; development, 119–33; estimate of character, 130 seq.; language, 8 f., 11, 15, 169 f., 179 f., 189 f.; social structure, 59 ff.; terms of relationship, 47 seq.; theory of personality, 119 f. *See also* Adolescence, Baby, Childhood, Kinship, &c.
United Church of Canada, 10, 221.
Uterine descent, 42–6.
Uterine nephew, *see* Mother's brother, Sister's son.

Vakuacisoko (organized age-groups), 114 f.
Village, 25 seq.; census, 28–31; court of justice, 36; headman, 36 f.; moving of, 37 ff.; plan of, 27 f.; social life of, 32–5; types of, 37; wards of, 25; work of Church in, 65 seq. *See also* Kinship, Social structure.
Villagers, 28 f., 30 f.
Virginity, tests for, 113.
Viye, kingdom of, 168, 198, 199; traditional history, 272 ff.; 'Ngangela' stock in, 175; linguistic differences, 190 n.; military occupation, 210.

Wagon road from Benguela to Caconda and Viye, 209.
Wambu, kingdom of, 168, 178, 198; traditional history, 176.
War, a royal function, 21; war-leader, the (*kesongo*), 21; war v. trade as occupation, 21, 197, 200.

INDEX

Water (ceremonial), 20.
Water-buck, 43.
Weaning, 93.
West Central Africa Mission, *see* American Board of Commissioners for Foreign Missions, United Church of Canada.
Wit and humour as outlets for anger, 125.
Witchcraft, 148, 223. *See also* Sorcery.
Women, in social life of village, 32; eat in kitchen with girls and younger children, 98; teach small children fear of ghosts, 99 f.; teach modesty to daughters, 103 f.; as rulers, 178. *See also* Kinship.

Yankees on Angola coast, 191.

Zambezi, 3; expedition to head-waters of, 198.
Zanzibar, Arabs from, 204 n.
Zanzibaris, 191.

PRINTED IN
GREAT BRITAIN
AT THE
UNIVERSITY PRESS
OXFORD
BY
CHARLES BATEY
PRINTER
TO THE
UNIVERSITY